S T R, Capitalism and Postcapitalism

The Great Transition

S T R, Capitalism and Postcapitalism

The Great Transition

Anil Rajimwale

S T R, CAPITALISM AND POSTCAPITALISM: The Great Transition
Anil Rajimwale

First Published 2017

ISBN 978-93-5002-481-2 (Hb)

Published by
AAKAR BOOKS
28 E Pocket IV, Mayur Vihar Phase I, Delhi 110 091
Phones : 011 2279 5505, 2279 5641
aakarbooks@gmail.com; www.aakarbooks.com

Designed by
Limited Colors, Delhi 110 092

Printed at
Mudrak, 30A, Patparganj, Delhi 110 091

Contents

Introduction

This is the second book in the series on the social impact of STR (Scientific and Technological Revolution), the first being *The Particle and Philosophy in Crisis* (2013). The book examines the impact of STR on production and labour processes, capitalist mode of production, the basic concepts like value and use value, nature of commodity, and a number of other ones.

It also examines the changing nature of tools and machines, hardware and software, evolution of the computer and the satellite and internet system and their growing impact on the society structure and social institutions.

It studies the transition from the industrial and capitalist system to the post-industrial, post-capitalist one.

The 'Great Transition'

We are living in an age of transition from the industrial to the post-industrial. We are really fortunate to be witness to such momentous changes. It is our duty to grasp and interpret these transformations and to use them for the benefit of human society.

The great industrial revolution of the 18th century was a giant step forward for human society. It transformed human beings beyond recognition and shifted the centre of our motion from the rural to the urban, from the manual use of the tool to the machine use of it.

Today, we are going through another technological revolution, the STR (Scientific and Technological Revolution), a much greater, higher, broader, deeper, and a most important, a much faster revolution. It has brought out the forces residing within the atom as the new productive force, and is proving to be a deep-going social force, which is undermining all the socio-economic, political, conceptual, philosophical and cultural structures and processes. Nothing can remain intact before this all powerful and dissolving force.

It was an unexpected, unprecedented event. None of the existing theories expected this development and sudden turn of motion of history and society. These events cannot be interpreted by any of the existing theories, disciplines, outlooks and concepts, simply because all of them took shape during and as a result of the industrial revolution. They are unable to come to terms with the new electronic events. They fall short of the task of understanding and interpreting them, more and more so with the passing of time and events. They have already discharged their task during the industrial age.

The Great Task Ahead

The most important task before us is to grasp the new world and to interpret it. For this we need new tools of knowledge and analysis. Old concepts are helpful only to a limited extent. We need to develop new tools of knowledge to understand the post-industrial and non-industrial processes that are rapidly emerging.

The sub-atomic particle and wave as the bearer of new transformation compel us to re-orientate our theoretical tools in new directions and to develop new ones. These directions are dominated by the time factor. Time is the basic factor in the new stage of social motion.

Total Overhaul of Theory

Scientific theory must evolve, otherwise it will be dead. It won't be able then to grasp and interpret the world. Our tools and means of analysis have fallen behind. We are still heavily dependent on the industrial concepts and tools of knowledge.

So the greatest task before us is to update theory and develop new ones if needed.

In this book we have tried to examine the industrial revolution and its machine base from the perspective of the STR: at what points does the STR affect, change and dissolve the industrial links and objects. STR and FTR (Fourth Technological Revolution) are the decisive factor shaping the contemporary world.

We need to re-examine the very basic factors of formation and development of society and its structures. Things like tools and machines themselves are under change and dissolution. This is something novel. That will in turn need a rework of the social processes and movement into the future. The fact is that the tool itself is under threat.

The modern world is based on the machine, but the machine itself is undergoing drastic transformations and transfigurations. This changes the course of modern society.

We need to examine the role of science and technology in the great transition as the basic building factors. Subatomic forces unleash unlimited energies into the productive base of the society, bringing about fundamental changes driven by time and information.

The book observes that the mode of production is being replaced by the mode of information. Therefore, most of the basic concepts and assumptions formed in the industrial age are under threat. We need to develop new ones.

A whole new world is emerging. Democracy becomes all-pervading and universal due to the electronic motions and domination of information.

The book has tried to develop new theories that will be able to explain the new emerging world.

New Delhi
27 January 2017

ANIL RAJIMWALE
(M) 9868525812
Email: anilrajim@gmail.com

1

Industrial Revolution and Distinguishing Features of Industrial Tools and Machines

In this chapter, we will try to trace why and how the machines and machine tools developed, and developed in a particular manner. It will be interesting to relate the machines not only with socio-economic conditions but also with the nature of the raw materials, plants and other natural materials, mine-mill relationship, markets and so on.

This will help us understand the points of the industrial revolution which were acted upon or influenced by the electronics revolution. These are the points where the two revolutions come in contact with each other, interact and mutually penetrate. But the dominant pole is that of the electronics revolution which gradually dissolves the mechanical and tangible means of the industrial revolution. The industrial revolution created qualitatively new kinds of means of production, industrial in nature. After two to three centuries of development, the STR began to change and dissolve the links and structures of the industrial age. How? This we have to understand. We should discover those dialectical points vulnerable to electronics, computers and information. The STR simultaneously created new means of production and communications.

Cotton, Spirality of Fibre and Industrial Revolution

"What a royal plant it is! The world waits in attendance..." wrote Henry W. Grady.[1] He expressed the key object of modern industry and, consequently of machinery, as also of general consumption. It was with cotton and cotton and woollen textiles that modern industrial production emerged and spread. It was with cotton again, combined with industrial machinery, that the industrial society took shape. Cotton and cotton fibres form a rhythmic unity with human activities, both social and individual. The wavy nature of cotton thread fully accords with daily life, cultural and religious activities and periodic nature of human life. Not only economics, but literature, culture, dances, songs, family and personal life, fashion, the whole human movements reflect the wavy thread, to be seen only under the microscope. The nature of the single wave-like cotton thread determines the rhythmic motions of the industrial machines.

The word 'cotton' is derived from the Arabic *qutun* or *kutun*. It is an ancient plant, with samples found in India in 3000 BC. It was to be found among the Egyptians and the Chinese also.

In botanical terms it belongs to the genus *Gossypium herbacium* of the Malvaceae family.

A single strand of mature cotton seen under the microscope looks like a flattened tube with spiral convolutions. The length of the fibre is from 1000 to 3000 times the breadth. The diameter and the number of twists differ from species to species.

Spirality of Cotton Fibre and Nature of Industrial Tools/Machines

The spirality of the cotton fibre distinguishes it from all the other plant fibres. No other natural fibre has this quality. None of the man-made fibres have been able to reproduce the spirality so far. The spirality and elasticity of the fibre makes it the best material for craftsmanship and industry, *and for industrial revolution.* The fibre is actually seed hair of profuse nature, and highly spiral. *It is this nature that has ultimately determined the nature of tools and machinery* working with certain motion with cotton down the ages.

Cotton plants have been modified due to artificial cultivation and cross-breeding down the ages for commercial purposes and consumption.

The operations of cloth production emanate from the nature of cotton thread. Spinning and weaving are the basic functions of the cotton processing. The threads or the fibres of the cotton seed must be spun first to enable one to make the cloth ultimately. Thus, the nature of tools working with cotton emanates directly from the nature of cotton itself.

For inventions and discoveries in cotton textiles as also in woollen textiles, it is essential to understand the principles of spinning. The raw material is the mass of matted fibres. From this mass yarn has to be produced. The material therefore has to be cleaned and made parallel or 'parallelized'. The manual spinner drew the fibres by hand from a revolving spindle which twisted them, and then twisted yarn was wound around the spindle.

The spinners did not attack the problem, at first, of spinning out of the mass of fibres, twisting them and parallelizing them. Their first efforts in the course of the preparatory stages of the industrial revolution were to increase production over the best hand spinning then in existence. The efforts to spin and twist the fibre led in the middle of the 18th century or there around to the inventions of Hargreaves' spinning jenny, Arkwright's spinning frame, Crompton's mule and such other inventions.

Some of the basic inventions that constituted the cotton machinery and industrial revolution related with it were: the spindle, the bobbin, spinner, shuttle, spinning machine, weaving machine etc. The spindle spins the wavy thread into yarn. Its motion converts the filaments into thicker threads which consist of numerous filaments, which in turn are themselves spiral. Thus *the spiral nature of the material continues to direct the nature of the tool.* The bobbin is a store of thread to be used later. The material, the thread, is transferred from the spindle to the bobbin. Large numbers of spindles in a machine help the thread to be transferred to the bobbins.

The bobbin has been an important object of the industrial revolution. It is the connecting tool between spinning and weaving. There are hundreds of them in a spinning and weaving machine. The increasing motion of the bobbin/s lies at the core of new inventions and in increase in production.

Crude spinning wheels evolved over centuries into spinning frames, weaving into handlooms. By 1800 the spinning wheels were replaced by spinning machines and handloom by powerloom. Spinning and weaving mills had been built and put into operation. The *textile industry was truly born.*

The spinning wheel had been improved but still remained manually operated. It is interesting to note that in 1519 Leonardo da Vinci invented a flyer of upside down horse-shoe shape. Its legs extended on either side of the spinning spindle and helped twisting and winding of the thread on the spindle. In 1530 Johann Jurgen made a wooden flyer. The Brunswick spinning wheel was invented in 1533. The improvements continued till the early period of the 18th century, soon to be taken over by the steam power.

Now the problem was to modernize the warp and weft functions to weave a cloth. Both kinds of threads originate in the same manner, and they must be combined to a cross pattern. It is an interesting terrain for inventions and novelty of motion. The main motion is that of the shuttle, a tool central to weaving. The warp or the lengthwise threads are drawn forward. By raising one heald frame and lowering the other, a division of the warp yarns is secured. Through the opening ('shed') thus created, shuttle containing the thread of waft is passed from side to side. The practice of throwing the waft by hand (with thread in shuttle) continued till 1733, when the shuttle began to 'fly'! The flying shuttle was invented that year by John Kay. It revolutionized the cotton industry of England and the whole world.

He added two small boxes to the lathe of the weaving machine on either side. Their function was to receive the shuttle. Spindles were fixed in each of the boxes. On each spindle a piece of wood or leather was threaded, called the 'picker'. The two pickers are connected with fly cords which the weaver holds in his hand with a small handle called a 'fly pin'. The weaver propels the shuttle from box to box by a sharp jerk or flick of the fly pin.

Kay's invention increased the speed of weaving; consequently the demand for thread increased tremendously, and therefore there was pressure to improve spinning methods and particularly its speed. The time was ripe now for mechanical and automatic spinning mills. A number of innovations were already made, mentioned elsewhere.

Kay's invention did not put weavers out of work, contrary to their fears. But that became clear only later. At first they thought they would be rendered jobless, and they attacked Kay's house and destroyed all his machines. He fled to France, where he died ultimately.

But his invention stood the test of times to become modernized and automated in the present times. Today, 'shuttle-less' electronic machines have come into being.

For these reasons, the inventions in spinning concerned themselves with increased spinning rates.

Drafting or attenuating by rollers was invented in 1738 by Lewis Paul. Wyatt's name also comes up in this connection. His invention was very crucial and important. It paved the way for the subsequent inventions of James Hargreaves and others. Herein the sliver or the untwisted rope of fibres is attenuated to reduce the number of such fibres in the cross section. This will help spinning of more fibres into a yarn of certain firmness.[2]

This was an important step towards emancipation from production of yarn by hand.

Some of the textile machinery is a direct result of the wavy and spiral nature of the cotton threads.

Crompton's Mule

Crompton combined Hargreaves' and Arkwright's inventions and the 'cross' was called the 'mule'. The naming of the machines is interesting. Due to the fact that the flyer of Arkwright's frame gave out a whistling sound like thrush singing, it was named 'throstle frame'. It was also known as 'jack frame', and when it was operated by water, it began to be called the water frame. According to some authors, Crompton's Mule is so called because it is a cross between the 'jack' and the 'jenny'. Others say that it was so named because it could spin yarn fine enough for weaving muslin, which later was corrupted into 'mule'.

Crompton began his invention in 1774 and completed it in 1779. Crompton took Arkwright's system of spindles without bobbins, which in combination with the faller or the presser wire gave the twist to the yarn. The yarn in this type of machine is stretched and spun at the same time as it was in Hargreaves', but the action is automatic and involves the stoppage of the rollers when a sufficient length of roving has been paid out. The most noteworthy feature of Crompton's machine is the movable carriage which carries the spindles. The carriage was drawn out for a distance of 54 to 56 inches from the roller beam, known as the draw, to stretch and twist the yarn. Hargreaves moved his clasp out by hand, his spindles being stationary. When twisting is complete the carriage moves back towards the roller beam, the yarn winding on to the spindles in the process.

Within a comparatively short period between 1738 and 1779, many far-reaching improvements had been made. The production capacity of the spinner improved many times and the quality of the yarn greatly increased.

It has to be noted that the alteration in movement of direction of the mule carriage had to be governed by hand. Roberts in 1830 invented the self-acting mule. It removed the onus of governing from the spinner to the machine.[3]

Preparatory Machines

Cotton in bale form is a matted, tangled mass with dust, twigs, seed, leaves, and other foreign materials. The mass of fibre needs cleaning. The fibre must be disentangled and made parallel for yarn production. With the advent of spinning machinery, cleaning operations had to be speeded up and mechanized. This was the dialectics of the emergence of the cleaning and carding machinery. Lewis

Paul in collabouration with John Wyatt invented roller spinning and some other machines by about the middle of the 18th century. Edward Cave rebuilt a mill on the river Nene in Northampton in 1842 to hold 4 or 5 water powered spinning machines, each with 50 spindles. It was thus the first cotton mill.[4]

Lewis Paul also helped inventions of the carding machines. Later Richard Arkwright improved upon the spinning machines in 1769 and later. They included drawing or drafting frame, essentially comprising successive pairs of rollers running at increased speeds. There were three other machines: 'slubber', 'intermediate' and 'speeder', essentially with the same idea. The object of these machines is to reduce the number of fibre to the cross-section and to parallelize them.

A machine was devised to open the matted dirty cotton from the bale. It consisted of a hopper or bin into which the cotton was fed and into which a roller having a number of pikes was made to revolve. The spikes tore the cotton apart and a strong air current freed the cotton of most of the dirty material and the seed.

Snodgrass in Glasgow invented a better cleaning machine in 1797. Till today it is practically the same. It is 'scutcher' or 'picker'. It comprised three or four metallic blades revolving at 4000 to 7000 RPM (revolutions per minute). The material was shown or touched to the edge of a metallic feed plate to the running blades. The cotton got broken and the foreign material, got beaten out and dropped.

Another similar machine combined with a lapping machine was employed. This helped the cotton roll out in the form of a sheet and wrap around a central spindle or core. From the scrutcher the 'lap' proceeded to the carding machine. The early hand card was a simple arrangement of brushes with short pieces of wire at a certain angle. The cotton was laid upon the back of one hand card and was brushed or combed with another. Further on in evolution, its size and speed kept increasing. Various combinations of the movements of the two led to greater production.[5]

Lewis Paul invented the rotary cylinder in 1748, covered with card clothing or wire teeth and a set of stationary 'flats' or strips of wood fitted with card clothing placed below the cylinder. This was the genesis of the present day card. Now the cylinder moves at high speed and the cards move above the cylinder in an endless chain.

Mechanics of the Industrial Revolution and of Textile and Some Other Industries

It was during the 15th century that England definitely passed from being a producer of wool to the manufacture of cloth. The clothing industry became the decisive feature of the economic life in the country, determining the speed and direction of its development, as distinct from other countries. During the Middle Ages England was more rural than France, for example. Its towns were smaller, and never came into sharp opposition to the feudal lords and the mass of peasantry. At the same time rural England was more developed, peasantry freer and less exploited. It was this evenness of development, this weakness of a specifically urban and partially feudal production of the manufactured goods which made the development of a capitalist based textile industry relatively easy and rapid.[6]

The textile industry first developed in East Anglia, the eastern part of England, and in south-west England, around Norwich and the rural Stour valley. Even today, the tall multi-windowed houses and high churches bear witness to those times of peculiar prosperity. East Anglia faced Flanders directly across the narrow sea, and stood in a special relationship with it. Other parts of England had developed large-scale export of wool but East Anglia exported little. It shipped corn to feed the industrial population of Ghent and Bruges. Its agriculture was at various stages of backwardness, with poor sheep and very poor quality of wool.[7] In the course of time, the Flemish craftsmen began to settle in these areas of East Anglia and taught the natives superior methods of cloth-weaving. By the beginning of the 15th century great improvements had been made in methods of cloth making. Obscure villages like Worsted and Kersey were to imprint their names on the cloth labels later to become famous all over Europe.[8]

At first the Anglian cloth went to Flanders in half-finished form to be sheared and dyed. The greater part of the profits remained in Flemish hands. But a native body of merchant adventurers wrested control of cloth exports from the Hansards in 15th century; they set up a 'factory' at Antwerp in 1407. Their advantage was a free and uninterrupted access to the supply of raw materials, which they could buy cheaper than Flemings who had to pay a heavy duty. In 1434 Flanders prohibited import of English cloth; in retaliation the export of wool was prohibited, which was more damaging. The industry of Flanders continued to decline even after normalization towards the end of the 15th century. The Spanish invasion of the Netherlands and the consequent fierce wars completed the process. This started a settlement of new waves of craftsmen in England. Holland won independence but was the less industrialized part of the Netherlands. Consequently, it became a commercial rather than an industrial rival in the 16th century.[9]

Wool exports declined while the textile exports increased. In 1354 the exports of cloth stood at less than 5000 pieces. In 1509 it rose to 80,000 pieces and in 1547 to 1,20,000 pieces.[10]

The cloth industry was run on capitalist lines from the very beginning. With the rise of export markets, the small independent weaver fell under the control of the merchant who had control over the resources and knowledge of the market. Besides, the guilds could flourish better in the wool industry because they sold in bulk. But there were far greater divisions of labour in the cloth industry and finer differences with the wool industry. Therefore, the cloth industry could not be organized on the guild basis. The attempts of the Norwich guilds to control the weavers of the surrounding villages did not succeed.[11]

The clothier (as the wool capitalist came to be called) began to sell yarn to the weavers and to buy back cloth from them. Soon the clothiers had every process under their control. They bought raw wool, gave it out to the spinners (most of whom were women and children working in their cottages), collected it again, handed it to the weavers, dyers, fullers, shearers, etc. Each process was separately paid for at piece rate in place of selling and buying at each stage. A statute of 1465 stated, among other things, that the wages shall be paid 'true and lawful money' and not in 'pins, girdles, and other unprofitable wares'. It was known as the first 'Truck Act'.

The accumulation of capital was rapid. The industry spread from East Anglia to Somerset, West Riding and other parts of the country. The clothiers were gradually crystallizing into a nebulous capitalist class. They were more progressive and even revolutionary compared to the conservative forces of the guild organizations. Bristol, Hull, and in particular London, became the centres of new and renewed industrial productive activity.

A qualitatively new stage in technological and economic-productive concentration was reached when the clothiers collected a large number of artisans *under one roof* and carried on the entire *industrial process* in that place.

The practice became fairly common in the 16th century. The Act of 1555 sought to limit the number of looms a clothier might concentrate and take out of the weavers' homes. The extra profit gained by the concentration was perhaps not sufficient to drive out the weavers, and at the same time the machinery used was not so expensive to make secure the clothiers a monopoly control.[12]

The rising rate of profit, the growing commodity production and the increasing world trade created a currency crisis in Europe in the second half of the 15th century. Now gold and silver could be the only satisfactory medium of exchange. Thus there was a real famine of precious metals, especially of gold. It was the shortage of gold which provided the general impulse to find new sources of gold the world over and caused new geographical discoveries in the 16th century.

Columbus himself was conscious of this fact. His voyages were the signal for the commencement of the first and the most far-reaching gold-rush.[13]

New Discoveries, Preparing the Ground for the First and Second Industrial Revolutions

Columbus reached the West Indies in 1492 and Vasco da Gama anchored at Calicut seven years later, negotiating the Cape of Good Hope. The trade between Europe and Asia was carried along several routes: the easterly one through Trebizond up the Don and Volga and into the Baltic, with Hanse towns at the northern tip; the other through the Persian Gulf, Baghdad and Aleppo into Constantinople, Venice and Genoa on the sea; a third was on the Red Sea and overland to the Nile and through Alexandria to the Asiatic parts.

The cost of land transport was very high, and only the least bulky cargo could be comfortably and profitably carried. The trade was unprofitable for Europe which had no small commodity to trade profitably. It had to pay in gold and silver for spices and other goods, thus reducing its bullion stock. Only merchants of Italy and Hanse found it profitable and they guarded sea routes carefully.

Mongol and Turk invasions during the 15th century threatened these routes. The former overran Russia and the Turks drove the Arabs out of the Asia Minor in 1453 and captured Constantinople. The overland routes were now becoming increasingly risky and costlier, and the profits began to fall.

In the meantime, several nation-states were emerging, who did not recognize the established practices and wanted to develop their own routes. They also wanted to break the monopoly of Venice and Genoa. Among such states were Portugal and Spain who expelled the Moors, France emerging against England, and the Hapsburg monarchy rising in the course of struggle against the Turks in defence of east Europe.

It is important to note that the new routes were all opened by the state and not by private enterprise.

Ship-building and navigation reached an advanced state of development in the 15th century. The typical merchant ship earlier was a basin-shaped structure with a single mast in the centre. It was incapable of sailing against the wind. Before 1400, ships larger than 100 tons were seldom built. But then there was a rapid development in ship-building. In 1439 the government had several ships of 200 to 360 tons. In 1451 there were 23 ships of 200 to 400 tons. A little later there was a vessel of over 900 tons with a private merchant.[14]

The Spanish and the Portuguese developed the caravel for coastal trade. They were longer, narrower and with 3 or 4 masts. The compass was perfected and the astrolabe was adapted for the calculation of latitude. The map-makers began to replace mythical cities with a certain measure of reality. Step by step it became possible to leave the coast and undertake transoceanic voyages. The first attempts were made by Portugal. Vasco da Gama returned from India to Lisbon with a cargo 60 times the cost of his voyage. It was unimaginable and it shattered the power of the Italian merchant towns. The centre of gravity shifted to the Atlantic coast.[15]

Spain went to the alternative direction of the west, discovering a new continent there, as also huge deposits of gold and silver. The areas from Mexico to Chile turned out to be unfathomable deposits of these precious metals, and virtually rivers of them flowed to Europe. Despite efforts to contain them within the country by the Spanish, they flowed all over Europe and raised prices, which helped the merchants and markets of various countries. France, England and Holland gained most. The English merchants went west and north, to North America and Canada, though they did not prove to be profitable. They then turned their attention to north Europe, to Norway, etc.

In 1553 a group of London merchants formed one of the first joint-stock companies with a capital of 6000 pounds. This was the time of mercantilism, aimed at amassing the greatest amounts of wealth in their own countries. Corn exports were encouraged since it speeded up the development of agriculture and brought money. Home industries were protected with tariffs, a practice followed up to the industrial revolution. So long as merchant capital was dominant, money was regarded as the measure of national wealth and prosperity. With the rise of industrial capital towards the end of the 18th century money began to be considered as a commodity. The wealth of a nation was now measured by the volume of production of commodities.16

In the 16th century the main aim of England's export of cloth was to secure gold and silver and to find new markets for cloth. Its export rose steadily until the middle of the 16th century, when due to a number of reasons it lost many markets. As a result, many new markets were found. But capital was forced to find avenues in new industries, which in turn gave stimulus to what is known as the *'little industrial revolution'*.

Whole new industries came into being, such as better finishing of cloth, soap-making, brewing, ship-building, glass-making, gun powder, paper, saltpeter, sugar etc. They began to be made on factory scales and industrial basis. Many of them needed coal in large quantities. They were generally run by water-driven machinery.

This led to a rapid expansion of coal-mining, which went deeper, particularly in England. Deep mining methods were made possible by water-driven pumps. The ventilation methods were also improved. So instead of being just a scratch over the ground, the coal mine became a deep sinking one. Industries began to concentrate around the coal areas, which needed better transportation now.

This was the *First Industrial Revolution* of 1540 to 1640, roughly of a hundred years. It prepared the ground for the *Second Industrial Revolution* that began in 1760 in England.

England was involved in a long war with Spain in quest of gold and silver. These precious materials came in greater quantities now, though not fast enough for the capitalists. It was at this time that another important revolution took place in England, the agrarian revolution, which led to large-scale unemployment and contributed to the growth of the proletariat.

Industrial Revolution Through Technological and Material Economic Needs

Agriculture was the most important sector of the economy in the 18th century in England. The changes in technique and the distribution of classes among the rural population created conditions, without which the industrial revolution would have been impossible. Agriculture was transformed from subsistence economy to a capitalist industry in this period and the process continued throughout the next period of industrial revolution.

The steady export market together with considerable export of malt and barley and the provisioning of London provided agriculture with an outlet to the outside market. This acted as a stimulus for technological improvements. Enclosures were speeded up and reached inland areas. Corn, sheep-breeding and larger amounts of manure, all followed in their wake, leading to a spread of the market.

Each advance in one branch of agriculture led to advancements in other branches. Demand for meat grew, deep ploughing became essential and tools and implements improved. Oxen were replaced by horses for deep plough. By the beginning of the 19th century the iron plough became common. Jethro Tull was experimenting with a seed drill in 1750. He was known as an agricultural scientist, who contributed to the agrarian revolution in England. He had inventions of many implements to his credit, including the horse seed drill and others.

All these changes could be brought about only by investing a considerable amount of capital. These practices were incompatible with the primitive open field farming over half the country. It was also incompatible with the small-scale yeoman farming, which was in vogue in some parts. Among the pioneers of new technological innovations were Jethro Tull, Lord Townshend, Coke of Holkham and Bakewell. The breed of sheep was improved, for example.

The technological revolution developed side by side with and as a consequence of the social revolution. These processes changed the face of England.[17]

Nature of enclosures: The enclosures of earlier times were made with the aim of the transformation of the arable land into sheep pastures. The enclosures of the 18th century aimed at transforming the communal open lands into compact large lands. They were more suited to the scientific mixed farming with the aim of producing more profits. Besides, the traditional villages under customary rights of various usages were now enclosed.

The tenants in other parts of England were now gradually evicted or ruined by high rents. This resulted in large-scale displacement of the farmers and in their losing lands, forcing them to leave their traditional dwellings. In addition, heavy taxation also contributed to rapid increase in the size of land-holdings and to squeezing out of the small tenants. There was a marked decrease in the size of land-holdings under 100 acres and a marked increase of those over 300 acres.

The changes in agriculture increased the productivity of land, created a reserve army of wage earners along with a class of owners of capital, and created an internal market of commodities. Only on the basis of a strong home market, could an effective exporting industry be built.

At the beginning of the 18th century England faced an acute shortage of fuel, leading to a considerable increase in coal mining. At the same time, the destruction of forest went on at a high rate. Wood for domestic use became scarce. Many tons of wood were needed to smelt a ton of iron. Massive forests were destroyed all over England.

The Darbys of Coalbrookdale and Roebuck made a series of improvements in smelting: they showed that it was practical to use coke for smelting and with a blast sufficiently powerful to get rid of sulphur and other impurities, it was more effective than charcoal. Roebuck had established his famous works at Carron in 1760. From 1765 onwards the iron industry grew at an increasingly rapid rate and the number and size of blast furnaces increased. At the same time the production of pig iron increased substantially during the 18th century.[18]

"Without coal there could have been no modern, scientific metallurgy, and modern metallurgy is the technical key to large-scale industry."[19] Without this change, the "elabourate and delicate machinery"[20] needed by the textile and other industries could not have been constructed. Also the "strong and exact"[21] steam engines as the source of energy would not have been possible.

Iron soon began to spread and dominate life. The first iron bridge was built over Severn in 1779 and the first iron ship in 1790. At the same time the quality of iron was constantly improved, which improved tool-making in turn.

At the turn of the 18th century lathe was invented, with slide-rest and planer. This made it possible for the engineer to work with greater accuracy to the fractions of an inch. Without such accuracies, large-scale machinery was impossible. It also became possible to inter-change the parts of the machinery, which characterized mass production half a century later.[22]

The English iron industry generally had large capital. The iron masters of Sussex and the Midlands had a substantial number of people with a large capital, and thus the industry made easy progress.

Coal mining also grew rapidly and its production rose substantially in the 18th century. But coal deposits were concentrated in certain regions only. This fact combined with the growing iron industry gave impetus to the new transport leading to the railways, roads and canals.

Very few roads existed in 1700 in England along which wheeled traffic moved round the year. Lighter goods were carried on the backs of the horses. In 1759 an 11 mile long canal was built between Worseley collieries and Manchester, which was so successful that the price of coal in Manchester fell by half. The 19th century saw a boom of canal construction comparable to the railway construction. Canals remained the main channels for the distribution of perishable and non-perishable goods for a long time till they were overtaken by the railways.

The development of roads was extremely uneven and suffered heavily due to corruption. Their upkeep and conditions were extremely uneven and irregular, and depended very much on the local authorities. It was only in the initial years of the 19th century that the roads began to improve. It was the era of the stage coach and scientific road construction led by Macadam. They were interrupted by the railways, and picked up only when motor transport came into service.

The development of the wool industry to the semi-capitalist stage in the 15th and 16th centuries got arrested, and subsequently even moved slightly backwards. This was due to the absence of machinery, and to the restricted and insufficient market, all combining to prevent a growth of a real factory system. In some centres there was resistance to new innovations. This was illustrated by the reception to Kay's flying shuttle towards the middle of the 18th century. While in East Anglia it was opposed on the ground that it threw workers out of jobs, in West Riding it was welcomed by the domestic weavers because it contributed to their earnings. Here progress was made on a more purely domestic basis and not under the control of the clothiers.

New, more concentrated and decisively capitalist cotton industry in the meantime made decisive strides forward and left the wool industry behind. Cheapness and lightness gave them an edge and popularity, and the cotton imports from India and other countries helped them grow. It could more easily adopt and adapt to the new technologies and could be run better by the capitalists and overcome the resistance of the wool manufacturers. *The new inventions in technology in the 18th century were more easily absorbed by the cotton industry.*

The mass production of cotton cloth made it more amenable to application of industrial machinery, putting it on a capitalist basis and making it more receptive to the technical inventions.

The cotton industry was centred in Lancashire from the beginning. The reasons were that fact that wool for warp was available and the climate there was damp enough and exactly suited to spin cotton yarn.

The textile industry was clearly divided into spinning and weaving. Weaving was better paid and more prosperous, while spinning was a slow labourious process. Thus *a contradiction* in the process of development of the textiles developed, which had far-reaching implications for the future of the industry and for technology in general. It had always been difficult for the spinners to supply sufficient yarn for the weavers. The balance between the two was completely upset with the arrival of Kay's flying shuttle, which doubled the speed at which cloth could be woven.

Therefore, a radical improvement in the *methods of spinning* became an urgent objective necessity.

Hargreaves developed the spinning jenny in 1764 and a few years later, Arkwright invented the water frame. They were the products of certain technological and economic needs. Water frame spun cotton more rapidly and produced yarn of finer quality. Consequently, the cotton fabric now did not need an admixture of wool and linen. Crompton invented the mule, combining the advantages of both these machines. At this time Whitney's cotton gin arrived, which simplified the extraction of workable cotton from the plant. Thus the supply of raw material was speeded up. It led to an increase in fields under cotton as also to tremendous increase in slavery in the USA.

At this point the balance shifted dialectically in favour of spinning. Here onwards, there were continuous shifts, now in favour of this, now that. Cartwright's power loom brought about a favourable situation for weaving.[23]

Need for external power: The flying shuttle and spinning jenny were only an improvement of the handloom and spinning wheel. They did not need external power. But Arkwright's water-frame and other machines that came later required external power. At first it was supplied by water. Because of the nature of motive power, that is water, the domestic workers had to go out of their homes to operate them. As a result they gathered at one place. This gave rise to factories, where a large number of people worked. First the spinners went out and then the weavers. They were collected by the owners who paid them wages for their work and who owned the materials and instruments as also the place of work.

There were 143 water mills in Lancashire in 1788; abundant water power led to a further concentration of industry and population there.

Gradually, the need arose for a strong driving power for the machines. This need was fulfilled by the invention of the steam engine, which at a certain point was used to drive the spinning machinery, rapidly replacing water-power. Large coal deposits were discovered in Lancashire at about that time. This helped the capitalists to linger around and invest in coal. Spinning and weaving were freed from their dependence on water sources such as rivers. Mills, settlements and towns came up in and around the new favourable areas. Steam power now became the motive power for a growing number of industries. What was used till now to pump water from the mines was now used to drive industrial machinery. Industrial coal mining now got impetus as also the metallurgical industries. New pressures were created upon transport, leading ultimately to the development of the railways and ships.

Machine production was confined till about 1790 to Lancashire and to the cotton industry. It then spread rapidly to the woollen textiles. Hand spinners and weavers were deprived of their occupation or had to face a hopeless contest with the machine. The last decades of the 18th century and the first ones of the 19th saw a rapid rise in pauperization and of the emergence of the proletariat forced to sell their labour power at the cheapest rates. At the same time there was an extraordinary rise in the women and child labour, and in fact parents were more than willing to send their children to the factories and mills as an additional source of income. Illegitimate children as a result were widely welcome.

Britain entered the central phase of the industrial revolution (1793–1815) as an agrarian country and emerged from the incessant wars as an industrial one.

There was a heavy slump after the Battle of Waterloo (1815). Some three hundred thousand (3 lakh) demobilized soldiers joined the army of the proletariat and the unemployed, already under strain. Several blast furnaces went out of production due to a fall in demand and lack of exports. The historic and famous Luddite machine-breaking movements took place during this period, and many frames, mills and machines were smashed. The 'Peterloo massacre' took place August 16, 1819 in Manchester.[24]

Spinning

Spinning was one of the crucial points of the production process acted upon by the industrial revolution. Spinning is the forming of threads by drawing out and twisting various fibres. This simple act was in operation since time immemorial. The primitive spinning tool consisted of a wooden spindle tapered at both ends and given spin with the help of the thick wooden part in the middle surrounded by a perforated disk, thus constituting a whorl or wharve. It was made to spin by hands, and the pool of cotton at the top was notched in a notch like a bent finger. The movement spun the fine cotton natural threads into thicker artificial thread, which constituted the basic element of the cloth.

It was here that the development of means of production in the course of history of social development acted profoundly to transform it into modern machines, leading to the emergence of a modern society and mode of production based upon such new machines and tools.

In the course of the industrial revolution, the modern changes in the textiles had to be the following: 1) Mechanical and rapid means had to be provided to rotate the spindle and free the hands for other functions. 2) The drawing out of the threads had to be freed from hands and given over to a machine. 3) Large groups of spindles had to be worked so as to draw out several threads together.

The first improvement began the forward motion of spinning. It consisted of cutting a groove in the wharve, mounting the spindle horizontally in a frame and passing a band from a large wheel round the wharve.[25]

The next problem was imparting a rotatory motion to the spindle. Earlier it was given by hand, and in India it was quite common. The turn was given by the left hand and the right hand held the spool of cotton and allowed the threads to twist with the motion of the spindle into a thread. The further revolutions in technology increased the revolutions of the thread and its twisting and increased the speed of production, bringing in its wake a whole series of technical changes and revolutions. The thread was coiled upon the spindle, and thus gathered there in amounts. In England it was known as the 'bobbing wheel', in constant use till the beginning of the 19th century

Evolution of Weaving Machinery

The longitudinal threads of a fabric are called warp, while the transverse threads are weft. Weft is the thread or yarn drawn through the warp to create the fabric or the cloth. Warp is a longitudinal thread in a roll. It is a transverse thread. Weft does not have to be stretched on a loom. The weft is threaded through a warp using shuttle, air or gas or pressure jets and 'rapier grippers'. Warps were earlier raised by hands alternately, through which the wefts were sent flying, by hand, later by shuttle and still later by machine-propelled shuttle.

For weaving these threads into a cloth, the machine had to discharge at least the following two functions:

1. Shedding, means raising and lowering of the warp in a predetermined manner or sequence. This would enable formation of two lines of threads, between which the weft could be passed.
2. Shuttling the thread across the warps to 'weave' the two threads.

The woven cloth has to be rolled on a roller etc. But this is not the function of the weaving machine proper.

These are the processes acted upon subsequently by the electronics and computer revolution.

Textile Industry and Industrial Revolution

The industrial revolution did not actually originate in heavy industry and transport but took shape from within the developments in the textile industry. So to understand the industrial revolution, one must study the textile industry. It was the major industry at that time in England. Both the internal and external demand for cloth increased. First in Yorkshire and then in Lancashire, added advantages for processes such as fuelling and coal to help washing and dyeing were found. By 1750 the industry came to deal with a new fibre, that is cotton, which was grown in the American plantations and imported.[26]

"Cotton called for new techniques and was not bound by the old traditions of wool."[27] It needed a damp atmosphere and was worked up in the poor district of Lancashire on account of a damp climate. The demand soon ran out of the capacity of the hand-spinning devices.

One of the first examples of use of machinery in the textile industry was in 1719 when the stocking frame and Lombe's silk mill were used. They could not spread because of lack of demand. By the second half of the 18th century the demand rose to a point as to enable replacement of hand work by machinery. The great inventions like Hargreaves' spinning jenny (1764), Arkwright's water-frame (1769) and Crompton's mule (1779) fulfilled the objective needs of the motion of the tools and the machines. According to J.D. Bernal,[28] they made the first real breach in old hand techniques, first by multiplying the action of the hand and then by the use of power in spinning. After a time, the capacity of the streams was stretched to their limits, paving the way for mechanical machinery. This necessity was met by adaptation of Watts' steam engine in 1785.

Textile Revolution

The textile revolution was not just a technical revolution. It was also made possible by the social and economic changes of the early 18th century. For it, both capital and labour were required. Capital came from the merchant profits and capital of the preceding century. Labour was liberated from land through enclosures as also from the guild restrictions in the medieval times. Lack of labour at first was an incentive for technical changes and their use. Later, the rush of labour slowed down new inventions, even while spreading them.

"The market for textiles determined the outbreak of the industrial revolution...";[29] its conditions were met in Britain most fully. The market for textiles forced the use of textile machinery; machinery and textile processing stimulated demand for iron and chemical industries; they all demanded increased supply of coal, which in turn demanded greater extraction and supply from the mines.

Concentration of industry is very important and even crucial for the industrial revolution. Darby's invention led to a big increase in cast iron production. As a result there arose a shortage of wrought iron. The problem was solved by Cort's method of puddling introduced in 1784.

Owing to these developments, the age-old dependence on wood as raw material ended and "brought the iron industry from the forests to the coalfields, where so much other industry was already concentrated."[30]

Cast iron had been known in China since the first century BC, but it appeared in Europe perhaps independently. For

3000 years iron was made by low-temperature reduction with charcoal in small bloomery furnaces. The iron turned a pasty mass. Through the Middle Ages the furnaces became larger, being provided with bellows; they were ultimately driven by water power. A method then appeared in the Rhineland in the 14th century, in which iron was run in front of the furnace on the floor. It was run in a hollow, which came to be known as the 'sow', and the iron in it as the 'litter' of the 'pig'. That is how it came to be known as the 'pig iron'.[31]

Bloomeries gave way to the new blast furnaces. Iron, as a result, began to be poured out by the ton, instead of being beaten out in small amounts.

Now a new problem arose. Charcoal became the new hurdle in the path of further development: its amount now proved too small for the large quantities of iron being smelt. Sussex lost its predominance to Sweden and Russia, which supplied timber. Iron became a major factor of trade and war, which brought them into the world economy.

There followed a shortage of wood, which began to be cut out from farther lands. Soon pit coal and coal deposits began to be worked upon, such as in Northumbria, Scotland and Newcastle. Between 1564 and 1634 the annual shipments of coal from Newcastle increased 14 times to half a million tons. Mining went deeper, and along with it, more technical efforts began to be needed. Technologies of metal mines were now being used in the coal mines. They included improved pumps and wooden *railway* (15th–16th centuries), with the latter used for constructing tracks to truck the coal out of the mines.

Coal now became the centre of civilization, in the course of which more and more wood and forests were cut. Now it moved to the coalfields, and here Britain scored over other countries. Civilization got inalienably tied to coal and the coalfields for another 400 years or so. It became possible to change from wood and water-power technology to coal and iron technology as a prelude to the great industrial revolution of the 18th century. The earlier industrial revolution can be called initial or preparatory one, the 'first' industrial revolution of the 16th–17th centuries.[32]

Concentration of production, according to Bernal,[33] was the prime feature of the industrial revolution. Feudal and urban guild production were scattered over vast areas. The new mechanical industry was closely associated with the coalfields from the very beginning. Nearly all the new products were produced in Glasgow, Newcastle, Manchester, Birmingham, etc.

The architects of the industrial revolution were basically artisans, who along with the workers, with their small accumulations, established their place in the face of the merchants of the circulating capital.

All this qualitatively changed with the introduction of the steam engine in production. It brought light and heavy industries together in one stream. The steam engine was a conscious application of science, and thus science played an essential role in the industrial revolution.

The period from 1760 to 1830, particularly from 1770 to 1800, was *decisive in world history*. Those years were marked by the impact of machinery on the society and economy within the framework of the new capitalist industry. They impacted Britain and France, and then the whole of Europe decisively in the coming decades, and fundamentally transformed the life on the continent and in the whole world.

The changes in the sciences were also equally revolutionary: pneumatic revolution, Copernican, Galilean, Newtonian revolutions, power engineering, chemistry, electricity, astronomy, navigation, and so on. At the beginning of the 19th century science became a major element in the productive forces, and began to outlast the social forms of capitalism.

The ideas of science and technology were not always easily and smoothly digested. People played a positive role in France and elsewhere, but having achieved certain things, they turned into *mobs,* which refused to see the scientific reason and turned against scientific discoveries that threatened their established supernatural notions. They could be easily used against new scientific discoveries and technological innovations.

Machine Tool and Iron Age

The opportunities arising from the use of machinery led to the emergence of the machine tool industry. This in turn created a revolution in handicrafts. Going a step further, machines began to be used for making machines too.

The first and the most important was the Maudsley's (1771–1831) lathe machine. It had a slide-rest and screw-cutting lathes. A new worker, the mechanical engineer, emerged. It was made possible by the availability of iron and then of steel. They could be changed to precise shapes using planes, micrometers and screws.

Till then the tool had remained in the control and within the size of the human being. It continued to be hand or/ and foot-operated (as was the initial lathe). Therefore it still remained within the resources of the Ancients. But the steam-hammer of Nasmyth decisively broke down the age-old barrier of the Vulcan's forge: the building of machines became a machine-sized and no longer a man-sized job.[34] Out of this also developed inter-changeability of parts.

The history of engineering reflects a growing interplay and convergence between different branches of production and activities, between commerce and industry, and new means of operation: machinery, engines, materials for new uses. It was the need for more yarn and more cloth that led to the first introduction of textile machinery, for more coal and iron and steel and metals, faster and more efficient transport, and thus for the steam engine as the motive power. The steam engine, as has been mentioned, was first developed for pumping and was adapted next for blowing furnaces and hammering iron and then to supplant the water wheel in driving machinery. Still later it was mounted on a boat or a wagon.

The handicraftsmen tried out and developed ever new devices and absorbed as much science as they could. On their part the scientists learned trades to understand the underlying processes.

The industrial revolution produced ever new inventions and ingenious mechanisms. The constant improvement of the machines and engines, almost entirely of the steam engines, was the notable feature of the period. There were efforts to steadily increase the power of the engine per unit of the weight of fuel or prime cost through detailed improvements in design and improvements.

The new developments split the world of power generation into two halves: the internal combustion engine was to lead to light power units, to the motor vehicle and later to the aeroplane; the steam turbine led to giant ship propulsion and to generation of distributable electrical energy. They were to mark the nature and history of the 20th century.

The *age of iron* arrived, and then of *steel*. Reaumur in his publication of 1722 solved the mystery of steel-making, which was a closely guarded secret since the days of Chalybes. He showed that "steel is iron containing not too much and not too little carbon."[35] He found that he could do it by melting cast and wrought iron together. For some time nobody took notice of his publication.

Throughout the late 18th and the early 19th centuries, production of iron went on at full speed, leaving steel far behind. Improvements in furnaces helped iron throughout the period.

Then came the decisive break. The radical innovation of Bessemer discovered a way of making cast steel on a large scale. In the Bessemer converter, air was blown through melted pig iron, which burnt away the carbon. The carbon in the pig iron acted as fuel and some of its carbon combined with the iron to produce steel. His ingenuity lay in the continuously tilting design of the converter. It produced enough heat to keep the resulting steel in molten form. The method was developed by Henry Bessemer (1813–1898). The Bessemer process revolutionized the whole process of steel making.

Soon after the Bessemer process appeared (1856), another one came into being, known as the open hearth process in the name of Siemens. Temperatures were raised by using spent hot gases to heat the incoming air. Large chunks of steel could be melted. Here Reaumur's process could be used for pig iron, scrap and ore. Since 1867 the open hearth process became a serious rival to the Bessemer.

They both had a serious limitation: they could be used only with pure iron ores. The problem was solved with the introduction of basic lining to absorb the harmful phosphorus. This was done by Gilchrist Thomas in 1867. This invention had not only a practical magnitude but was a thoroughly a scientific achievement. Thomas was a police court clerk but knew precisely the points of innovations needed in the technological developments. Within three years his technical innovations assumed the form of mass scale production. It prepared the ground for industrial research in the next century.

The three factors mentioned above inaugurated the age of steel. It first rapidly displaced wood as engineering structural material, and then the cast iron for rails, ships and guns. Steel was to become the basis for imperialism of the future. Steel helped railways, ships, ports and docks to grow, and to help prepare naval and land warfare.

Iron and Steel

In the field of iron and steel, it was necessary to produce steel on massive scales. This was made possible by the invention of the Bessemer converter in 1856 by Henry Bessemer and its adoption on a commercial scale in 1870. Steel was known earlier too but its massive scales due to the changes in the second half of the 19th century tipped the scales qualitatively. Scientists and industrialists found ways to oxidize iron to make steel, which then revolutionized the railways and machine-making industry.

In addition to the growth of the industries, new means of transport were developed. While the 18th century was that of production, the 19th century was one of communication. Railways and steamships were the new means of transport. The railway was originally the product of coal-mining. An engine was put on the wheels on the rails and it became a locomotive pulling passenger and load car. The railways covered Britain in the 1830s and 1840s, and later spread to the rest of the world.

The mid-19th century was not one of radical technical innovations but of their spread and gradual improvements. The cheap goods now had to be transported and communicated about. Therefore, there was a great need for new and faster transport. It acted as the incentive for the railways and telegraph.

The idea of transforming water into steam and using the pressure to drive a system had constantly been in the minds of scientists and practical people since the 16th century itself. There were repeated experiments and a considerable number of people, who attempted such experiments.

But it was Captain Savery (1650–1715) who succeeded in designing and financing a workable fire-driven pump. Thomas Newcomen of Dartmouth made a more successful and practical engine in 1712, using a piston depressed by condensing steam in a cylinder.

In the meantime, heat began to be an important area of scientific investigations with the gradual spread of industrial activities. Joseph Black in 1754 carried forward the work of Jean Morin (17th century) and others. As a result, theories of specific and latent heat were developed, which came in handy in the development of the steam engine.

The first practical application of the discovery of the latent heat was made by James Watt. He hit upon the idea of making a condenser with the help of Black, while repairing a model Newcomen engine. Watt entered into a partnership with Matthew Boulton, the Birmingham manufacturer. Watt had made a number of other improvements in his model, leading to the more or less final one of a steam engine. With the use of his engine, the products of metals and coal spread over a wide area and became cheaper and more easily available.

By combining flywheel, throttle and centrifugal governor, Watt made an engine which could drive machinery at a steady speed. "This device in itself is the first example of feed-back or *cybernetic* control in industry."[36]

Before, Watt, the steam engines were used only in mines well away from the coalfields. The Newcomen engine was useful only in pumping coalmines.

Still the Watt engine was useful only for mine and factory purposes. It was heavy and used too much coal. Lightness and high power was needed for the *locomotive* engine. The answer lay in high-pressure engine, which gave up condenser and blew out exhaust steam into the air. It began to run on rails, which emanated initially from the coal-pits. A self-taught colliery miner's son George Stephenson solved many details of running on the rail tracks. His most important invention was turning the exhaust steam into funnel steam, providing enough power for the wheels, and getting a speed of 20 miles an hour. In the Rainhill trials of 1829 on the Manchester-Liverpool line, the Rocket took the prize. Four miles from St Helens in Lancashire four locomotives took part in the competition and the 'Rocket' designed by Stephenson came out the best.

Revolutionary Changes in Technology and Application of Sciences in the 18th–19th Centuries

The 18th and 19th centuries were those of revolutionary transformations in the technological base of production, leading to the machines as the main means of production. The period saw a series of new and inter-related inventions. They were not simply the result of discoveries and inventions by the great scientific minds. They were the products of the inherent mechanism, contradictions and the dialectical logic of the technical and technological systems themselves. One led inevitably to another. It would be very interesting to trace the development of, for example, the spinning and weaving machines to illustrate the point. New inventions increased the production of thread, forcing acceleration in the rate and nature of machines. The single individual spinning instruments were brought together in numbers, propelled by increasingly powerful motive forces. The motive parts were at first provided by wind and water, later, after the use of steam, by the steam power/engines, qualitatively transforming the modern base of production. One thing led to another. When spun threads passed ahead of weaving operations in production, changes in weaving resulted. Hand-thrown shuttles were improved due to the invention of the flying shuttle invented by John Kay. Still later, the flying shuttles began to be thrown across by special 'throwers'. Still later, automatic machines helped by steam, diesel and electricity helped the shuttle and the bobbins to acquire even high speeds.

This inherent logic is true of the steel industry too.

The Mill

The development of the machine led inevitably to the emergence of the mill, which represented the modern industrial scene.[37] Certain economic and technical changes in the 18th century led to the development of the machinery and the mill. The technical improvements and innovations constantly responded to the need for increased production. John Lombe learned the secrets of Italian silk spinning machines in Italy itself. He then, with his brother, created a mill in 1717.

The flying shuttle invented by the weaver John Kay in 1733 became widespread after 25 years. Between 1740 and 1770, the consumption of cotton rose by 117 per cent. Consequently, there was a sharp rise in the development of weaving. As a result, there occurred a scarcity of thread. In 1764, James Hargreaves, who was a weaver, developed the spinning jenny. It was a hand-operated spinning wheel in which several threads could be spun at a time.

Almost at this time, in 1767, Thomas Highs, a wool-comber, and in 1768–70 Arkwright the barber, invented the water-frame by using the energy of running water to run spinning wheels. The use of spinning jenny gradually spread among the workers in the home. These two inventions were combined by Crompton into the spinning mule. He was a spinner and a weaver. He combined the two inventions by Arkwright and Hargreaves into the mule jenny in 1779. As a result, spinning mills began to be set up along the waterways.

The first spinning mill run by the steam engine was constructed in Nottingham in 1785. At this time, weaving was lagging behind the abundant production of thread. Cartwright, a pastor, made a mechanical loom the same year. It was put into operation by the end of the century. Simultaneously, technical changes, advances and inventions were taking place in other branches of textiles, like the threshing, carding, rough spinning, bleaching, dyeing, as also in other branches and industries.

As a result of these inventions and developments, a *new form of production, known as the mill,* came into being. It was basically a collection of machines, run on a source of power or energy (water, coal, steam, etc). The central source of power distributed its energy and motive power through the motive mechanisms placed with each machine or group of machines. The steam engine provided the main breakthrough for the whole series of inventions, and changed the very nature of production. It made possible the emergence of fully-formed modern mills, upon which the *modern economy and society* is based. For the first time, the centre of production shifted from the village and the agrarian economy to the city and the industrial system. An *industrial society* now began to take shape.

Spinning mills were built and set up within brick buildings. These buildings used to be some 4 or 5 storey high. They employed several hundred workers. In Derbyshire, in the three Arkwright mills, there were 1150 workers.

Around 1800 there were about 500 steam engines in service in England.

Iron Works

During the early 18th century, the Darbys, ironmasters at Coalbrookdale, produced improved versions of cast iron with mixtures of coal, peat and coal dust with the help of powerful blowers. In the mines, steam-powered atmospheric engines were used to pump out water. In 1735 the Darbys smelted iron with coke. This practice spread to the whole of England by 1760. Huntsmann in Sheffield made cast steel in small quantities.

The use of iron rose by 50 per cent between 1730 and 1760. During this very period, James Watt invented the single-effect steam engine, which was being used by the industry by 1775. In 1776 the first iron rails were produced, which were used in the mine. The first iron bridge was made in 1779, and the first iron boat was floated in 1787, which was an incredible development for many. By the end of the 18th century, the use of the steam engine invented by James Watt became commoner.

Decarburation of cast iron by Henry Cort and Peter Onions was carried out in 1783.

In 1783 itself, Watt invented the double-effect steam engine.

Reasons for Technological Innovations

Here we would like to discuss a very crucial point, and that is about the driving force of innovations and discoveries. The problem can be presented as follows: does the source of innovations lie in the socio-economic conditions or in the technological motion or both? The posing of the question may appear to be mechanical but it has been necessitated by long-drawn discussions and debates among the authors.

Many of them, including J.D. Bernal, tend to argue that the source of innovations and discoveries lie almost or entirely in the socio-economic conditions, without which they would not have developed. For example without certain economic conditions such as the emergence of capital and capitalistic exploitation, no steam engine and such other inventions would have been possible.

On the other hand, there seems to be another extreme view, according to which technological inventions are entirely the result of the development of sciences.

The matter is not so simple, and there seems to be much truth in both the views.

One point seems to have been totally ignored in the course of these debates is the fact that human beings always try to improve their work, reduce burden and difficulties and finish jobs in as little time as possible. This is a very important individual, cultural as well as social factor, along with the others. Since time immemorial, humans have been improving upon the stone implements, tools, means and equipment. One may say that during the stone age, for example, the primitive humans and their society constantly tried, both consciously and without their knowing it, to better facilitate their work and fruits of it, to produce more and better. This tendency and endeavour has not disappeared but only increased. The primitives always tried to better dig out the roots or kill their prey or grow plants better and more. This took centuries and millennia, of course, but it undoubtedly was a constant attempt. The stone implements became smaller and sharper with the passage of time. The same thing happened to the means to kill not only the animals but also human beings.

That is how new implements came into being through the different stages of the Stone Age. It cannot be attributed entirely or even mainly to the social needs and social structure. The social needs contributed undoubtedly, and the need of distribution of produce, for example, also speeded up the process. Still later, the need to produce more from agriculture and still later to store and store better would also accelerate the process. And in the class-divided societies or structures and relations, the needs of exploitation and acceleration and increase of it act as added factor. But they do not replace the internal dialectics of the individuals and the society and of the implements and tools themselves. The tools themselves have their own dialectics, which is a major source of their development and improvement.

We have already discussed certain points in the context of the dialectics of machine development.

A new innovation or discovery in technology or science always forces itself to be worked upon and used in a social and individual manner. Of course, for a major discovery to be used or a major innovation to be implemented, certain social and economic conditions are essential, particularly in the modern-day society. But the point is that the tool continues to evolve on its own, irrespective of its social conditions and demands, even on a purely individual basis or in an individual area. Every individual is always trying to improve the nature and productivity of the tool and/or improve the conditions in which it is worked with.

Therefore, the tool is in constant motion, and that is the secret and source of social motion. Besides, a tool has its own dialectics. A stone tool may be improved in one direction by sharpening it in a particular place and thus become a better tool. But by so doing, the human being only sharpens its internal dialectics. Another area or part of the stone is left behind even more; the distance and difference between the two is increased rather than decreased. This is resolved by making certain other changes, for example, by smoothening a part or area to fashion a better hand-holding area. Thus goes on the dialectical development of the stone implement or the tool.

Such processes are more visible in the implements with several elements or parts, such as with the artisan's work tools and implements. An artisan's work is an ideal object to study the dialectics of the implements, the weaving machine, for example. It has several constituent parts, and each part has endless possibilities for constant improvement. A series of historically evolved weaving systems and tools can be seen throughout the world.

A potter's wheel will always evolve through dialectical solution of problems of speed, width of the wheel, the nature and form the stick that moves it, the way mud is made and used, its amount and so on endlessly.

Of course, it is related with the market or the demand and in case of greater demand, it has to increase its productivity and speed. But even within its own limits, within the limits of the family and the home itself, the potter will continue to improve it.

After all, one improves one's hut and its endless aspects, so as, for example, not allow rain-water to enter it or to get more and better light or in case of the summer season, to get less of it, etc.

Similar things can be seen in the case of cars or such other machines such as steam engines, etc. At first each of the parts of the car or machines like the sewing machines are separate. They originate and evolve separately, each with its own history and social background. For example, the lamp has its own history, the wheels have a long history deep into antiquity with fascinating evolution reaching up to the railways and even airplanes, the seats have their own, and the most important, the engine has its own background, with sources in pre-steam, steam, oil, petrol and other sources of energy as the driving force of the system.

Now each one of these components comes together to be driven by the petrol engine, which is qualitatively a new invention enabling them to be part of a system and driving them as a vehicle or machine. In the course of evolution, they begin to lose their separate identities and histories. They become increasingly merged in one. For example, the car-lamp becomes more tuned to as an inalienable part of the car. It more and more becomes difficult to find a separate lamp; only the bulb can be separate, and now that also is disappearing into the electric and computerized system. These inventions almost go together because of their separate and collective dialectics. A 19th century bulb case and bulb cannot be fitted into the present-day car. It is more a part of the car than a separate object. It is merging into the overall object. Similar is the case with the steering wheel, doors and other parts.

The merger process goes on more deeply in the engine, in which all the parts become one and today almost the whole thing has to be replaced if something goes wrong.

But the car or the stem engine can be used only in particular socio-economic formation, say in an industrial society and not in the primitive stone age. In this sense, an invention or a discovery is a product of a particular social condition.

Both the processes go together supplementing each other.

The work of the artisan is another apt example of development from undifferentiated to differentiated labour processes and of evolution of different parts of an object. Work of the weaver at first proceeds as an individual and family work. His means of labour and production are undifferentiated yet, and are run simultaneously or one by one by an individual. The product, say a piece of cloth, is the product of the unified labour of that particular individual or the family.

In the course of historic development and evolution, each type of labour gets differentiated. Not only spinning, weaving, wrapping etc each get separated and differentiated; each function on the loom gets differentiated. The loom gets extended into a mill, wrapping of the thread, preparing the bobbin, putting the bobbin into the frame, spinning, warp and wafting, taking out the cloth, etc., all become separate specialized jobs. The tool develops accordingly into separate specialized ones. This point is extremely important for the subsequent discussion of the post-industrial production process.

Another important and crucial development is the involvement of a large body of workers in the spinning and weaving processes. Wafting and warping is not only done by a large number of workers but their work becomes more specialized. They are not supposed to be bothered about related processes, which are now done by others. The work of the individual/family is broken up into separate jobs among a whole group of workers, and the group keeps growing as the industrial revolution proceeds. In an assembly plant, each worker has a strictly limited job on the assembly line, down to the fitting of a nut or bolt in the automobile and engineering plant.

It is to run such a complicated specialized production process that the steam engine comes in handy as a driving or propelling source.

Each of these labour processes and each of the tools has its own history, which merges into one common history of the machine, with the tools becoming part of the steam-driven system. A new history begins.

Thus it is that the tool and the machine and parts thereof have their own dialectics and source of development.

The scientific and technological developments in the 18th and 19th centuries are exemplified in the material development of the society as also in the qualitative change in thought and way of life. Science began to grow faster than the economy and occupied a more important position at the end of the period than at the beginning. In the early 18th century it provided a motive force for the industry in the form of the steam engine that was still largely based on traditional techniques. More of practical experience and ingenuity was involved and less of science as such.[38]

Towards the end of the 19th century new and major industries were based entirely on science. At the beginning science learnt more from industry; at the end the existence of industry was based on science.[39]

In the scientific revolution of 16th–17th centuries, little was drawn from science except astronomy and navigation. In the second period a whole range was developed on the basis of science: power, transport, mechanism, chemicals, munitions, etc. The science of the first period was concerned more with the development and use of instruments, such as: telescopes, microscopes, barometers, thermometers etc. In the second period instruments became part of the machines, tools, engines, dynamos, motors, etc. They tended to not just know the nature but to change it.[40]

Science passed on from playing a passive to an active role.

Marx's point: In this regard Karl Marx raises a very interesting point, with the help of other authorities. The employment of machinery presupposes not a scarcity but an abundance of hands. He says: "Only when there is a superfluity of labour powers, does machinery intervene to replace labour."[41]. According to him it is only in the imagination of economists that machinery assists the individual worker. It can only operate with a mass of labourers. "Machinery is not introduced to make up for a shortage of labour power, but to reduce abundantly available labour power to the necessary volume. Only when labour capacity is available in large quantities is machinery introduced."[42]

This is a very important point that needs discussion.

Marx quotes Ravenstone, by contradicting Lauderdale as follows: "Machinery can seldom be applied with success to abridge the labours of an individual; more time would be lost in its construction than would be saved by its application. It is really useful when it acts on great masses, when a single machine can assist the labours of thousands. It is accordingly in the most populous countries where there are most idle men that it is always most abundant. It is not called into action by a scarcity of men but by the facility with which they are brought together."[43] Here Marx makes a comparison between the relationship of an individual to the machinery and the mass of labourers to the machinery. He is obviously referring to the giant industrial machinery created by the industrial revolution and rightly points out that in relation to one individual the machinery would take very long to realize its cost of production. That is why the machinery can stand only in relation to the mass of labour power.

This point cannot be applied as it is to the present-day STR and electronics. The electronics revolution is producing smaller and smaller scales of tools and machinery. Since the trend of the scales of machinery has reversed, the machines are getting smaller and are therefore establishing a one-to-one relation with the individual or are moving in that direction. The mobile is an example of the direct relation of the equipment with the individual. The computers are also becoming individual-friendly. The cost of production and the price of these machines are falling fast. Individual production is getting the upper hand.

It is a new trend in the machine development.

References

1. Henry W. Grady. (*Encyclopedia Britannica,* on 'Cotton and Cotton Industry')
2. Based on *Encyclopedia Britannica,* Section on Cotton, etc.
3. Based on *Encyclopedia Britannica.*
4. From Lewis Paul, in Wikipedia.
5. *Encyclopedia Britannica.*
6. Based on A.L. Morton, *A People's History of England,* Aakar Books, 2014, p. 126.
7. Morton, ibid.
8. Ibid., p. 127.
9. Ibid., p. 128.
10. Ibid.
11. Ibid., pp. 128–29.
12. Ibid., pp. 129–30.
13. Ibid., p. 131.
14. Ibid., p. 132.
15. Ibid., p. 133.
16. Ibid.
17. Ibid., pp. 278–80.
18. Ibid., p. 283.
19. Ibid., p. 284.
20. Ibid., p. 283.
21. Ibid.
22. Ibid.
23. Based on Morton.
24. Based on Morton.
25. See, *Encylopaedia Britannica.*
26. J.D. Bernal, *Science in History* (4 Vols.), Penguin Books, England, 1974, Vol. 2, p. 521.
27. Bernal, Ibid.
28. Ibid.
29. Ibid., p. 523, (Vol 2).
30. Ibid., p. 523.
31. Based on Bernal pp. 412–13.

32. See Bernal pp. 413–14.
33. Ibid. p. 523.
34. Based on Bernal pp. 594–95 (Vol 2).
35. Ibid., p. 596.
36. ibid., p. 582.
37. The following is based mainly on Mechel Beaud, *A History of Capitalism, 1500–2000,* Aakar Books, 2004, pp. 70–74.
38. Based on Bernal, pp. 657–58.
39. Ibid., p. 658.
40. Ibid.
41. Marx and Engels, *CW* 29, p. 88.
42. Ibid.
43. Quoted in Marx-Engels, *CW* 29, pp. 79–80; also in *CW* 28, p. 325; original caps, etc. removed and simplified.

2

Machine and Dialectics of its Development

We have seen from the previous discussions that the machine has its own inherent dialectical logic of development. It is through the operation of this logic and solution of contradictions as and when they arise that the machine undergoes changes, transformations and development, both quantitative as well as qualitative. The job of the industrial revolution is to modify, change, dissolve, create and revolutionize those key points which are crucial for further development.

Industrial revolution creates an increasing number of knotty points and hurdles within the system of the machine. They are resolved in the course of time, and consequently the machine evolves through ever new levels.

What is a machine, first of all? This must be absolutely clear. A 'machine' or the fully developed machinery has three basic or essential components[1]: "All fully developed machinery consists of three essentially different parts, the motor mechanism, the transmitting mechanism, and finally the tool or the working machine."[2]

Here, it needs to be noted that each of the components has its own mechanism of motion, as well as totality of motion in consonance with the other ones. One affects the other. One may go ahead leaving the other behind, which then tries to catch up with it, bringing in its wake necessary changes in its structure, nature and function.

It is also essential to note that the tool is *the most basic component* of the system of the machine, determining ultimately the very nature of the society. It would be interesting to note the transformations in the tools, first in the course of the emergence of the industrial society, and then in the course of the transition from the industrial to the post-industrial one. The tool, in the final analysis, determines these historic shifts.

The motor mechanism puts the whole system in motion. With the industrial revolution it generates its own motive power such as the steam engine, electric and electro-magnetic engine, diesel engine, etc. Earlier it used to get impulses from outside in the form of muscle power or the natural forces like water in the form of water-wheels, windmill, etc.

The transmitting mechanism consists of fly-wheels, shafts, gears, straps, bands, conveyors and so on. The motions are changed, for example, from linear to circular and are spread all over the system.

These two parts basically set the system in motion.

The third, tool or the working machine, is the part with which *the industrial revolution* of the 18th century *began.* It continued to serve as the starting point, whenever a handicraft, or a manufacture is turned into an industry carried on by machinery.[3] Elsewhere[4] Marx says that "The machine ... is the starting point of the industrial revolution..." He further says that it sets in motion a number of similar tools, in contrast to the workman who handles a single tool.

These two are not different starting points of the industrial revolution. They have their own contexts or aspects. The industrial revolution began when the tool went out of the hands of the workman and became part of the machine. But, on this basis, the industrial revolution could not continue beyond a certain point. The machine cannot handle several tools and accessories, unless there is a powerful motor mechanism. This was provided by the steam power revolution and the steam power-driven engine. That really started the industrial revolution on a massive scale. With the industrial revolution, handicrafts and manufactures turned into industry. The interesting and important thing is that they are transformed from being human elements, worked and operated by the humans, into implements of a mechanism, of the machine. This will prove to be a very important point for the subsequent history and for the discussion of the STR on the tools and the machinery.

The transformations take place in two essential ways, although there could be other intermediate variants. One is that the old machine or the system changes as a whole, for example, in case of the handloom which becomes powerloom. All the constituent parts more or less change together. The other path of development is that the constituent parts are fitted gradually into a new frame, as in the case of spindles, mules, needles etc. A needle is operated by hand in the ancient traditional way. Gradually a hand or hand and foot-driven system comes into being *which drives the needle*. Still later, mainly because of the industrial revolution, the needle is fitted onto a machine and is driven by the steam engine as part of a system of machine. This system takes the form of the mill in developed cases. Thus, there is a complete transformation of the base of the production system.

Consequently, a complicated dialectics arises between the tools and the main body or the body proper of the machinery, causing the evolution and development of the machine as a result of the inherent contradictions and conflicts due to one or the other part falling behind the other and trying to catch up with the rest.

The tool thus goes *out of the limits of the human body* and begins a limitless movement through innovations and inventions. Human beings can only operate a limited number of tools in a limited manner; the machinery frees the production of this limit. In Germany, an attempt was made to make the spinner work with two spinning wheels at once, but it failed to work. On the other hand, the jenny, since its very inception, spun with 12–18 spindles. The stocking loom knits with many thousands of needles at once.

The steam engine in itself did not give rise to the industrial revolution. It was the machines that made possible a revolution in the form of the steam engine. The steam engine was invented during the manufacturing period at the close of the 17th century and continued in existence down to the 1780s. The human being instead of working with the tool or the implement on the object begins at a certain point to work as a *motive power* for the whole system ('machine'). Here the machine begins to become independent and in certain senses 'self-acting'. It is not a mere accident that the human being is converted into a motive force: he or she becomes a motive force through convergence of historical necessities/tendencies. It is again through the operation of historical trends and necessities that the human being ceases to be the motive force. *From now onwards he can be replaced by any other force:* wind, water or the steam power.

Increase in the size of the machine and in the number of the machine tools *necessitates a massive mechanism* to drive it. It needs a mightier motive power than that of the human beings or any other. It is interesting to note that horse was used extensively during the infancy of the modern machinery to drive the machine. Water-driven Arkwright's throstle-spinning mill was used during the manufacturing period. Water was not the ideal motive power because it could not be sustained and could not produce its own motive force and could not be increased at will.

It was the invention of James Watt's second and double-acting steam engine that changed things entirely. It was the prime mover that helped run heavy machines and spread machine production. It produced its own force through consumption of coal and water. It was entirely under human control, was mobile, and was the means of force and locomotion that was really urban, making it possible to concentrate production in the towns. The water-driven system could only work in the rural areas where rivers, etc. could be found.

In the specification of the patent of the engine in April 1784 the engine is described as universal and not for any specific purpose. His successors, Boulton and Watt produced in 1851 engines of colossal proportions for the ocean steamers.

As soon as tools had been converted from manual implements of human beings to the implements run by machines, the motor mechanism also needed an independent form. It needed to be emancipated from the restraints of human strength. Consequently, the individual machines disappear into the system of machinery as mere factors in factory production of innumerable machines. Now one motor mechanism drove many machines at the same time. This mechanism grows and controls an increasing number of machines, and thus the transmitting mechanism becomes a rapidly spreading apparatus.

Increase in the size of machines and in the number of tools creates the need for more massive motor mechanism to drive the system. Consequently, a mightier motive power than the human being is needed. Besides, the human is an imperfect instrument for producing uniform motion continuously.

In history motive powers like the horse, water, wind, etc have been in use. But they all clearly had several limitations of their own. Steam power removed those limitations at once.

Having thus traced the evolution of the machine, Marx then proceeds to distinguish the cooperation of a number of machines of one kind from a complex system of machinery. In one case, the product is made entirely by a single machine. It performs all the various operations performed previously by one handicraftsman with his tool. The weaver's loom is one example. In the manufacture of envelopes, one man folded paper with folder, another applied the gum, and the third turned the flap, and so on. Later one single machine could perform all these functions.

At a certain stage of development, modern industry becomes incompatible with the basis provided by handicraft and manufacture. An organized system of machines, to which motion is communicated by the transmitting mechanism from a central automaton, is the most developed form of production by machinery.[5] The isolated machines are replaced by a central and giant mechanical driving force filling the whole of the factory with slow and measured motions breaking out into a fast and furious whirl of countless working organs.

"There were mules and steam engines before there were any labourers, whose exclusive occupation it was to make mules and steam engines."[6] It is like the humans wearing clothes before they became tailors. The various inventions became practical because a considerable number of skilled workers were provided by the manufacturing period. As inventions grew in number and the demand for machinery increased, the machine-making industry grew and split up more and more into independent branches. The division of labour in these manufactures grew rapidly.

Thus "we see in manufacture the immediate technical foundation of modern industry."[7] Manufacture produced machinery by means of which modern industry abolished handicraft and manufacture in those spheres of production which it seized first.

Thus the factory system was raised on an inadequate foundation. When the system attained a certain maturity, it had to root out this old foundation and create a new one corresponding to its nature and methods of production.

"A system of machinery, whether it reposes on the mere cooperation of similar machines, as in weaving, or on a combination of different machines, as in spinning, constitutes in itself a huge automaton, wherever it is driven by a self-acting prime mover."[8] As soon as a machine executes all movements without human help, needing only attendance from him, we have an automatic system susceptible to constant improvements in details.[9]

Thus the automatic system accelerates its motion through its own internal needs. This is an important dialectics of the machine.

"An organized system of machines, to which motion is communicated by the transmitting mechanism from a central automaton, is the most developed form of production by machinery."[10]

This is a key to understand the motion of the machine, which leads further on to a transformation into the modern machine system in the 20th and 21st centuries.

Modern industry was crippled in its development due to its features derived from handicrafts and manufacture, dependence on muscular and physical strength, personal skills, and so on. "Modern industry became technologically incompatible with the basis furnished for it by handicraft and manufacture."[11] It breaks those fetters one by one and reaches new levels.

One is interconnected with the sector of production and of machinery. Spinning by machinery made weaving by machinery a necessity, and both together made mechanical and chemical revolutions, as expressed in bleaching, printing, dyeing, etc.[12]

Machinery in the course of its development, must fully liberate itself from human limits of the worker's labour, and attain unhindered growth. This is achieved in the production of the means of production. "The most essential condition to the production of machines by machines was a prime mover capable of exerting any amount of force, yet under perfect control."[13] Manual implements reappear on a cyclopean scale.[14] "The implements of labour, in the form of machinery, necessitate substitution of natural forces for human force, and the conscious application of science, instead of the rule of thumb."[15]

Science thus enters the production of the means of production as an important and then as the decisive factor. In manufacture, the organization of production is purely subjective, a combination of details labourers; in modern industry, the production system is purely objective, with the labourer as a mere appendage of the material conditions of production.[16]

This objective character imparts an independent motion to the machinery and parts thereof, and makes them subject to and susceptible to the subsequent electronics revolution.

Individual parts of machinery are produced with increasing accuracy, and this constitutes a crucial basis for the future post-industrial revolution, in which accuracy is a crucial factor at every stage.

Each step and constituent part of the industrial production process is worked upon, individually as well as collectively by the electronic and computer revolution, transforming them into computerized software system.

Information is becoming the crucial vehicle for the post-industrial revolution.

References

1. Based mainly on Karl Marx, *Capital,* Vol. I, 1974, Moscow edition, Chapter on 'Machinery and Modern Industry', p. 351 onwards.
2. Marx, ibid., p. 352
3. Marx, ibid., p. 353.
4. Marx, ibid., p. 355.
5. Marx, ibid., p. 360.
6. Marx, p. 361.
7. Marx, ibid.
8. Marx, p. 360.
9. See Marx, ibid.
10. Marx, ibid.
11. Marx, ibid, pp. 361–62.
12. Marx, ibid.
13. Marx, ibid., p. 363.
14. Ibid., p. 364.
15. Ibid.
16. Based on Marx, ibid.

3

Marx's *Grundrisse* and Dissolution of Labour and Production Processes

Grundrisse, an extraordinary work by Karl Marx,[1] is of immense help to unravel the underlying sources of transition in the mode of production from the industrial to the post-industrial. It provides certain key hints to uncover the meaning of STR for machine and tool development, and labour and production processes. The work is more relevant today than ever before. *Grundrisse* brings out the characteristic features of the capitalist mode of production *in the conditions of automation.*

In this chapter, we will study certain key concepts of *Grundrisse* to understand the dissolution of labour and production processes today. It helps us discover the secret of their dissolution, to know why and how exactly it happens. In this light we will try to understand where and how exactly the processes are worked upon by the STR.

It is crucial to remember that Marx was a critic of the political economy of his times. The very title of his book is *Grundrisse* or *Outlines of the Critique of Political Economy.* ('Grundrisse' simply means 'outlines'.) He carries forward the work of Adam Smith and others to critique the workings of capitalist economy and in particular its political economy. He developed and used the labour theory of value to show the inherent contradictions of the capitalist mode of production, and he could thus discover surplus value as the source of exploitation.

But Marx was in no way bound by political economy and its concepts. In *Grundrisse* he analyses the labour process and is able to reach *the very limits* of the capitalist mode of production, where the labour process just transits into a secondary, even unnecessary, process. According to his prediction, *production would proceed without recourse to the labour process*.

This was a great discovery of his, at least in the form of a hypothesis, which is being proved correct today.

The '*work by machine*' concept, replacing the concept of work by labour, changes the entire perspective, with which economists and theoreticians had been working. The mode of production itself is transformed. In that case, in what way will the concept of socialism/communism be modified, what will be the nature of the future society and its structure? Where and how should we place workers, and what will be the nature of the working class, etc? Marx has not given any indications or definite answers to them.

Grundrisse versus *Capital*

It is somewhat strange and even intriguing that certain concepts like the above-mentioned ones are not mentioned at all in Marx's *Das Capital*. It has to be emphasized that while the centre of gravity in *Grundrisse* is, among others, on the later stages of capitalism and on the dissolution of the labour process itself, in the celebrated and far more popular and known work *Capital*, the centre or the subject of analysis is the capitalist mode of production itself. *Grundrisse* tends to tackle the *industrial* mode of production rather than the *capitalist* mode of production. There are various combinations of the two in the latter work. Consequently, it deals more with science and technology.

A few words about *Grundrisse*. A new stage began in the economic work of Karl Marx after the failure of the European revolution of 1848–49. Marx moved to London in the autumn of 1849 and resumed his studies of political economy. The reason, among others, also was that in his opinion, political revolution could not be understood without properly studying the economic base of the society. Until July 1857 Marx collected and studied an enormous wealth of material on economics.

Thus came out the *Outlines of the Critique of Political Economy* or in short *Grundrisse* (*Grundrisse der Kritik der Politischen Oekonomie*). Later on, it became popular simply as the *Grundrisse* ('outlines'), which has seen a revival in the recent years and is the subject of many commentaries and reviews. Volume 28 also contains the *Economic Manuscripts of 1857–58* or the 'first version of Capital'. Thus the volumes 28 and 29 of the *Collected Works* of Marx and Engels (Moscow edition of 1986 and 1987) basically contain the Outlines (*Grundrisse)*, the *Economic Manuscripts* and a few other works.

Grundrisse has become popular and even controversial, particularly because many concepts, passages and expressions are not to be found in the final versions of *Capital*, leading to serious speculations and controversies. There are strong grounds for these controversies.

It is surprising that Marx does not make a detailed evaluation of this question in *Capital*. On the one hand, it is not surprising because he was engaged, so to say, in the laboratory study of commodity production and the related questions, and therefore the above-mentioned problems did not really form part of the study. Yet, on the other hand, it would have helped had he made some sort of important reference to unravelling the processes connected with automation, as he did in his *Grundrisse*. Perhaps, it did not fit in and in those remote times, capitalism did not properly display such tendencies as prominently to draw attention.

Anyhow, the reasons are not fully clear. Had he analysed and mentioned them in *Capital* and some of his other works, much of dogmatism, sloganism and formulaism of subsequent history could have been avoided. The sloganism against capitalism, irrespective of the situation, has done much damage, and *Capital* was used extensively for it. It took the form of ideology and thus diverted far from science and scientific method. Even then, the Marxist movement and theory has left the problems unresolved and thus has let the scientific method and study suffer heavily with the passage of time. The Marxist scientific methodology has itself suffered. Dialectical materialism has increasingly become mechanical materialism and mechanistic method. The questions related with the changing nature of the working class, that of the separation of the labour process from the productive one, the proletariat as the one 'who has nothing to lose but its chains', etc. have become slogans, truisms, and replacements for concrete and dialectical scientific method. Concrete analyses of capitalism are replaced by slogans demanding the downfall of capitalism. This is strange considering that capitalism is a society as normal as any other, and is today showing signs of vigorous growth and development of the productive forces. One therefore cannot urge its 'downfall', whatever that may mean. It should change and evolve, as is happening today, and should be made to change and evolve.

Labour and Production Processes

Here we will examine some of the concepts in the *Grundrisse* and compare them with the results of the present-day electronics revolution. The concepts are of great help to understand the STR and its social impact.

First of all, labour becomes part of the machine production system and then in the course of history after a full cycle of development it goes out of the process and simply disappears. *We cannot escape this conclusion.* Objective scientific facts prove it without doubt. The machine and labour become *opposites* of each other, and then *this opposition disappears through their mutual dissolution.* The productive labour develops to a point where it *negates* itself by dissolving *into* the machine, by becoming superfluous. The sphere or area of production gradually constricts to a point where the productivity of labour is *handed over* to the productivity of the machine.

Marx says precisely this: "Once included into the production process of capital, however, the means of labour passes through a series of metamorphoses until it ends up as the *machine,* or rather as an *automatic system of machinery...* this automation consists of a very large number of mechanical and intellectual organs, with the workers themselves cast in the role of merely conscious members of it."[2]

We inevitably reach the conclusion that the capacity of labour is *biologically and historically limited,* and as such it must at some point in the development of history, hand itself over to the self-acting and more productive automatic systems. Today the latter are represented by STR and ICR, driven by the electronics. This is precisely what the electronics revolution is about.

Working capacities are converted and concentrated into the lifeless machines and expressed as fixed capital. With electronics, they take on far greater freedom and become much more detached because the 'electron' movement is more brain-like and akin to consciousness than to the physical labour processes. Machines and tools are getting identified with the brain processes, something that did not happen during Marx's time.

The object of the machine is not to mediate between the worker and the object. It is not the means of the individual labour. It is labour itself, of the worker, who is a mediating factor. This is a very significant point with far-reaching implications for the present and the future, which needs tracing and discussion. Says Marx: "On the contrary, the worker's activity is posited rather as merely mediating the labour of the machine, its action upon the raw material—he watches over it and guards against obstructions... the machine... possesses a soul of its own in the laws of mechanics, which determine its operations; and to maintain its continuous self-motion it consumes coal, oil etc. as the worker consumes foodstuffs. The activity of the worker, restricted to a mere abstraction of activity, is determined and governed in every respect by the movement of the machinery, not vice versa. Science, which compels the inanimate members of the machinery, by means of their design, to operate purposefully as an automaton, does not exist in the worker's consciousness, but acts upon him through the machine as an alien force, as the force of the machine itself."[3]

This is a very important passage; one is surprised at the extraordinary genius of Karl Marx. He virtually anticipates the basic results of the electronics revolution, wherein the worker and his consciousness are being replaced in their essentials by hardware/software of the computer. Marx interestingly talks here of the '*labour* of the machine'. Today, the electronics revolution is taking over the growing number of labour functions: the 'labour of the machine' is spreading rapidly, proving the abovementioned formulation correct. It is more appropriate today. While the labour of the machine is taking over, the labour of the worker disappears to that extent. This is precisely what is happening today.

The electronics is today creating a system of the *thinking machine,* and in this it is far more and qualitatively advanced than the machines of the industrial revolution.

Secondly, Marx makes a very interesting statement about the '*soul of the machine*' in the form of the laws of mechanics. The machine has self-motion. Today, mechanical laws have been replaced by the laws of the electronics, by extraordinary powers or energy of the forces within the atom and by quantum mechanics. A whole revolution has been unleashed with science as the motive force of history, as the productive and information force. The 'soul' is taking over almost all the conscious functions replacing the traditional machine and its functions. The 'machine' is matching the human being limb for limb. It can even 'murder' the live human beings, as has actually happened in some cases. The 'soul of the machine' has become far more lively and expressive!

Thirdly, the concept of *abstraction* of labour is crucial. We see today that labour works not with the tangible objects but with *their images*. The living labour is restricted and reduced in every respect by the growing electronic machines and the fast-spreading computers and micro-processors. They work with images, particles and waves, and as such, they compete with the human brain and mental labour. The physical labour is simply not needed.

Besides, these images are active elements, and therefore function as bits of consciousness. The images direct the labour/productive and other processes. The 'product' of the industrial revolution, the tangible one, becomes an adjunct of the system of production of the images and information. Labour is rendered superfluous, with information taking over all functions.

The labour/production process is an actual material process converting the object. Image is the opposite of the labour process, reflecting it, replacing it all the while, and usurping its powers and functions, and thus replacing the labour and productive processes. This historic negation results in the dissolution of labour itself.

Any conversion of the productive (tangible) into image-creation is a negation of labour, its very antithesis. Image in turn guides creation of objects.

Therefore, the question arises whether the further evolution of machine accords with the nature of capital? Marx replies that the machine is the most appropriate form of fixed capital. *Further, fixed capital in its use value goes beyond the definition of capital.*

This is very appropriate to the ongoing electronics revolution.

The question consequently arises whether use value and value stand in opposition to each other. Has use value acquired a form to which capital is totally indifferent? In other words, is capital unable to use values generated by the quantum revolution? Is the concept of fixed capital relevant? Is it not jettisoning its tangible forms in favour of the energy forms and getting united with (dissolved into) labour forms? And in this way, is capital not losing its character in production even while maintaining itself in exchange?

The point is that under the impact of the electronics revolution, commodity and capital as also labour, are undergoing fundamental transformations. Capital finds use values useless to itself; the use values by being deprived of value are ceasing to be the source of profit and of capital proper. The use values created by the quantum revolution do not match the nature of capital. It is difficult to keep in place the concept of fixed capital because signals, rays, signs and images do not fit in with it.

The extraordinary increase in the productivity has brought the commodity to the periphery of production and into the sphere of exchange, and thus there is a separation and division between use value and exchange value. To use Marx's expression the machine itself enters and dissolves into the produced commodity, which no more remains a commodity. Production is rendering use value and in particular the exchange value increasingly irrelevant. They are going out of the circuit.

With full development of capital, labour, labour process and means of labour become part and parcel of the production process. And in that case, the production process itself becomes an application of science which instantly transforms into technology. The living labour just becomes a moment of production. As the labour time becomes less and less and disappears as the determinant of value of the commodity, labour loses its importance and value, and it is the science and technology that converts the commodity. This forces, has to force, capital, to lose itself because labour loses itself.

"The value of fixed capital is only reproduced to the extent that it is used up in the production process. If it is not used, fixed capital loses its use value, without its value passing on to the product. Hence the larger the scale on which fixed capital develops… the more *the continuity of the production process* or the continuous flow of reproduction becomes a compelling external condition of the mode of production based upon capital."[4]

"In this respect too, the appropriation of living labour by capital takes on an immediate reality in machinery: on the one hand, it is the analysis and application of mechanical and chemical laws—originating directly from science—that enables the machine to perform the same labour as was previously performed by the same labour. However, the development of machinery takes this course only when large-scale industry has already attained a high level of development and all the sciences have been forced into the service of capital, and when, on the other hand, the machinery already in existence itself affords great resources. At this point, invention becomes a business and the application of science to immediate production itself becomes a factor determining and soliciting science."[5]

"But in the degree in which large-scale industry develops, the creation of wealth becomes *less dependent upon labour time and the quantity of labour employed* than upon the power of the agent set in motion during labour time. And their power—their POWERFUL EFFECTIVENESS—in turn bears no relation to the immediate labour time which their production costs, but depends, rather, upon the general level of development of science and the progress of technology, or on the application of science to technology.."[6]

Marx further says that the real wealth manifests itself, as revealed by large-scale industry, in the immense disproportion between the labour time employed and its product, and similarly in the qualitative disproportion between labour reduced to a pure abstraction and the power of production process which it oversees. Labour no longer appears so much as included itself in the production process, but rather man relates himself to that process as its overseer and regulator.... No longer does the worker interpose a modified natural object as an intermediate element between the object and himself; now he interposes *the natural process,* which he transforms into an industrial one, *as an intermediary* between himself and inorganic nature, which he makes himself master of. *He stands beside the productive process, rather than being its main agent.*"[7]

"Once this transformation has taken place, it is neither the immediate labour performed by man himself nor the time for which he works, but the appropriation of his own general productive power, his comprehension of nature and domination of it by virtue of his being a social entity—in a word the development of the social individual—that appears as the cornerstone of production and wealth. The *theft of alien labour time, which is the basis of the present wealth,* appears to be a miserable foundation compared to this newly developed one, the foundation created by large-scale industry itself. As soon as labour in its immediate form has ceased to be the great source of wealth, labour time ceases and must cease to be its measure, and therefore exchange value [must cease to be the measure] of use value. The *surplus labour of the masses* has ceased to be the condition for the development of general wealth, just as the *non-labour of a few* has ceased to be the condition for the development of the general powers of the human mind. As a result, production based upon exchange value collapses, and the immediate material production process itself is stripped of indigence and antagonism. Free development of individualities, and hence not the reduction of necessary labour time in order to posit surplus labour, but in general the reduction of the necessary labour of society to a minimum, to which then corresponds the artistic, scientific etc. development of individuals, made possible by the time thus set free and the means produced for all of them."[8]

This is one of the most extraordinary passages from Marx, fully applicable to the present-day electronics revolution. It needs application to the contemporary and future technological revolutions and their impact.

This is partly quoted by Mark Poster also but he misses its crucial importance after having taken up the thread initially.[9] Marx clearly states that a stage in the development of fixed capital may reach when labour will cease to be the source of wealth and capital, labour time will then cease to be the measure of wealth and hence of exchange value itself. Thus the development of fixed capital and of large-scale industry returns to itself but on a higher level where it dissolves labour and thus value-creation itself. In this way the old basis of production ceases to exist. No more exchange value and use value with value contained is created.

The labour process separates out of the production process and dissolves itself. The very basis of capitalist mode of production disappears or is dissolved.

The electronics revolution is precisely bringing into being such a situation where labour separates out of the production process and consequently no values are being created any more. The question of the nature of production then needs a separate treatment, which we will do elsewhere.

The following statement is quite relevant today:

"By striving to reduce labour time to a minimum, while, on the other hand, positing labour time as the sole measure and source of wealth, capital itself is a contradiction-in-process. It therefore diminishes labour time in the form of necessary labour time in order to increase it in the form of superfluous labour time; it thus posits superfluous labour time to an increasing degree as a condition for necessary labour time. On the one hand, therefore, it calls into life all the powers of science and nature, and of social combination and social interaction, in order to make the creation of wealth (relatively) independent of the labour time employed for that purpose. On the other hand, it wishes the enormous social forces thus created to be measured by labour time and to confine them within the limits necessary to maintain as value the value already created."[10] The electronics revolution reduces labour time to the barest minimum. All the predictions and observations of Marx come out here as more than true. Today, when labour input is reaching the minimum, the value and price of commodities are sought to be measured in the old, industrial way. Giant MNCs and financial circles seek to maintain prices and values of the commodities at their usual level in order to 'calculate' them so as to garner massive profits which are not due to them at all. Prices and values of every commodity must come down in a drastic way. They are no doubt coming down, yet are sought to be kept high artificially.

"The development of fixed capital shows the degree to which society's general science, KNOWLEDGE, has become an *immediate productive force*, and hence the degree to which the conditions of the social life process itself have been brought under the control of the GENERAL INTELLECT and remoulded according to it."[11]

Here we will have to replace fixed capital with the means growing smaller in the form of electronic gadgets. Today, there is an explosion of science and technology. Science, and technology, have become immediate productive force, replacing labour. They both have not only become the productive force, but much more than that, information force, driving the production and spread of general information. The conditions of social life have been brought under the control of 'general intellect', which includes not only human intellect, not only science, but also the electronic machine systems which act *as intellect.*

Knowledge, information and science mould social structures and their motion. The electronics revolution is dissolving the fixed capital, replacing it with electronics, which are no more creating tools and machines, but the electronic and electromagnetic forces to act as the 'means of production and information'. Science has developed to such a high level that it *no more* needs tangible, fixed means or fixed capital. Electronic signals replace them. Therefore, the transition to immediate productive force is immediate and instant, *without the mediacy of tangible means.* Science itself is an information and productive force.

With the development of electronic and quantum sciences, all the need for industrial and capitalist means of production disappears.

"There is yet another aspect from which the development of fixed capital indicates the degree of development of wealth in general or of the development of capital. The object of production directly aimed at use value, and similarly directly at exchange value, is the product itself, which is intended for consumption. The part of production aimed at the production of fixed capital does not produce immediate objects of enjoyment or immediate exchange values; at least it does not produce immediately realizable exchange values. *So it depends upon the level of productivity already attained—upon a mere part of production time being sufficient for immediate production—that an increasingly large part of production time is employed in producing the means of production."*[12]

This provides a key to the production of the means of production. Here it would be necessary to analyse the STR and point out that this trend has been reversed. The STR has led to a situation where production is losing its primacy; wealth is less connected with the production of means of production, more is produced in less time, with less cost, at an intensified rate. As a result, capital is fast moving into the domains of the production of the consumer goods and proportionately less in the production of means of production.

Now for production, 'a mere part of production time' is no more being used. That mere part is sufficient not only for production but also for information production. Increasingly a larger proportion of 'production' is being used to create the totality of hardware and software, the sources of information systems that overwhelm now the entire tangibility of commodities.

This point needs to be studied in greater detail. The point here is that increasingly less time is being spent on the production of the means of production. This is because the means of production themselves are becoming smaller and information-oriented. As such Marx's prediction regarding growth of large-scale machines has to be modified here. The tools and means of production are produced in an instant due to the electronics revolution. It has become much easier to produce consumer goods and 'immediate objects of enjoyment', practically in no time.

This is being done at no value; no value is being added to the commodities produced and production thus is being sidelined.

"This presupposes that society can wait, can withdraw a large part of the wealth already created both from immediate enjoyment and from production intended for immediate enjoyment, and employ it for labour which is *not immediately productive* (within the material production process itself). For it to be able to do so, productivity and relative excess must already have attained a certain level, and indeed a level directly proportionate to the scale on which circulating capital is transformed into fixed capital. Just as the *amount of relative surplus labour depends upon the productivity of necessary* labour, so the amount of the labour time employed on the production of fixed capital—living labour time as well as objectified—depends upon the *productivity of the labour time intended for the direct production of products.*[13]

Today, due to the STR it is *no more necessary to withdraw capital from consumption to production of fixed capital.* The size of the means of production is becoming smaller, and its industrial nature is being reduced. Consequently, capital goes more and more into non-production and thus into areas *where capital is not being created at all.*

Surplus Product, Surplus Population and Fixed Capital

"*Surplus population* (surplus from this standpoint), like *surplus* production, is a condition for this, i.e. the result of the time employed upon immediate production must be relatively in excess of what is immediately required for the reproduction of the capital employed in these branches of industry. *The less* the immediate yield of *fixed capital,* the less fixed capital engaged in the *immediate production process,* the larger this relative *surplus population and surplus production* must be; i.e. more relative surplus population and surplus is required to build railways, canals, waterworks, telegraphs etc., than to make machinery used in the immediate production process. Hence... the continual over-and underproduction in modern industry reflecting the continual fluctuation and convulsions in the disproportionate—now insufficient, now excessive—transformation of circulating capital into fixed capital.

"The creation of an abundance of DISPOSABLE TIME apart from necessary labour time, for society in general and for each of its members...this creation of non-labour time appears under the conditions of capital, and at all earlier stages, as the creation of not-labour-time, free time, for a few. What capital adds is that it increases the surplus labour time of the masses by all the means of art and science, because its wealth consists directly in its appropriation of surplus labour time; for its direct *aim is value,* not use value."[14]

Here an interesting source of the expansion of the infrastructure is to be discovered. Due to less involvement of fixed capital in the immediate production, larger relative surplus production is made; that only means the population is shifted from making of machinery to building railways etc., and the proportion of population engaged in production is getting reduced due to this process. Today, due to the STR, a massive proportion is precisely being shifted from production to construction of the infrastructure. This is a *historical tendency* of capitalism, *leading it away from capitalism itself.*

"Hence it is INSTRUMENTAL, despite itself, IN CREATING THE MEANS OF SOCIAL DISPOSABLE TIME, of reducing labour time for the whole of society to a declining minimum, and of thus setting free the time of all [members of society] for their own development. But its tendency is always, on the one hand *to create* DISPOSABLE TIME, *and on the other* TO CONVERT IT INTO SURPLUS LABOUR. Yet if it is too successful in the former, it is afflicted with surplus production, and then necessary labour is interrupted, as *no* SURPLUS LABOUR can be utilized *by capital.*"[15]

This again is an extraordinary passage from Marx, particularly in the present context of STR. He has identified a historical tendency of capitalist production which is *actually taking shape* today, and this is one of a post-industrial nature. Marx rightly points out that capitalism has a tendency to reduce the necessary labour to a declining minimum: the tendency applies to the *whole* of society. This is extraordinary, and is a key to understand the transition from the industrial to the post-industrial society. And what is that? If it becomes too successful in creating the disposable time, then surplus labour cannot be used by capital.

And this exactly is what is taking place today.

Further. "The more this contradiction develops, the more obvious it becomes that the growth of the productive forces can no longer be tied to the appropriation of alien SURPLUS LABOUR, and that the working masses must, rather, themselves appropriate their surplus labour. Once they have done so—and DISPOSABLE TIME HAS THEREBY ceased to possess an *antithetical* existence—then, on the other hand, necessary labour time will be measured by the needs of the social individual; and, on the other, society's productive power will develop so rapidly that, although production will now be calculated to provide wealth for all, the DISPOSABLE TIME of all will increase. Then wealth is no longer measured by labour time but by DISPOSABLE TIME. *Labour time as the measure of wealth* posits wealth itself as based upon poverty, and DISPOSABLE TIME only as existing *in and through the opposition to surplus labour time;* or the whole time of the individual is posited as labour time, and he is degraded to a mere labourer, subsumed under labour. *Hence the most developed machinery now compels the labourer to work for a longer time than the savage does, or than the labourer himself did when he was using the simplest, crudest implements.*"[16]

Here, Marx traces and analyses the inner dialectics of the machine development in terms of time. Interestingly he traces the growth of the productive forces out of the necessary time and into the disposable time. The development of the productive forces is a continuous process. They therefore move towards creating disposable time on a larger scale compared to the necessary time. From the ancient times to the present, production tends to be for the whole of society. Marx continues:

"Just as with the development of large-scale industry, the basis on which it rests, appropriation of alien labour time ceases to constitute or create wealth, so, as this development takes place, *immediate labour* as such ceases to be the basis of production. That happens because, on the one hand, immediate labour is transformed into a predominantly overseeing and regulating activity; and also because, on the other hand, the product ceases to be the product of isolated immediate labour, and it is rather the combination of social activity that appears as the producer."[17]

Immediate labour is transformed into an overseeing activity, and at the same time, the product becomes social and ceases to be the product of isolated labour. This is another clue to what is going on now. Due to the development of STR and to the electronic processes, labour does not remain a direct process but an overseeing one, and that means it ceases to be the labour process. At the same time labour becomes social and thus continuously falling in value: the commodities need less and less labour, leading ultimately only to the production of use values, shedding the exchange values.

"...in the production of large-scale industry, we see, on the one hand, that the productive power of the means of labour developed to an automatic process presupposes the subjection of the natural forces to the social intelligence, *and on the other hand, that the labour of the individual in its immediate existence is posited as superseded individual, i.e. as social, labour. Thus the other basis of this mode of production is abolished.*"[18] "In the degree which production directed to the satisfaction of immediate needs becomes more productive, a larger part of production can be directed to satisfy the needs of production itself or to the production of the means of production. In so far as the production of fixed capital aims directly... neither at the production of immediate use values, nor of values required for the immediate reproduction of capital...but aims at the production of means for the creation of value, hence not at value as an immediate object, but at the creation of value,...—the production of value materially posited in the object of production itself as the purpose of production,...—to that extent *capital posits itself as an end-in-itself*—and is active as *capital—in a higher potency in the production of fixed capital than in that of circulating capital.* Therefore in this respect too, the magnitude which fixed capital already possesses, and which its production constitutes in overall production, is the measure of the development of wealth based upon the capitalist mode of production."[19]

These passages provide keys to several points. They show the *increasing distance* of the means of production under capitalism, that is of the fixed capital, from production as such, as it moves away from the 'production of immediate use values', from the immediate production. The more it moves away, the greater its distance from the *capitalist mode of production* itself. This distance is combined with another distance. From the production of value, it moves to the production of the means of production of value.

The problem is that today everything is transformed into circulation and services, and the distance from production is increasing rapidly. The means of production are acquiring higher productivities and therefore fixed capital is getting converted into the means of services and information. Service is a new field encompassing production and distribution, but more importantly the information about them all.

Here and in some other passages, Marx analyses the very *motion* of *the mode of production based upon machines.* The motion has its own logic. It is interesting to note that Marx is analysing the existing mode of production based upon the machine and follows it to its very limits. Marx clearly says: "Thus the other basis of this mode of production is abolished."

Capitalism to Post-Capitalism

This is crucial. The machine goes through a process whereby it gradually takes over the functions of the labourer and renders him/her as an onlooker/overseer. The very source of value creation disappears, leading to several questions, because the very *theft* of alien labour ceases to take place.

The contradiction *inherent* in the capitalist mode of production creates or moves towards its own negation. The modern-day STR has taken the development of fixed capital, of the means of production, to a point of its dissolution. The fixed capital (means of production) has crossed the border-line where values are not produced as values; they were not the purpose *any more* of the production process and since they not the purpose, what takes place is the production of *the image of production* rather than production itself; images are being produced as images ***post**-fixed capital.* The quest for greater profits and for development of the means of production has led capital to produce what is 'not-object', and therefore '*not*-value'. *This development is definitely post-industrial.* Production aims not to produce its own basis: everything turns away from production and into non-production. Every production takes place as, converts immediately into, non-production, that is, as a constant negation of production, as information. Production constantly expresses itself, explains itself, as and in the form of and through, information. Information, meant initially for production, actually turns out to be non-production, even anti-production.

At a certain point in its development, capitalism sheds its industrial form, and is transformed into image, signals and intangible forms, and becomes post-industrial, post-capitalism.

For the first time in the history of social development, production is dethroned as the centre and cause of social motion, and becomes a secondary source of motion. It is no more the main source of dialectics and motion, it does no more drive the society; it more and more shifts to being an end product.

That this tendency is inherent in capital itself is clear in the above-mentioned passages from Marx. Only, that was the industrial age, and Marx went to the very edge of that age in the course of his studies. Today, the electronics revolution completes the process of both capital and labour going out of production and creating a *new sphere* of circulation dominated by information, services and the internet.

In today's context, the electronically mediated information is the means by which production is sought to be increased. Information and not the object, not thing, is the 'object of production' in an increasing number of fields including production itself. But this new 'object', new means of production, that is information, actually turns completely away from production itself and enters the arena of communications and information transmission. *Production of almost every kind is jettisoned.*

Thus, capital and the process of production of capital have many 'weak spots' upon which the information-based new industrial revolution works to dissolve and thus to dissolve production *as such*.

Historic cycle of capital: STR and jettisoning the industrial for the post-industrial. Not Marx's *Capital*.

These ideas from the *Grundrisse* are extraordinary, more so because they emanate from the 19th century. Today they are actually happening. Karl Marx reaches the very pinnacle of intellectual exercise.

Marx presents an invaluable formulation[20] saying that capital increasingly comes out of the sphere of circulation and enters that of production. The whole industrial age has been one of capitalization in and through production.

In fact, capitalization can only take place in the course of production cycles.

Emerging features of post-industrial society: non-production

Today, things are moving in the opposite direction, going beyond production cycles, into the world of information production. Capital is no longer being invested in production but in circulation. It is coming out of production and getting involved in the services, transmission, information and distribution of consumer goods, etc.

From this point of view, capital *can no longer be termed as 'capital' in the strict sense of the term.* It is no more 'capital'. A whole cycle of historical development is getting completed. Production has not only completed in its full cycle covering the entire social (human) development; wealth ('capital') is jettisoning its former form and *re-entering* the sphere of circulation, but *at much higher levels*. Wealth is giving up the form of 'fixed' capital ('fixed property'), *in fact the form of production itself.* Let us remember that capital had begun its journey as a *moving property* or as exchange value. (Exchange value has a whole history, covering almost the entire history of human society except the very beginnings. The humans have always exchanged goods which step by step became established as commodities, reaching the highest form in the capitalist mode of production.)

Now once again, capital is acquiring the form of exchange value, of circulation, but at a higher level. The production form has been given up and circulation (services, market, information etc) has been acquired.

This means capital is being exchanged at a time when the production base is constricting while simultaneously acquiring extraordinarily higher productivities. Consequently, the proportion of capital in production is getting reduced and that in the non-production rapidly increasing. The *production form of capital* is being *jettisoned* due to the scientific and technological revolution.

This is not '*Marx's Capital*'. His capital was the product and base of production. He had followed the transition from circulation to productive capital and the source of surplus capital (value).

Today, the situation is undergoing a change. In the post-industrial society production is disappearing, and information and transmission are becoming the decisive. Consequently, most of the concepts created during the industrial age are getting obsolete. ***At a time when capital is giving up its productive form, it cannot be termed 'capital' in its strict sense.***

This liberation from labour time is the *most significant* liberation of the human being. The human becomes the most important productive force affecting the existing productive forces. Humans themselves become fixed capital as a replacement of the functions of the fixed capital.[21]

This is an *extraordinary statement by Marx* wherein capital leads to self-negation and results thus in the negation of capital and capitalism itself.

This is what Marx has to say:

"The saving of labour time is equivalent to the increase of free time, i.e. time for the full development of the individual, which itself as the greatest productive force, in turn reacts upon the productive power of labour. From the standpoint of the immediate production process, it can be considered as the production of *fixed capital,* this fixed capital BEING MAN HIMSELF."[22]

"It is self-evident that immediate labour time itself cannot remain in abstract antithesis to free time, as it appears to do from the standpoint of bourgeois political economy.

Labour time cannot become a game...Free time—which is both leisure and time for higher activity—has naturally transformed its possessor into another subject; and it is then as this other subject that he enters into the immediate production process." This process is both discipline with respect to the developing human being, and material and experimental science with respect to the developed human being whose mind is the repository of the accumulated knowledge of society.[23]

"Just as the system of bourgeois political economy unfolds to us only gradually, so also does its negation of itself, which is its ultimate result. At this point we shall be concerned with the immediate production process. If we consider bourgeois society in the round, it is always society itself, i.e. man himself in his social relations, that appears as the final result of the social productive process. Everything that has a solid form, like the product, etc., appears merely as a moment, a *vanishing* moment in this movement. Even the immediate production process itself appears here merely as a moment. The conditions and objectifications of that process are themselves, to an equal degree, moments of it, and it is only individuals that appear as its subjects; yet individuals in relation to one another, which they reproduce just as much as they produce them anew. Their own continuous process of movements, in which they renew themselves to just the same extent as they renew the world of wealth which they create."[24]

The creation or emergence of moments really become moments with the electronic revolution, where **everything**, literally, becomes momentary. What this transformation does is to convert *everything,* every process, into a 'vanishing moment'. This is possible only with technologies based on electronics. Electronics has the capacity to convert every material, objective process/thing into electronic signals or the tiniest symbol, and thus create not only a momentary image but images into endless divisions of that moment. It is a technology which has the capacity to convert a thing into the endless series of expressions as images in order to better explain it/them. The subject, as a result, assumes the nature of a transitory or temporary subject.

These are extremely significant passages from Marx, and they do not fit in with the usual Marxist impressions. The society in the last analysis is driven by production, but as the production develops, its time and place and importance is reduced and that of the individuals increase. In the context of the social being, production and the associated things become just a moment. What is most interesting and shockingly pleasant is his characterization of production and solid forms of objects as vanishing moments. This is extraordinary for its time, and is fully applicable today. This is exactly what is happening: the electronics revolution is rendering production as the vanishing moment.

Marx then quotes Robert Owen to the effect that workers and capitalists develop in *real terms only with the large-scale production.*[25] This implies that these classes begin to disappear with the dissolution of large-scale production in the course of STR.

Here is another important passage from Karl Marx: "In fixed capital, capital exists, physically too, not merely as objectified labour intended to serve as means of new labour, but as value whose use value is the production of new values. The existence of fixed capital is therefore above all its existence as productive capital. Hence the level of development already attained by the mode of production based on capital—or the extent to which capital itself is already presupposed, has presupposed itself, as the condition for its own production—is measured by the existing volume of fixed capital. Not only by its quantity, but by its quality as well."[26]

"Finally: In fixed capital, the social productive power of labour is posited as a property inherent in capital; the SCIENTIFIC POWER as well as the combination of social forces within the production process and finally the skill translated from immediate labour into machines, into lifeless productive power."[27]

Production Ceases to be 'Production': Emergence of a Post-Production Society

The new technology has shifted the basis, nature and method of production to such an extent that its very nature has changed fundamentally: *production ceases to be 'production'*. And that is the biggest break, the leap, the drastic change that has taken place during the STR. Production now equals *production of information*; that is not what was meant to be, but that is what exactly has happened. And this has completely transformed the nature of production, which is now *led by* information.

Things are now upside down. Production of information, information about production, overthrows production as production, the very engine of society and of social development. The means becomes the aim, imperceptibly, unconsciously, unknowingly, known so late that it now needs extensive research to understand the process of the entire transformation.

Henceforward, it is social development caused and fashioned by information and its production. A new era of social development has begun, increasingly caused by production of information. It is moving towards a post-production society.

A post-production society does not depend on production for its existence and growth; it is liberated from production, its greatest liberation. The aim of the society now is to create as much information as possible. Every individual tries to produce and collect an increasing range of information. Production is no more the main concern of society; it has now become a by-product, as natural by-product as any.

Social relations and structures are being re-organised around information, with, of course, heavy dose and survival of the industrial age. Communication between human beings through electronic means has become the main activity of the individual and the society. Thus society has begun a new history on an entirely different basis. It is a new beginning, on qualitatively different basis from what society based its development upon, so far.

Industrial society has classes, state, government, production, distribution, nation, economics, politics, groups and so on, organized around industrial production.

The post-production society has groups, communities, new workers and worker-intellectuals, porous state, weakening of national borders and nations, electronic media taking over functions of government and parties, domination of information, struggles around immediate solution of concrete problems, individuals and society organized around information, loss of place for production, universalisation of democracy, new direction or directions for democracy as the way of life for humans, etc.

Marx's analyses, mentioned above, reflect a process of change similar in some key elements to the one described here. But with him, the nature of the means of production, of the machine is still industrial, quite different from what it is today. Therefore, he has a historical limit, a limit determined by the nature of the industrial age. Marx goes to the very edge of his age, tracing and foreseeing many future trends to their very possible limits.

Transformation of Mode of Production into Mode of Information

Information about production creates growing distances from production itself, and grows and congeals, solidifies into a new mode, *the mode of information,* unexpectedly for production and for the theories based upon it. Production is mediated through information and information-production. All our basic theories were based upon production and its elements. Our consciousness was derived from that reality. But now consciousness is created directly from images and not from solid objects; consciousness is created from the consciousness-like reflection of the solids. It is this that drives production, this information-based consciousness. Therefore, production is indirect, not direct.

The very basis of society is changed. We have to re-work everything, including the future history which will not be based upon 'material' production but upon the production of images.

The questions related with value, work, labour and labour process will have to be re-studied from this vantage point. For example, information will not be, cannot be producing values and commodities. Information is something that does not require labour and even time. It is instant. Therefore, the category of the 'commodity' needs re-examination for its being 'non-commodity'. We are not producing values; we are producing *commands,* which themselves are becoming automatic and instant.

For example, let us examine and re-examine this passage from Marx: "We have previously noted that the productive power (fixed capital) only imparts value—because it only possesses value—in so far as it is itself produced, is itself a certain quantity of objectified labour time."[28]

The passage should be examined from the viewpoint of a comparison of Marx's time with the present-day STR. Marx identifies productive power with the 'fixed capital', which is a certain quantity of 'objectified labour time'. In other words, fixed capital is the product of production process, and has the power to produce. The fixed capital can be 'un-fixed' if it is not the objectified labour power, that is, no labour is required to produce it. This can happen only under the STR, *where no labour is actually required to produce a commodity,* with the labourer standing 'beside' and not within the labour and production processes. And as there is no labour power and labour time, the object produced by information only possesses non-value or has no value. It is futile to convert non-value into value. The base of the fixed capital disappears, and capital and production lose their original character. What is objectified? Not labour time or power but image, and images are produced in no time and in a million copies! It is as simple as that.

Does the machinery requiring production of images need labour and has value? It does. But in the course of time all that is realized completely, at the turn of the change. Soon it is cancelled out and further development does not require any labour and labour time.

Here is another very crucial passage from Marx:

"In *fixed capital,* capital exists, physically too, not merely as objectified labour intended to serve as the means of new labour, but as value whose use value is the production of new values....the level of development already attained by the mode of production based on capital...is measured by the existing volume of fixed capital. Not only by its quantity, but by its quality as well." "Finally: In *fixed capital,* the social productive power of labour is posited as a property inherent in capital: *the* SCIENTIFIC POWER *as well as the combination of social forces within the production process, and finally the skill translated from immediate labour into machines.* In circulating capital, on the other hand, it is the exchange of labours, of the various branches of industry, their intermeshing and formation of a system, the coexistence of productive labour, that appears as the *property of capital.*"[29]

These lines from Marx provide several clues to the post-industrial nature of the new productive forces. First of all, the nature of fixed capital is to produce new values. The latest productive forces are more capable than ever before to produce new values *without recourse* to labour, and therefore the new values are without value proper. *The new productive forces do not produce value at all.*

Besides, there is the important point of the productive forces being the scientific power. Today, this scientific power is becoming the dominant factor of social development, leaving behind the 'social combination of forces'.

Thirdly, the immediate labour is being transformed into machines, into 'lifeless' productive power. It is lifeless, yet it is productive power. It is clearly a transition from live labour to the 'value'-producing automatic system in the form of the electronics-driven technological revolution, that jettisons labour, and thus the production process becomes the information-driven process. It is a technological revolution of social nature.

Is a merger of fixed and circulating capitals taking place today? Is the electronics and electronically mediated communication a form of this merger and thus of dissolution of capital as productive? The answer can only be in the affirmative. It is a new kind of 'capital' which reduces production as a **mere** function of information processing. Circulation being instant, production completely gets transformed into a post-industrial process, wherein information plays a dominant role. Production also is becoming **instant**. 3-D printing, for example, has this potential.

Therefore, production as such ceases to be the driving force of social development.

"If valuable machinery were employed to make a small amount of products, it would not be operating as a productive force, but would render the product infinitely more costly than if it had been produced without the aid of the machinery. Machinery produces surplus value, not because it itself possesses value—for this is simply replaced—but only because it increases relative surplus time, or diminishes necessary labour time. Hence, in the proportion in which the volume of machinery employed increases, the amount of products must increase and the living labour employed must relatively decline. *The smaller the value of the fixed capital in relation to its effectiveness, the more does it correspond to its purpose*. All non-necessary fixed capital appears as 'overhead costs of production', just as do all unnecessary circulation costs. If capital could possess machinery without expending labour on it, capital would raise the productive power of labour and diminish necessary labour, without having to buy labour. Hence, the value of fixed capital is never an end in itself in the production of labour."[30]

This is exactly what is happening during the STR today in the following manner:

- necessary labour time is being diminished to the barest minimum;
- living labour being employed is decreasing, even replaced entirely;
- most important: the value and the size of the fixed capital are decreasing very rapidly.

Today, we are going through a historic phase wherein the *size* of the means of production, apparatus, equipment, etc. is reducing fast, in some cases even moving towards *miniaturization*. This is a very important and crucial point. It is on the size and the tendency of the size to grow or reduce that the nature of society, its classes, their nature, the form and structure of the state and government, the concept of nation and country, the dissolution of the individual into the class and his/her crystallization as an individual, the nature of democracy, nature of socialism, nature of the industrial production and industrial society, the state of capitalism, etc. depend. The size and the nature of the tool/machine are crucial to the speed and direction of social development.

In such a situation and scenario, in the midst of such a motion, it is impossible to act in an industrial way and to talk of industrial production. This is one of the basic dilemmas of the modern phase of human development. It is, at this point torn between two most major revolutions in human history. The giant industrial revolution put human society on the machine and urban basis, run by physical and mental labour, in which increasing human functions were handed over to the machine. This transference is important: human being did not simply use the means and the tool; he/she began to operate the tool and the tool-system as part and parcel of the machine system, because the tool became a part of the machine. It was a giant step into the future.

The other, present, revolution is transferring all the human functions, including the mental and logical ones, to the computer and the software. This is a revolution of a higher order. It involves creation of parallel 'humans'. The tools and machines are disappearing or are becoming temporary and transient. The human consciousness created till and in the industrial revolution is being handed over to the computerized system. Thus this system is becoming part and parcel of the human biological and social system. By so doing the human being is being thrown ahead far into the future, as if by a sling shot. The human is no more dependent upon the machine and the tool, is liberated from them almost entirely, and is making them a natural part of its own existence through necessary technological and scientific changes. In future the human will be inseparable from mechanical, electronic, bio-electronic, nano and other systems and will add those to its own being. The human being in that case will stand redefined.

We are living with smaller tools and machines with far greater productivity. *This constitutes a major new feature of the post-industrial society*. It is impossible to pose any problem without first recognizing the fact of ours being a post-industrial society.

It is also a distributive society, wherein the social structures are created according to the needs of and in order to facilitate distribution and not production. This is increasingly becoming clearer from the rapidly constricting productive base.

At the same time, we have to look at the new features of circulation. The skill is translated into lifeless productive power. Not only this; the skill is getting converted into something else: into skills of distribution, services, information, transmission, etc. Thus the skill is coming out of the bounds of production and acquiring endless other forms, thanks to ICR and STR. Abstract labour can be converted into any image possible (and into what was till now impossible).

The Future: Instant Conversions

Any object and any image can be converted into any other, and *it is no more necessary to go through 'production'*: this is the future, a future wherein *instant conversions* will replace the process of production. The conversions can be made into endless copies and re-converted into new objects of use or admiration. The inventions in the field of 3-D printers, distant production, robots, computerized production, brain-computer interface, usage of nanotechnology, etc. bear this out. The sphere of circulation has acquired *new meaning*. It is today an area of endless conversions and dissemination of images. These images are almost enough for us to convert them into the objects of use. *Thus anything can be made from anything else and from any image*. The image can be used as templates or commands to create a new or desired object. Manipulations of tangible objects, molecules, atoms, sub-atomic particles and forces have opened out endless possibilities for us to create new things and processes in future. It will virtually be a manipulation of production and the image, particularly at the micro and sub-atomic level.

There can be no doubt now that today we live in an age of 'instant' production, 'instant' labour and most importantly instant information. It is the last one that determines the nature of the present era.

We are moving towards production of commodities which are use values only and not really commodities.

Electronics Revolution, Abstract and Concrete Labour

Scientific and technological revolution (STR) is operating directly upon the labour process and is *dissolving it*. It would be interesting to see how the interaction and dissolution are taking place. The STR is leading to conversion and merger of various kinds of labour, that is, of the concrete labour. It is through and in the images that the products of labour are being converted. That means 'concrete labour' is converted into images, while 'abstract labour' into signals/language of the process. Both work simultaneously. The language of the computer or the software is the equivalent of 'abstract labour'. It does not matter what is constituted of it: it can constitute an image, photo, video, still picture, words and sentences, etc. Abstract labour is dissolved (converted) into binary language of the software. It then transmits its instructions to the processes concerned.

At the same time, software language always constitutes something; it cannot work in abstract. The result is the concrete forms and images.

These processes then rapidly *recede from* the actual labour process. Therefore, there is a *vanishing* relation with labour and the labour process, as the system becomes automatic and electronically driven. But the particularity of this automation is qualitatively different. This labour takes it away from actual labour. Computer language is involved in this process, which guides both human labour as well as the material processes of production. The computer thus takes over increasingly human functions of guidance and labour. In fact, it first takes away the labour process and then and at the same time the guidance. In other words, the functions of the human brain are being taken over by the electronics system in the course of production.

This disappearance of the labour process is actually a unification, an identity of electronics and brain functions.

Thus, labour, and the functions discharged by labour, are being shifted to/are being taken over by the machine. The labour dissolves. With this, dissolves the hitherto created and existing society, to begin its further development anew.

In the relation between our brain and the computer, labour tends to be abstract and superfluous.

Self-motion of information: dissolution of production into information

We have to take up the thread from two ends to trace the development of fixed capital and of electronic means of production.

First, we should trace the development of large-scale production ('fixed capital').

Second, we have to trace the emergence and development of production based on the electronics revolution or the electronic means of production.

It is clear that the industrial means of production *have reached their largest and the highest scales ever*. Thus the very limit of the industrial revolution has been reached. Massive plants and industries, giant production centres, the so-called infrastructures, and such other centres of production have not only reached their largest ever scales but also in many cases have acquired full automation even without the intervention of the electronics. Giant textile mills, engineering works, paper production, iron and steel works and so on have in their most advanced stage been automated.

When we use the term 'fixed capital', it essentially refers to the solid, tangible, large-sized, large-scale machinery and factories. Hence the word 'fixed' capital. They are the products of the industrial revolution; they are the 'industrial' means of production. It is around the *industrial* means of production alone that the industrial and capitalist mode of production (and capital) is built up. This mode of production naturally contains a certain kind of relations of production.

These relations of production begin to be under stress and take on a different nature with information becoming the dominant factor in fashioning means, tools and medium of production. While information is sought to be used as a means of production, it more and more *ceases* to be so: the more you use information as the means of production, the more it tends to disappear as such. Simultaneously it appears as the means of non-production and dissemination. It gets converted into means of information, leading to the emergence of the mode of information.

Any further development of industrial means of production can only take place in the direction of and with the participation of information. For further development, the machine is equipped with microprocessors, computers and such other electronic devices, which necessarily convert all the processes into information. The production process automatically keeps converting into the information processing process.

With this development the mode of production is converted into the mode of information. It is difficult for fixed capital to sustain itself as fixed capital; inroads are made into it by information. A new mode takes shape.

The separation of the labour process from the production process has already become operational in these industries, which have consequently begun to *lose* their capitalist nature. The fixed capital in industries is also losing its basic character, and as such can no more be called fixed capital. This capital is getting automated and self-acting through the introduction of electronics. Fixed capital is becoming the carrier of information, and thus is losing its centrality in production. Production is being rendered the nature of information production. Consequently, their motion towards bigger scales has been reversed towards smaller scales.

Besides, the fixed capital is no more 'fixed': it is amorphous, dissolute, smaller and smaller, is in the form of particles and waves, etc. There cannot be any fixed capital, and therefore any tangible capitalism.

Electronics is deeply impacting the scales of fixed capital, downsizing it. Smaller and smaller tools, machines and means of production are emerging.

Due to the dissolution of the labour process as well as of production process, the labourer is set free as non-labourer, converting him/her into an observer. Thus we already have a mass of labourers who are, strictly speaking, non-labourers. The labour process is undergoing a serious and historical process of dissolution *for the first time in human history.*

Thus, the capitalist *mode of production* is seriously undermined by internal contradictions. It is becoming something else. It was meant to be augmented by information, but has been superceded by it. It has been undermined by the same inherent logic that had so far propelled its development.

This process is seriously limited or slowed down, restricted, by the existing social, political and economic structures. The superstructure of the society does not easily reflect these new tendencies displayed by the capitalist/machine mode of production. The social structures fail to reflect the mode of information properly; they reflect it in a distorted, *ideological* manner.

It has also to be remembered that similar tendencies are displayed by the 'socialist societies', if one can refer to them as so. They too are basically industrial societies. Thus now the capitalist (as well as socialist) mode of production is crossed by the industrial mode of production, which in turn is being negated by the information mode.

The second aspect is the emergence of the electronics revolution from within the industrial society. It is interesting to note that the electronics revolution is something antithetical to the industrial revolution, through whose negation it has evolved. The STR is undoubtedly an unexpected development, and stands in opposition to the industrial revolution in every way. It, the STR, is basically a product of the emergence/unleashing of the atomic and sub-atomic processes within the industrial domain.

The electrons have become messengers of information.

So when we talk of the electronics revolution, we refer and have to refer to the rapid motions of particles and forces inside the atom being transformed into productive and information forces. A new driving force of production comes into being in the form of information generated as instant pulses of energy and particles. It is this that is being put to use in the present-day production and information systems.

The computer not only controls the signs and symbols, words and numbers, but through them, the machine itself by producing and regulating information. Thus information enters as the increasingly decisive factor in production and in the evolution of society itself.

In the course of automation, the labour process separates out of fixed capital. In the process of separation, abstract labour no more takes place and therefore is no more the source of exchange value. This separation is not so much related to the *nature of the social system as to the nature of fixed capital* as a product of the industrial revolution. Quite often the separation may also take the form of alienation. The replacement of capitalist ownership by collective ownership in the form of the state does not bring about any *basic* change in the position of the owner of labour power.

The owner of labour power remains as such even within the collective and socialist ownership and faces the same problems as those under the capitalist mode of production. Its relation with the rest of the society and with the mode of production remains as it is. It has to spend itself in the course of production and has to run parallel with and as part of the production process. Socialism does not bring any separation of the labour process from the production process, nor its dissolution. Socialism brings about a change in the *ownership* of the means of production and in the nature of *distribution*. The nature of ownership accords with the industrial nature of the means of production, more particularly with the large-scale fixed 'capital' or machinery.

Yet, labour power and labour process remain an independent domain, which will dissolve only when a society of abundance or 'communism' arrives. In the society of abundance labour will become an accidental form of activity and *only to the extent* that the society and the individual need it. It is then transformed into a source of use value only and not of exchange value.

All these linkages of industrial logic will drastically change when electronics and computerization grips the socialist society or the society of equality. A society of equality based on electronics will be quite different from an industrial socialist society.

A drastic change in the mode of production deeply affects fixed capital, the production process and labour process. This separation and dissolution of the labour process depends on the nature of the industrial revolution which now converts into electronics and the computer revolution.

It was the industrial revolution which gave birth to labour power and labour process in their purity. It is the replacement of industrial processes by non-or post-industrial processes/ revolution that causes labour process and therefore labour power to dissolve.

The dissolution of the labour process continues till technology loses or jettisons its industrial nature. An analysis of capitalist and socialist modes of production shows that the nature of labour and labour process remains the same. *From this point of view,* there is no difference between these two modes. In this context we have rather to talk of *the industrial mode of production.*

Collective ownership in itself does not eliminate the division between necessary and surplus labour time. The production of surplus and surplus product from surplus labour power continues to take place. Social equality and justice, and social good can be established to an extent but only in the social domain. It will largely be a combination of the subjective act and objective necessities, including the large scales of means of production, which favour collective ownership.

Today we can discern the beginning of the end of the industrial age and its replacement by the post-industrial mode of production. This fact modifies the nature and features of future socialism.

Karl Marx says at one place[31] that capital crystallized out of circulation and entered the sphere of production. In the course of time, capital became part of the means of production giving rise to the capitalist mode of production.

Today, capital is *jettisoning/ giving up* its fixed and tangible form. Capital is crystallizing out of the production form and is getting the information/services form, which partially combines the circulation form. The cycle is getting complete, but at a higher level: capital is once again getting transformed into circulatory wealth, capital and values. *It is in the process of ceasing to be capital.*

Proportion of capital in production is getting reduced and that in circulation/services is increasing. The process is based on the higher levels of science and technology and their post-industrial usage. Capital is giving up its productive form; thus *it is not capital in the strict sense of the term any more.*

This is not the capital of *Capital* of Karl Marx. In Marx, capital is mainly and characteristically in production, a product of production, capital produces production, is its production. Marx analysed transition to productive capital, and consequently of labour power and surplus value and exploitation. That is how commodity production was carried on. *Surplus value is the product of production and production alone.*

This process is undergoing a qualitative change today.

The electronics or the post-industrial revolution based on STR has the capacity to convert every tangible and solid object and process into signals and images. It is in this respect very near, almost identical with, the mental and consciousness-related processes. It is like reflection of the material world on the brain, which converts them into images. Thus revolution in production is actually turning out to be *dissolution* of production. It is a revolution into image. In this new revolution one must create the image of the thing and only then the object. Image creation is the chief feature of the new revolution, a negation of the creation of solid objects. Thus it is a double negation. It is through separation from the object, through creation of the opposite of the object or the 'job', that the object is created. Though information (image) is supposed to serve and enhance production, it is actually converting production into a secondary process, a byproduct and a side result. Image creation is becoming the main purpose of production; production is getting converted into its opposite. Only then the image again gets converted into product (production). Thus the opposite of production is dominating the whole world of the mode of production, reducing it to a mere moment of social development. Non-production is the dominating and driving production, with instant communication overcoming production.

Objectification is the denial (negation) of the object into its image form to create it anew. Image instead of helping the product actually directs and guides it. Image and the world of images have the capacity to pre-empt production by producing in the world of information (virtual reality) the whole of production, which then selectively gives shape according to the needs of society, while the rest of the images and information is surplus accumulation of little use and to be used whenever needed. Wastage of images is no wastage. It is like the cameras and their images from out in the space. An endless number of images are produced from the space, with infinitesimally small amount used, if at all. The rest is floating as the brain of the earth, never to be known or used.

Negation as assertion is the philosophy and practice of the electronics revolution.

Human beings for the first time have separated themselves from the material world in order to create the material world. Information and consciousness play a central role in foreseeing and then creating the tangibles. But the tangibles are created through the intangibles. Even the solid key-board has disappeared, re-emerging as and in the form of software, as its own momentary representation. The unreal must be brought to the fore to drive the real. It is like invoking the images to drive the material forces. This is because electronic signals as the carrier of information *manipulate* material structures as in chemistry and physics. We have the examples of nano-carbon, etc. in which even the atoms can be moved at will.

This is because of handing over of the mental processes to the machines, the very essence of the information revolution.

Marx says, "...the means of labour in the strict sense serves only within production and for production, and has no other value."[32] This is a statement of great significance, helping us to understand certain key points in the STR and dissolution of the labour process. Outside production, labour has no value at all. This is a key development today.

Since the value of labour is now dissolved, it is replaced by that of the scientific and technological revolution. *We are compelled to reach this conclusion* because there can be no other source of production. And this forces us *to fundamentally amend and change the conclusions* of Marx's *Capital.*

We are also compelled to reach the conclusion that labour is replaced by instant electronic, light etc. signals, which cannot have a value. They 'are and are not'. Rays and signals replace the means of production and tools, and they have the quality of instant conversion into the tangibles and the intangibles. It is very near the functions of the brain and consciousness. There can be no doubt at all that we have come out of the tangible demarcated limits of production and have entered into a world of unlimited and intangible realm of the images and information.

The information revolution is *an anti-production revolution* which upsets the mode of production and thus the very history of society. The tools are for the first time converted into information. As soon as we use rays and signals as tools, they act as carriers of information rather than as tools of production. Therefore, production itself is carried as and in the form of information. ***The history of society begins anew.***

Information transmission is not magic or a figment of our imagination; it is a particular configuration of particles and waves converted into both computer and human languages. These configurations and programs presuppose precise productive and other activities and their results. They are production in advance, an anticipation of production. Information/signals presuppose their opposite, which is the production. The polar opposites are exchanged, and the pole of information now dominates mainly because of speed (time) and absence (superfluity) of space. Space is unimportant in production-less production. Human productive activity for the first time breaks out of *the limits of time and space.* Therefore it is not production in the strict sense of term. Production gets included, subsumed, within information, within the time existence and therefore cannot really exist. To exist, to serve as production and to serve production itself, time must be made to slow down, and be limited within the space. This is done by a series of manoeuvres leading ultimately to the conversion of information back into production, which actually is an attempt to become a natural force. It is a conflict between the natural and the unnatural, which decides the motion and direction of the human being.

Production is converted into moments of information, which now reproduces the human society and the individuals in innumerable images. The order of things is reversed. The purpose of information transmission goes far beyond production; now it reproduces society endless times in order to provide its changing identity. Information keeps society alive.

Does Capital Exist? Information and Consciousness

Information becoming a factor of production changes the entire human history, almost beginning it anew. The moment information becomes a factor of production, the production starts its journey towards being non-production. This is a peculiar turn of history, *a non-physical one*. Information has to do with consciousness, and it emanates into production from the use of non-natural forces. So far, history and production have been built upon and developed on tangible productive forces, using naturally-occurring materials. Thus the use of a particular type of material is also important as shown by human history and the turn in it. Use of tangible materials kept it within the confines of the body. Use of non-natural forces take it out of the body and into the consciousness. Information equals consciousness or the beginning of it. The brain is conscious being, the consciousness, and therefore once it enters production, production itself is disrupted into non-production as the driving force of humans. Now we have to interpret history and economy in terms of consciousness as represented by information, and therefore society moves out of the mode of production. Consciousness/ brain/information drive the machines towards non-machines, towards their dissolution. A system driven by consciousness (information) cannot be production because information generates the tangibles increasingly and only as by-products. Consciousness/ information can lead only to the production of the images of production which then are copied into the tangible use-values. The tangible objects, which were earlier the products of labour, now are *products of images* generated by the mode of information. Thus images drive human society and economic activity. Information and images do not have measurable values, and thus one has to keep *using the past,* that is, old methods of computing the values which are not really measures.

The information revolution signifies the collapse of the hardware, of the machine itself.

References

1. Karl Marx and Frederick Engels, *Collected Works (CW),* Volumes 28 and 29, Progress Publishers, Moscow, 1986, 1987.
2. Karl Marx, *C.W.,* Volume 29, p. 82, first two emphases original; underline added.)
3. Ibid., pp. 82–83, underline added.
4. Ibid., p. 89.
5. Ibid., pp. 89–90.
6. Ibid., p. 90, italics added; caps in the original.

7. Ibid., p. 91. Both the italics and the underline added.
8. Ibid., p. 91; italics in the original; underline and bold emphases added.
9. Mark Poster, See his *Mode of Information,* Polity Press, 1990.
10. Marx, Vol. 29, pp. 91–92.
11. Ibid., p. 92, all the emphases in the original.
12. Ibid., pp. 92–93, emphasis in the original.
13. Ibid., p. 93, emphasis in the original.
14. Ibid., pp. 92–93, emphasis in the original.
15. Ibid., p. 94, emphases in the original.
16. Ibid., p. 94; emphases in the original.
17. Ibid., pp. 94–95; emphasis in the original.
18. Ibid., p. 95; emphasis in the original; underline added.
19. Ibid., pp. 95–96; emphasis in the original.
20. Ibid., pp. 95–96.
21. See for example, ibid., p. 97.
22. Ibid., p. 97; caps and emphasis in the original.
23. Ibid., p. 97.
24. Ibid., p. 98, emphases added.
25. Ibid., p. 98, emphasis added.
26. Ibid., p. 100.
27. Ibid., emphasis original.
28. Ibid., p. 99.
29. Ibid., pp. 100–01, emphasis in the original.
30. Ibid., pp. 124–25, emphasis in the original.
31. Ibid., pp. 95–96.
32. Ibid., pp. 80–81.

4

Microelectronic and Computer Revolution

Towards Dissolution of the Machine

The new technological revolution (or microelectronic and computer revolution) has begun a process of the dissolution of the tool and the machine. We shall try to find out how the process has worked in the course of the STR.

The STR basically uses the forces within the atom first on technological and then social scales. Consequently, it has become a powerful social force. These forces include quantum, electronic (electron-related), particle and wave, light and other energies. The revolution based upon the use of the electrons is generally known as the electronic or micro-electronic revolution. For the first time in history they have become the productive force and by extension the information force. This revolution is qualitatively different from the industrial revolution based upon the use of steam power and steam engine. Still later electricity and oil was used as the energy sources.

The computer revolution is based on a very interesting, new type of 'machine', based on logic, and therefore it approached intelligence (hence the problem related with AI or 'artificial intelligence', an unprecedented event). It is the computer program that drives the 'machine', with the human becoming an observer. Computer basically 'computes' and converts the processes into numbers, characters and images. *It is having an epoch-making impact on human nature, history and society.* Every process is converted into uniform system of signals based upon binary 'language', popularly known as the 'software'.

Without going into all the major and minor details, we will trace main outlines of computer development and stress particularly the aspects different qualitatively from the industrial qualities.

Radio and Modern Information Revolution

Charles Babbage created a mechanical computer in the 19th century, based upon wheels, pulleys, gears, etc. Modern information revolution began with the invention of radio. Radio was born out of the most theoretical field of science, that is, electro-magnetism of physics. The German scientist Heinrich Hertz (1857–1894) discovered electro-magnetic radiation. He was the discoverer of radio waves, which are part of the electro-magnetic waves. He showed through experiments that electric charges and sparks could be transmitted between electrodes 20 metres apart. This discovery earned his name a permanent place as the unit of radio frequencies, which are measured in terms of "Hertz".[1]

In 1888 Edward Branley invented the radio conductor transmitting electro-magnetic waves. Electric alarm and telegraph relay could be activated with its help from several metres.[2] Oliver Lodge invented apparatus to increase or decrease frequencies and thus to send signals; that was in 1894.[3] In 1895, the attempts to set up antenna were being made: A.S. Popov enabled a vertical pole to receive radio waves. Popov increased the capacity of the Lodge resonator to 250 metres. He used radio-electric Morse to transmit through radiogram the words "Heinrich Hertz", on March, 12 1896. It was Popov who created the first radio, followed immediately by Marconi. The same year (1895) Giulimo Marconi used Morse code to send radio signals far off.[4]

This came to be known as the 'wireless' because no wire was involved in the transmission of the messages.

Invention of 'Valve' or 'Tube'

The invention of valve qualitatively changed radio transmission. Valve or cathode was invented towards the end of the 19th century. Electron rays are released in vacuum from a cathode, reaching anode. Such a vacuum is also called diode, invented by John Fleming in 1904. A grid in between would work as amplifier, which would make it possible to hear the radio signals (triodes).[5]

Cathode ray tubes made it possible to hear a wide range of radio frequencies. Later, transmitters and receivers were invented. Loudspeakers and microphones came into being. The triodes later helped the development of TV, radar and initial forms of computers.

Thus the valves and tubes were important steps in the development of communications, which were to drastically change exchange of information.

Initial Steps Towards the Computer

Development of electronics gradually pushed electro-magnetic machines to the background. Events and discoveries in the quantum, electronics and computers helped replace giant machines with smaller and smoother ones, run on different principles. The 'empire' of the industrial, oil, electric and electro-magnetic machines began to crumble, their domination began to crack up.

The intellectual, theoretical and scientific base of the computing revolution was created by computing science which was the part of mathematics. George Boule put forward some theories of modern number computation. Claude Shannon proved in 1937 that the logical system of Boule provided the basis for electro-mechanical circuits with 'switches' and relays. They could be used in creating the logical systems: the computer thus evolved as a 'logical system'.

Alan Turing created the famous 'Turing machine' in 1936 by proving that if a question or a problem was converted into symbolic algorithm, or a program, the computer could solve it. The problems and solutions were punched on paper tapes and run in the machine. Turing invented the "Colossus" in 1943 for the British army to break the codes.

John von Neumann is another important name in this field. He invented the high-speed numeric computing machine in 1945 with a 'memory'. It was the first time that the binary code or language of 0 and 1 was used. The internal parts were made not of electro-mechanical but electronic parts. It had a central processing unit or the CPU, and it was freer from human intervention. That is why the modern computer is also known as the von Neumann computer.

In 1944 Howard Aiken created Harvard Mark I, simply called Mark I, computer with the help of the IBM, but it did not have memory. He realized that a computer was conceptually different from a calculating machine. It was meant to calculate ballistic trajectories for the US navy. It was called ASCC or the Automatic Sequence Controlled Calculator.[6] In 1947 the IBM created the selective sequence electronic computer or the SSEC.

The ENIAC was created in 1946 by John Presper Eckert and John Mauchly. "The first fully electronic general purpose computer had been built. "[7] It was created for the purposes of the US army, but it was to play an important role in the subsequent history. Its full form is Electronic Numerical Integrator and Computer. It was the first full-scale computer based upon 19000 vacuum tubes or valves. It filled 1500 square feet and was equal to a building of 4 to 5 storeys. It had electric wires running several kilometres. And it was considered a 'small' computer!

Its program was wired through switches, plugs, wires, cables etc, and needed a great effort to reorganize the components for any change. Mathematician John von Neumann was introduced to the ENIAC in its early stages, and he realized its limitations in programming. He concluded that if its program were treated just like any other data and reduced to numbers, they could be stored within the machine. This idea, which was to prove historic and futuristic, was incorporated into the second computer of the Moore's School of Electrical Engineering, EDVAC (ENIAC being the first). But it never got completed. The idea of program was built into the BINAC of 1950. By then Kilburn and Williams had introduced the stored program into Manchester Mark I and Maurice Wilkes did the same with the EDSAC machine.[8] In 1949 Zed-3 computer was invented which for the first time had a controlled program and its language was binary.

Neumann began creating EDVAC or Electronic Discrete Automatic Computer in 1949, which was completed by 1952. It used binary language. To run the program it used 4000 vacuums and 10000 crystal diodes.

Several other experiments and constructions in the field of computer technology helped constant evolution and improvement of the 'computer'.

Transistor Revolution: Creating the Ground for the Information Revolution

Then the transistor revolution happened without which the microchip and computer revolutions were not possible. The transistors came to replace the valves, a crucial development.

We have already talked of the valves or the vacuums (vacuum tubes). Their job was to regulate electric currents, signals, radio waves etc to pass or to prevent their passage. That is why they came to be known as the 'switches' or the valves. A number of them could be connected with wires and a signalling system could thus be created, as in the ENIAC or the EDVAC. Used as codes the passage of signals, or otherwise, could be used to represent characters constituting numbers, words, images and so on. Besides, the valves were used in the radios to amplify, oscillate and resist (as resistance), and as signalling devices.

There were several problems with the valves (or 'vacuum tubes'). They could undoubtedly be produced easily and cheaply. Yet the valve was bulky and fragile, and relatively slow in transmitting electronic signals. Besides, because of its incandescent filaments, it consumed relatively large amounts of electricity.[9]

The vacuum tubes (valves) were too heavy and big, they were expensive and needed constant watch and repairs, which were quite frequent and a big headache. Quite often, more time was spent on repairs than on actual work. The electronic signals used to slow down.

Further researches led to the discovery of the 'semiconductors', which replaced valves by the middle of the 1950s. The semiconductor was the product of the solid state physics of the 1920s and 30s. Its first generation was constituted by transistors. The transistor was made in commercial quantities by etching circuits on germanium and later on silicon wafers by electrolyte jets.[10]

The semiconductors led to the invention of the transistors.

Good conductors let the electricity pass easily; bad conductors do not let it pass or let it pass with great difficulty; 'semi'-conductors, as the name suggests, let electricity pass selectively.[11]

The discovery of solid semi-conductors straight-away led to the transistors. In December 1947, William Shockley and his two associates demonstrated a new semi-conductor device. They attached two wires to a germanium foil and used it as a switching and amplifying system. It was a kind of diode, and was precisely known as the 'point contact transistor'.

A name had to be found for this new electronic device that conveyed the process of the transfer of electric charge through the crystal. They decided to name it 'transistor'.[12] It was announced on July 1, 1948. The newspapers announced that the transistor contained no vacuum, grid, plate, or glass envelope to protect it from air. The active parts of the component consisted of two thin wires running to a piece of semi-conducting metal, the size of a pin-head attached, to a metal.[13]

Later silicon was used for making transistors. A transistor has three regions divided by junctions. That is why they are known as the triodes. The middle one is known as the base; the other two are the emitter and the collector. Some impurities are mixed in the transistor to increase its conducting qualities. The collector collects the electrons and the emitter allows them to pass. Thus a 'gate' system is created.

The micro-electronic revolution began when:

1. The transistors began to downsize to very small dimensions.

2. The transistors began to be embedded on the chips, made primarily of silicon.

The revolution began towards the end of the 1950s and gathered speed in the 1960s and 70s. As a result, *the world began to come out of the industrial era.*

The transistor replaced the valves over a period, and became embedded on the chip. This brought about a fundamental transformation of the signalling system and enabled the micro-chip revolution. The replacement of the huge, by the later standards, valve by transistor made it possible for the devices to collapse to much smaller sizes. This was crucial for the future course of development. It was an immense shortening of space in particular. The external parts began to be internalized.

Now the transistor and the chip began to replace the valves, and this made the electronic revolution possible; the computer got converted into a chip-based device.

The main basis of this revolution is a very common element found in the sand known as the silicon (Si). In the language of chemistry, sand is silicon oxide. Oxygen is removed through chemical processes and we get silicon crystals. *The silicon is the very basis of the ongoing new electronic revolution!* Silicon crystals are cut into thin foils and then into very fine square chips. Specialized machines and equipment are needed for the purpose. Very small chips or pieces result ultimately, the size of finger-nails or even smaller.

These very chips are the basis of the micro-chip based *electronic revolution.*

In 1959 several transistors were embedded on to a chip and inter-connected. A little later the transistors and the circuits began to be etched onto the chip itself. They were called IC or the integrated circuits. Thus began the present-day electronic, information and communication revolution

(ICR), a new stage of micro-electronic revolution. The etched gates on the chips act as the doors and pathways for the electrons. With the passage of time the number and complications of the circuits and the number of transistors increased exponentially. If an electron passes the gate, then this represents 'one'; if not it is 'zero'. Thus, various combinations of 1 and 0 result, constituting the software or language of the computer.

It is now common knowledge that a combination of number of ones and zeroes constitute various numbers, words and images. Things are simplified down to the binaries of 1 and 0. Today the computer language and the software programs have developed to a high stage where they cover vast domains and even act as the commands for human beings.

We can witness these processes on the screen, which has become a central field for today's information revolution.

The techniques of etching the circuits and transistors in the growingly smaller silicon chips are becoming miniaturized, creating immense possibilities for the future. Now replacements for silicon chips are being probed to the extent that atomic and light guided software is being visualized. This is going to bring about fundamental changes in the computer.

Even electron microscopes are being used to etch the circuits on the chips. The etching was begun with that of the transistors and semi-conductors. At a certain stage, the transistors were not embedded onto the chips but were directly etched on them. Thus begins the 'chip-based revolution'. In the advanced stage of etching no wires or parts are attached but are etched onto the chip directly. This is an extraordinary event signalling an end of circuit, wires, bolt, parts made of metals, etc. Only circuits *in the form of etches* through photography are used.

Thus these developments signal *the end of solid parts,* replaced by the electronic circuits. This is a crucial qualitative change. Mechanical physical sciences cross the Newtonian sciences and laws, and are replaced by the quantum forces within the atom.

The transistors on the silicon chips are imaged through photolithography and etching. With the development of the techniques the size and shape of the transistors become smaller and simpler. This increases the capacity of the chips very rapidly. Electron beams or light is used in the process. Deposition lithography is used to join the various parts. X-ray lithography is also used. In the last decades the concentration of etched circuits has been doubling every 18 months. (Moore's law)

Some impurities are added to speed up the electrons and to render the silicon chip more conductive. Thus the electron speeds are controlled and regulated. Therefore the chips are called semi-conductors.

A silicon chip may be 2x2 mm and 0.25 mm thick. It is possible to etch one lakh (a hundred thousand) components on a chip, the majority of them being transistors. Each transistor is 6 microns in size (one micron is one millionth of a metre).

The chips constitute the *brain* of the computer. They perform all the logical and mathematical operations and issue instructions to other parts. Then there are memory chips retaining data and information.

By 1965 small-scale integration (SSI) had begun. The chip contained ten transistors. Between 1963 and 1971 the chips contained 24 and 64 transistors. In 1969 there were 1000 components and in 1975 32000. This was the MLSI which later led to large-scale integration or the LSI and BSLI.[14]

The further development of the chips led to the development of microprocessors which contained a very large number of transistors and circuits. Owing to the developments in the microprocessors the development of the micro-computers became possible and one of the most important and momentous developments took place, that of the microprocessor-based 'PC' or the personal computer. The development of the PCs changed the whole face of the computer revolution.

The microprocessor and PC revolution began in Paulo Alto of California, which came to be known as the Silicon Valley. The first microprocessor was created in 1971. Ted Hoff created a chip on which an entire CPU or the central processing unit had been etched. Another chip acted as the ROM or the 'read only memory'.[15]

Thus two very big units of a computer were accommodated in a very small space. The microprocessor chip of Hoff contained 2300 transistors. The computing capacity of this one chip alone was equal to the computing capacity of the ENIAC computer. Its size was only 1/8 x 1x6 of an inch. In 1974 the general purpose microprocessor was created which contained an entire computer on a circuit board. It used to carry out 29000 commands per second. The chip capacity quickly increased from 8 kilobits to 64 KB. The hardware was now ready for a PC revolution.[16]

Till 1974–75, the big companies had the monopoly over computing. Mini-computers and PCs broke this monopoly, and the role of the individual increased rapidly as never before. While the mainframe computer was the result of the processes set in during the Second World War, the mini-computer was the contribution of the 1960s and the PC originated still later and outside this process.[17]

The year 1981 may be considered the first year of the PC. The PC revolution was accompanied by the software revolution, which fitted in with the needs of the PCs and their rapidly increasing computing powers. The new software was facilitated by the great and exponential increase in the chip capacities. By 1989 chips contained 160 million information units.

This writer had the opportunity to witness the transition from the mainframe to the personal computers in JNU, New Delhi, during the 1970s to 1990s. The Computer Centre of JNU had installed the very first mainframe in the university. It was the centre of attraction. It was installed in a huge air-conditioned hall, where a big magnetic tape was installed connected to so many terminals. It was an efficient system with the data produced at the terminals fed and preserved in the mainframe. They were very smooth and efficient.[18]

Yet, it was a centralized system, in which the scholars and operators had very little freedom and manoeuvrability. Data though was quite safe and there was no problem of virus etc, as there was no Internet during those days.

It was a system stable at one place, and one had to come to the place to work. Yet, it was highly efficient and useful. On got prints on demands for the text.

Gradually one heard of the PCs or the personal computers and desktops, which at the beginning were difficult to grasp. The mainframe began to lose its importance and became increasingly subject to the vagaries and irregularities of maintenance. The 'desktop' and the PCs were absolutely novel, difficult to fathom at first. Gradually one leant that 'all that the big computer could do', can be done on one small computer! What a magic! Gradually people learnt to cope with it, and there were several of these smaller and small wonders, which used to be issued to the scholars. It really took a long time to grasp the real significance of the PCs. The magnetic tape and all that disappeared, and their functions were carried on by a different kind of equipment.

The present-day computer surpasses the giant offices of twenty years ago. The electron waves take less than one second to travel and they are calculated in nano and pieco seconds. A nano second equals one billionth of a second and a pieco second is one hundred thousandth of the one millionth part of a second.

Today everything is based in the PCs and laptops, which have become a common means of information exchange and generation and even the means of production.

A new society is taking birth and the industrial society is fast transiting to the post-industrial society.

The Microprocessor Revolution: Emergence of 'Memory'

Integrated circuits or the ICs first appeared in 1959, ushering in a *new technological revolution*. They have immense potentialities including managing new emerging technologies. One of the firms, the INTEL or the Integrated Electronics Corporation concentrated its efforts on the manufacture of semiconductor memories, particularly the RAMs. It was the first time that 'memory' emerged as a regular feature of a system. The memory became a fundamental discovery, which determined the future course of development of the computerized system. The RAMs (memory chips) were just replacing magnetic cores as random access memories in computers. The magnetic core memories were physically large in size and slow in operation. So, the semiconductor memories or RAMs were a boon to the development of the computers. The semiconductor RAMs helped reducing the size of computers, while simultaneously speeding up their operations.

In the ENIAC electronic computer of 1946, the program had to be stored *externally*. Thus the steps of the program could be executed only at the speed at which instructions could be read by the rather primitive card or paper tape reader of those days. von Neumann introduced a major conceptual change. He introduced the concept of 'stored program control', thus 'internalizing' it. The detailed steps of the computer were coded and fed into the computer along with the data. This acted as the memory of the computer entered or stored into it. They or their sub-programs could be called any time or 'retrieved'. To solve a new problem, a new program or software was prepared and entered into the computer along with the data.

In the centre of the computer system is the CPU or central processing unit. It processes the inputs of data as per commands. The CPU has three parts: ALU or the arithmetic-cum-logic unit, the control unit (CU) and memory. ALU does the actual computing and performs logic operations, and CU decodes instructions to generate command signals. It sends instructions and regulates flow of information.

The memory in the CPU is mainly RAMs. The data from the main memory is held in an internal memory till necessary. Data flows follow what is known as the 'bus' system. Data is in the units of 'bits', which may be 8, 16, etc. It is fed into the computers by the keyboard. The results of thc processing are displayed on the screen.

The theory behind the first and second generation computers was that they managed mathematical problems, and their functions ranged *from running a computer and machine to running a factory*. These functions needed different and appropriate programs. Data on a punched card was given to the expert and he would solve the problem in a few hours.

By the end of the 1950s the computers began to collapse in size. It was mainly because of the use of ICs. These smaller computers became more amenable to the smaller organizations. They were the 'mini'-computers. They could be used to solve specific problems related with the control of electrical machines, power stations, controlling numeric machine tools, chemical reactions and processes, advanced instrumentation systems, and so on.

In early 1970 INTEL got a contract from a Japanese firm for electronic calculators. The order was for a new generation chips. According to an idea of Ted Hoff at the INTEL, instead of a separate chip for each function, there was to be a general purpose one. It could then be suitably programmed before assembly for each particular kind of calculator. After supplying the Japanese company, Hoff went ahead and created integrated arithmetic and logical processing elements on a single chip. He incorporated 2250 components on a single chip.

This was a revolutionary development. Most of the functions of the CPU now were contained on a chip of 4mm square. When the chip was connected to other ICs with memory and registers, attached to input-output units, it became a tiny computer or a microprocessor. The first microprocessors used the words of 4 bits; the new versions went up to 32 bits. They had a speed of 100 megahertz, which is basically the frequency of the crystal oscillator generating clock pulses required to operate the microprocessor and the associated circuits.

The advantage with the microprocessor is that by bringing together a few chips, one could accomplish more computing power and storage than the computers of the 1950s. They functioned as the microcontrollers of various processes with particular programs, such as, digital measuring instruments, electronic games, cash registers, microwave ovens, automobiles, traffic lights etc.

Microprocessors are being used in the petrol engines, replacing mechanical controls by microprocessor based electrical system. The inlet petrol valve, the spark ignition and the piston start are all done precisely by the chip or the microprocessor. This makes the car fuel efficient.

The microprocessor integrates the whole of CPU and its input-output functions on one or a few ICs, which greatly reduces the size of the CPU and also the number of electrical connections. Earlier the initial forms of CPU were using racks of circuit boards arranged or embedded on to the card-boards with small and medium scale circuits. The microprocessor unites them in a few large-scale ICs. The microprocessor is a multipurpose programmable device with input-output devices attached. It works on the principles of the binary language system.

The number of transistors is very important. The microprocessors have been going through various phases of development and continue to evolve. They have gone through 8, 16, 32, and 64 bit chips. Now multi-core microprocessors can be embedded on to a single microprocessor chip. The main characteristic of these developments is that while the size and number of chips keep coming down, the number of transistors and other accessories keeps increasing rapidly. This is the process of miniaturization.

Bits and bytes: A bit represents a single numeric data like 1 or 0. It encodes a single unit of digital information. Byte equals a series of bits; usually 8 bits equal one byte. Bits are grouped into bytes to facilitate the work of hardware and computer functioning.

What is 'New' in Electronics Revolution: A Discussion

Many people including prominent scholars treat the new technological or electronics revolution as one of the usual changes with *nothing qualitatively new.* For them it is just another industrial revolution, different from the earlier industrial revolution only in quantity and scale. The earlier one was based on the steam power, this one on electric and electronic sources. That is all the difference. For the rest the impact is the same. They think that, some new, faster and more efficient machines have come up, helping us better in the usual jobs. Otherwise, there are no changes in the usual industrial activities. Even the more advanced, intellectually developed people think that all the categories and concepts of the industrial revolution can more or less be used as it is, and that there is nothing basically new. Besides, we continue to face the usual exploitation, the daily labour, wage and salary problems, the troubles of daily life, etc, and those more partisan or involved in abstract economic and political thinking observe that it is another case of capitalism at much higher levels, with our problems and ways of life more or less intact. They look upon the electronic or the computer revolution as providing a more efficient and intensive mechanism of exploitation by capitalism.

So for them, these developments are more a quantitative change rather than qualitative. And even if they are qualitatively new, they are basically within the old framework of exploitative capitalism and imperialism.

The industrial society and capitalist order of things are more or less intact. Our thoughts and ways of life do show some changes but our problems, troubles, poverty, unemployment, price rise, exploitation, and such other issues are more or less intact. Therefore, the problems of the capitalist system continue to trouble us. Till there is exploitation, there is no basic change in the nature of capitalism. The technological revolution is the only another means to enhance exploitation, and it does not solve any problems of our daily life, so the argument goes. The problems can only be solved if the capitalist society is overthrown. For them, the capitalist mode of production has basically not changed. Only, today, information as a new factor has become part and parcel of capitalist economy and production.

This is something we have to discuss properly throughout the book, and we will surely be taking up at least some of the points for discussions.

It is little realized, in fact not realized at all, that we are fortunate to be witness to the greatest event in human history, so far. We are participating in the unprecedented scientific and technological revolution (STR) or the new technological or electronics revolution, whatever you may call it. The world has changed beyond recognition in the last 4 or 5 decades. It is an all embracing revolution affecting every single aspect qualitatively. The way we live and work has changed. All the existing concepts, theories, philosophical conceptions, etc. have been proved obsolete. This is exemplified by the quantum revolution and quantum philosophy. Politics has changed drastically. We are using new means of production quite different from those provided by the industrial revolution. The computer and mobile are fundamentally different means of production and information. In world politics and economics, who would have imagined a growing integration of the European states and countries? Religion is being given up by a growing majority of population of Europe.

We are using information-driven equipment. Electronics has become part and parcel of our life. The very composition of the society and of various classes and sections is drastically changing and changing very fast. We live in a world increasingly dominated by images, where time and space are collapsing and where the internet is increasingly dominating our consciousness. All the established notions about the subject, consciousness and ideas are collapsing and we have to re-work every single concept.

Means of production and information are reaching every individual for the first time, creating new and novel possibilities. We are shifting from mode of production to mode of information.

Environment and the destruction of nature have become universal problems, and for the first time humans are having to cooperate on a holistic issue.

Rapid Spread of STR

In the last three or four decades the STR has spread extremely rapidly all over the world and into the backward and developing countries like India. When one talked some years ago about STR and electronics and their impact in India, most of the people pooh-poohed the idea as 'European'. They thought it is something 'foreign', confined to Europe, America and the advanced world. Not any more. Even those who talked in this way are now either silent or are admitting that the STR is a reality in India. Some of the people though try to adjust their traditional or existing views to the new developments or try to fit in the new in their fixed and rigid old ideas.

Not very long ago, just a few years earlier, we used to see a large number of PCOs and used to go there to phone or make long-distance calls. Making STD used to be so difficult and costly, and there used to be long queues, generally. How times have changed! We are talking of 'those times' which were not very long ago, just a decade or two back or three at the most. The scenario of 'those times' has changed completely. And that is due to that small gadget called mobile to be seen in almost every hand! The person concerned may not have proper food for himself/herself and their family, but must have a mobile, a vital connection with the outside world. Ideas, consciousness and communication have become far more important than food itself! Trade and exchange, buying and selling is being carried on even where there is no road, no transport, no other facilities.

It has to be admitted that the whole thinking and behaviour pattern of the people have undergone drastic changes. Without doubt the role of the individual has increased, rightly or wrongly or both ways. The new means of communication have given a new sense of independence and freedom to act to the person.

These means of information are also quite often if not always the new means of production. It is often difficult to differentiate between the two unless one really looks at the actual production process.

In other words, human beings are already using the revolutionized and absolutely new means of production. This aspect has far-reaching implications for human life and thought. The tools and means are getting smaller rapidly, faster than we visualized. Mobiles, PCs, laptops, notebooks and their varieties like the 'tablets', GPS system, increasing usage in transport, new means of transport, ATMs, drastic changes in banking, collapse of functions into and towards the mobile, and endless other applications and gadgets threaten to overthrow the existing society and history.

Now the world is talking of the 'fourth industrial revolution', which was the theme of the World Economic Forum at Davos in January 2016. 3–D printing, bio-technology, merger of electronics, physics and biology, nanotechnology and such other developments have rendered the events of the last four decades, even two decades, obsolete. We have entered into new levels of technological revolution. In fact, it will be erroneous to call it industrial revolution at all; it is a new level of the post-industrial revolution.

Let us consider the industrial machine. Let us take the example of the lathe machine. Different tools are attached to this machine according to need and nature of job e.g.: cutting, planing, boring, grinding, drilling, shearing, etc. Lathe is a multi-dimensional multi-functional machine. The worker for example attaches a cutting tool and the metal piece to be worked upon, and then switches on power. The production process begins. The operator arranges and adjusts the tools and the job as per the need, changes their angles, position, speed and so on. At the same time he arranges the electric supply, oil and oil-flow, raw material, corrects any defect etc. Although the worker does not do everything with the help of the machine, yet he does many physical and mental jobs with the help of machines and tools. At the end of the process, which combines production and labour processes, he gets the required piece of finished product.

Now let us assume that a microprocessor or a microchip is attached to the lathe machine and a screen is installed. This immediately brings about several changes in the nature of the machine and in that of production, labour and the labourer himself. What are the changes and what is their nature? Information enters the production/labour process as a new factor. The microprocessor has the capacity to collect information about any related process, to examine things and to give commands or to convey them. All the information about the position of the tools, the job, temperature, chemical composition, state of oil and lubricants, thickness or otherwise of the job, various angles, length, width, thickness etc of the objects concerned, all these and other information can be available on the screen. At the same time, commands can be given about any required changes in position, angles, speed, temperature, etc. Any defects are immediately brought to notice on the screen. The operator has now to keep a watch on the screen, follow the trends and act accordingly. Nowadays, increasingly, even this is not required as the commands can be auto-commands or the corrections can be auto-corrections.

The worker/operator intervenes in the production process through the screen: his relationship with the machine, tool and production process undergoes a drastic change. It becomes indirect and via the use of information.

The Post-Industrial Machine

In other words we are witnessing the operation of *a different kind of machine altogether, qualitatively different from that under the industrial revolution.* It is *no more an industrial machine.* There are aspects now that separate it from the product of the industrial revolution, and may broadly be termed a 'post-industrial' machine. This machine has not only taken over the physical functions of the worker but also the mental ones. The introduction of the chip has transformed the lathe into a machine driven not by the industrial mechanical method but by electronic information. It is a program- and software-driven system, not a simple mechanical one. This (computerized) automation is qualitatively different from the industrial automation, with all the physical and mental functions having been transferred to an automatic system which also carries out logical functions. The human being becomes generally free of the labour process and is only an overseer of the production process.

The new technological revolution begins with scientific and technological changes in information, its gradual emergence from production and then domination over production and in the method of its emission and transmission. That is why the new technological revolution is also an information revolution. The information of the production processes travel at the speed of light or of electrons, etc. It is in this respect that the main characteristics of the information revolution reside. The relationship of the machine with the worker undergoes a fundamental transformation and conversion in the sense that the worker is now related most of all with the information and not with the value creating machine system. This relation is temporary, transitional and intangible. The worker for the first time is not related with something solid, visible and concrete. He/she is working with something that keeps disappearing, something that is only an image of the solid job or visible process. On the shop-floor, the worker stands redefined.

With the STR it is a transition from the tangible to the intangible. It is the intangible that is the basis of production and information transmission.

As in the example of the cutting tool in the lathe machine, the microprocessors can be used in any machine and can replace a number of jobs and concentrate production processes in large numbers on the screen. Today, the processes in the textile industry, weaving, spinning, tailoring, processes in the iron and steel and engineering industries and so on are being computerized. The present author had the opportunity to see the production process in the paper mills in Rajahmundhry in Andhra Pradesh in the early years of the century. It was a revelation in many ways. All the processes, from the shop-floor stand to winding, are to be seen on the screen/s. All the furnaces are connected to the screen. Thus every chemical reaction, the thickness and other conditions of the paper rolls, etc., the defects, and other major ingredients of a process can be watched on the screen and modified as per requirement 'insisted' upon by the state of process as displayed by the computer system.

Electronic Information and Death of the Machine

Another trend is to be noted in the development of the machine. We should not think it is a case of *just attaching* the microprocessor to an older machine or to any machine. The attachment brings about a fundamental transformation in the machine. The microprocessor step by step forces changes in the nature and functioning of the machine, tools and flow of information. It is the flow of information which brings about a collapse and reorganization of the machine and machine tools. The chips begin a process of reduction in the size of the machine because so much space is redundant. The machine is becoming smaller and handier. The machine now requires much less of the nuts and bolts, pulleys, shafts, gears, pistons, etc., and on smaller scales. The computers render such parts superfluous as the information about things reach the screen directly.

Information and the chips render the tangible parts increasingly superfluous and unimportant.

The application of the chip at one point transforms the nature and functioning of the entire factory, machines and even industry. This is because the particular job/ jobs performed earlier by the worker is now being performed by the computer. For example, it is the computer which detects the break in thread, which was earlier done by the worker. Even its repair can be done by the computer itself. Addition or reduction of chemicals, gases, liquids etc are done at the commands of the computer. This entails certain necessary changes in the structure of the machine and the tool.

The use of chips and computers in spinning and weaving machines have changed the nature of these machines and therefore of the groups of workers operating them. Even before the use of computers, the gas and water-jet driven shuttles were being used. The process has developed further and computers have taken over. As a result the job of throwing shuttles has been taken over by the computers and many of the earlier parts and machinery have disappeared.

This change from the mechanical to the computerized automatic system spells death for many industrial parts and elements and for the industries themselves. Now the machines occupy less space and are more handy, attractive and lighter.

The bobbins are attached and ejected automatically.

We may take another example. The computers have drastically transformed the newspaper and book publishing and production. The previous printing methods and technologies were qualitatively different. The letters were arranged by the compositors separately and the printed matter was printed on the flat press etc. Then came the 'lino' or arranging matter by lines, where the metal got melted in a separate tank, to come out as new lines. Still later the matter was photographed and printed as 'bromide' and so on. Page correction, page making, putting ink, printing, folding, arranging in various other ways etc involved tangible work by a large number of workers and employees.

Today, all this has changed completely. For example, for composing, proof reading, page making, etc no solid materials are needed and they can all be done on the screen itself, and for these jobs just one or only a few persons may be enough. Books and newspapers may be sent direct to the press, where they have simply to print the matter on the paper. The various labour and production processes are simply merged together, having become one and the workers, employee, proof reader, editor, writer, etc are all in one. Even in the printing press, the printing machine may be run by a computer command. Even folding and arranging in final book or paper form is done by the machine. This is a very high level of logical automation.

Many other examples may be given, e.g. of paper, textile, steel, and others. Now robots are dealing with the automobile industry, and they have reached very high levels in countries like Japan and many others. The science and technology of the robot is producing wonders.

The basic and crucial point is that the introduction of the electronic computer not only changes *the nature of machines and tools but also of the workers,* employees and *of the society itself.*

The new technological revolution is distinguished from the industrial revolution on several counts; some of them are discussed as follows:

- In the course of the STR all the physical labour and more and more mental labour is being transferred to the machines. Our mental labour is trying to keep ahead of the computer and it is becoming increasingly complicated and logical.
- The computerized system has the great advantage in terms of extremely rapid speeds. This speed relates with the job of computing and logical calculations and computations. Therefore, it is in a far better position to show directions to the processes. *Never before in history was a system created which works out the logic of production and information processes,* and thus these logical machines are the new means of production and at the same time the means of information driving the machines; *they are the very driving force* of the machines, production and the society.
- Computers and the electronic machines are nearer the brain than anything else that the human beings have ever created. This is an unprecedented unexpected development, with endless implications and potentials.
- The trend of development of the means of production has been reversed. So far the industrial revolution had created machines, factories and industries that were

becoming larger and larger. All our previous concepts were based on this trend. The size of the machines and tools are becoming smaller and more compact. Their productivity is at the same time increasing.

- These machines are rapidly becoming personalized, distributed and decentralized. They are to be found almost *everywhere* in the society. They are not fixed or rooted to one place. By acquiring growing mobility, they are becoming a kind of power in the hands of the individual. In the last four or five decades, the computers and the electronic systems have shrunk drastically. These developments have far-reaching implications for the future of society, humankind and the individual.
- These electronic systems and the microprocessors are being introduced in the most unexpected places e.g. in agriculture with the plough, the tractors, for field levelling. etc.
- The STR is *acting upon* various critical points of the historically created machines and tools. For example the tools have acquired a temporary nature. For example, light can also act as a tool. The computer, its software, screen and command system, etc. *are not tools and machines in the strict sense of the term.*
- The hard, solid and the tangible parts are fast getting dissolved into software, symbols, images etc. For example the keyboard is making *a transition from hardware to software*. The *hardware is fast losing its form as representation of the bygone ages* of the industrial age, and is more and more being represented by, getting converted into, software. This event represents a dialectical conflict between the industrial age as reflected in the hardware and hard tangible parts and elements, and the software represented by the

binary language. It is a historic contest, which signals *the end of the industrial age in a decisive manner, and beginning of a post-industrial age* in an equally decisive manner. *A new history thus begins.* The dissolution of the hardware and its conversion into software *closes the entire previous human history and begins a new one.*

- Information is becoming the crucial factor of production and communication. We have as a result begun to live in an age of information. *We are transiting from the mode of production to the mode of information.*
- The worker is being ejected from the position of worker to that of overseer.
- The labour process is for the first time getting separated out of the production process and getting dissolved.

The *industrial objects are disappearing* into history. The machine had the tool as the key element. Without the tool, one cannot produce. The industrial revolution attached the tool to the machine, having taken it away from the hands of human beings or the worker and the artisan.

Today the tool is dissolving under the impact of the electronic information revolution. This is a strange, unprecedented and most unexpected transformation and transfiguration, which never occurred before in history. This dissolution is one of the major historical acts dissolving society itself.

The tool is losing its independent existence. Hammer, pin, lathe tool, shuttle, spindle and several other tools and associated objects are losing their functions and even existence as tools. Their functions are being taken over by non-tool processes, by rays, waves and particles. In other words, *for the first time in history, the tools as such are disappearing.* It was on the basis of tools and their making and fashioning that the human society arose and evolved.

Therefore, their disappearance has deep implications.

To take an example, for boring a metal piece, laser rays instead of actual solid tools are being used. If the machine emanates laser, it is not a tool, only a tool-function. This tool is temporary, non-solid and intangible. The difference between the lab and the productive machine is reducing. Either the tools are disappearing or becoming an insignificant part of the machine.

The trend of the tool is towards disappearance and dissolution. Robot is a tool-less system, being used widely.

Thus the tool has not only gone out of the hands of the human beings; it is also disappearing from the machine itself.

In the textile processes, the process of transfer of thread from the bobbin to the cone is guided by the microprocessor. The smallest production unit of the factory becomes a self-reliant information machine. All the processes in the spinning and weaving units get connected with and controlled by the chips, which actually reduce the role of the tools if not entirely eliminate them. But soon the tools themselves will go out of the production, replaced by information, which guides the remaining parts and elements of the machine.

Every loom, even every bobbin, has now sensors attached to it, whose motion is recorded on the microprocessor screens. The width, length, thickness of the woven cloth, the state of threads constituting it, the need for any changes, speed, the nature and thickness of the thread, the speed (RPM or revolutions per minute) and so on and so forth are recorded constantly by the microprocessors and the computer screens. There are hundreds of bobbins, cones and shuttles and innumerable threads and their endless aspects; they are all recorded on the computers and are either adjusted automatically or with some amount of human intervention. Obviously human beings, the workers and the engineers would be unable to discharge such extensive of jobs.

Thus, these are the jobs transferred to the electronic systems, which have taken over not only simple jobs but also increasingly complicated logical functions.

We may take one more example, that of the watch. The microelectronic revolution has brought about fundamental transformations in the watch, use of watch, in our attitude to watch and to the concept of time itself. The earlier watches used to be *mechanical* systems, and this is a very important point. It produced a mechanical world-view. In fact the watch represents *the nature of the industrial revolution* in many ways. *It represents mechanical industrial time*. It has shaped the contemporary attitude to time. With the passage of time, the various times have gradually merged together, universalized and become uniform, leading to country-wide and world-wide time zones. Our whole routine of daily, monthly and yearly life has been divided into particular zones.

It is interesting to note that we are now so used to the watch and its time that we have forgotten the real nature and meaning of time, as if it is not we who created seconds, minutes and hours but the other way round: it is the divisions of time which have created us! The mechanical concept of time, basically developed in the industrial age, has actually shaped our thoughts and even determined our philosophical approach. Today we are going through a quantum revolution, which has produced a quantum concept of time, modifying our philosophical concept of time and space and our world-view.

The characteristic feature of the mechanical watch is that it converts the mechanical energy or power of the spring into the motion of the indicators showing hours and minutes. The indicator moves about the pre-fixed time indicators. This kind of watch has given rise to a whole watch industry producing all kinds of mechanical dented wheels, springs, small and fine wheels and so on. The Swiss watch industry became particularly world famous for its finesse and high technical levels. Smaller scales of mechanical watches and their fine parts became a source of competition the world over.

The mechanical watches and their production and distribution were once dominated by giant world companies and certain countries like Switzerland.

But now this has changed and that kind of monopoly has drastically weakened, thanks to the electronic revolution in the watch industry. The advent of electronic watches has changed the scene. Now such watches are produced in almost every house. Introduction of electronics in watch-making has dispensed with the necessity of manufacturing small parts and detailed elements of a watch. The electronic watch contains almost no spare parts. It is just a small circuit reflecting its flow of energy or electrons in the screen. Nowadays any device like the mobile or the laptop or any computer can show the time because it is easy to introduce the system of flow of waves into any device. Time display has thus become highly simplified.

We are still working with the old concept of time division, but even here some changes are to be seen and are bound to come. Now further divisions of a second are easily shown on various devices. We can easily find the time of various places on the earth and thus reduce the time differences and have a better and relative concept of time. We are now working not only according to our own local time but also as per the time of the concerned country or place or the whole earth. Cultural, sports and other events, news of various happenings etc can all be received together. Thus the previous barrier to time limits is breaking. Even the work hours are becoming staggered.

The shift to electronics is bound to give rise to more floating and flowing concepts about time, which was highly limited and bounded earlier. This is due to the electronics revolution.

Spread of Electronics and Information Revolution

With the development of electronics the information revolution is spreading very rapidly. It becomes difficult to tell whether a particular productive activity is a *production or information* process. Electronics is information activity. Information in turn regulates the process of production and its various elements. This aspect was not to be found in the industrial process.

The information revolution began about five decades or so ago. Today it has engulfed the whole earth. The satellite system has qualitatively changed the place and role of the information system, and it has become a worldwide phenomenon. It is information that drives our lives today.

Let us take some facts and figures to get an idea of the advance of the information revolution. The number of telephones in 1890 was 480 000; it rose to 20800000, in 1950, to 7 crore 53 lakhs and in 1985 to 62 crores 50 lakhs. Obviously these figures are old and much greater spread has taken place since then.

The first 10 crores of telephones were introduced during 80 years from 1876 to 1956; the second 10 crore phones were introduced in only 10 years from 1956 to 1966; the third part in 6 years, the fourth in 4 1/2 years, fifth in 4 years and the sixth 10 crores in only 3 years. According to older figures the number of telephones was increasing at the rate of 1 lakh (one hundred thousand) per 24 hours!

Optic cables arrived in the 1980s and 90s, which operate using light waves. These cables are thinner than human hair and can carry 140 million units of information per second. Electric currents are converted into optic waves.

The use of the optic fibre has revolutionized information transmission because the information travels at light speed.

The satellite revolution of the 1970s has played a decisive role in making the information revolution a world-wide phenomenon. It is because of the increasing number and capacities of the satellites that it has been possible to connect the increasing number of computers of the earth into one network or network of networks. As a result, the earth is enveloped in a layer of information ('consciousness'), which is today growing by the hour. This is one of the major developments affecting the nature of society and human beings, the full import of which is yet to be worked out. Whereas in the 1960s and 70s there were only a handful of satellites orbiting the earth, today there are hundreds, even thousands. An increasing number of new countries is joining the 'space club'. Most of the countries of the world are now part and parcel of the *satellite information system.* Some of the satellites are the geostationary type, which orbit the earth or orbit with the earth at 32 000 kilometres. They are crucial to the information system.

The satellites reflect and transmit beams of information in various forms to and from the earth. They thus engulf the whole earth in the increasing complexity of information threads. It is for the first time that *human consciousness surrounds the earth* in growing layers, engulfing the living bodies. The development has very important technical, social and philosophical implications. The humans are in contact with *their own consciousness* on such a massive scale for the first time, made possible due to signals being transmitted at near-light speeds on hundreds of beam reflectors. This is the 'noosphere' that Vladimir Vernadsky talked about, who was the founder of the concept.[19]

There is no doubt that the growing layers of information are becoming the decisive factor in production and financial processes, and are fashioning the development of the individual and social actions. The world has totally changed in the last four decades or so: information and circulating consciousness has become *the decisive factor in human development,* changing its trajectory.

Earth Engulfed by Information

The planet earth is being rapidly engulfed by layers of information, so much so that we will soon be reassessing our identity. Let us look at some facts and figures to get an idea of the extraordinary levels of the spread of information on and around the earth.

When the Sloan Digital Sky Survey began to function in 2000, its telescope in New Mexico collected more data in the first few weeks *than in the entire history of astronomy.* At present, a decade later, its archive contains 140 terabytes of information; one terabyte being equal to 1000 gigabytes. Its successor telescope, to be established in Chile in 2016, will accumulate this quantity every five days.

Such scales of information can be found on the ground as well. The retail company, Wal-Mart, handles more than a million customer transactions every hour, feeding databases more than 25 petabytes, that is, the equivalent of 167 times the books in the American Library of Congress. One petabyte equals 100 terabytes. Facebook is home to 40 billion photos. Decoding the human genome took ten years the first time in 2003, but can now be done in one week!

The world contains unimaginable amounts of digital information getting vaster ever more rapidly. They can be used to do newer things in all fields of life, not possible earlier, if put to proper use. Yet despite the abundance and types of tools, e.g. computers, mobiles, sensors, etc., the information already exceeds the available storage space. Besides, the security and privacy of data is becoming a major problem. Storage capacity is half the information created, making it impossible to access much of it. In other words we are going through a rapid and extremely rapid data revolution.

The business of information management is growing extremely rapidly. It helps organizations to analyse, interpret and make sense of data. The industry of data management and analytics is growing roughly twice as fast as the software business as a whole. A new kind of professional has emerged, who combines the skills of software programmer, statistician and artist-story-teller, whose job is to make sense of the mountain of data available.

Information Explosion

There are many reasons for information explosion, the most important being qualitatively new advances in technology. Every available item of information, past or present, is being digitalized. The capabilities of the devices are soaring and their prices are falling rapidly. Besides, many more people have access now to the devices than before. There are, for example, 4.6 billion mobile phone subscriptions all over the world. This already massive number is growing, even after adjustments made for various factors like one person having more than one connection etc. 1 to 2 billion people using the internet.

Many more people use the available information. Between 1990 and 2005, the population of the middle class grew by 1 billion. People are otherwise also becoming more literate, which means many more are using information.

"Revolutions in science have often been preceded by revolutions in measurements."[20] Microscope transformed biology, electron microscope changed physics; similarly the present data are turning the social sciences upside down.[21] Researchers are now able to better understand human behaviour, not only at the individual level, they are able to understand it at the population levels too.

According to Moore's law, processing power and storage capacity of computer chips double every 18 months. At the same time their prices halve in the same duration. As a result of this and other factors, the amount of data increases tenfold every five years.

Vast amounts of information are being shared over the internet. By 2013 the traffic flow over the internet per year will reach 667 exabytes. One exabyte equals 1000 petabytes or equivalent of 10 billion copies of the journal *The Economist*.

Quantitative to Qualitative Change

The society is shifting towards an information society. There is a surfeit of information, and it is the new raw material of the economy. Managing data better is becoming the basic necessity today and going to be more so in the future. Sophisticated quantitative analysis is being applied to almost all the aspects of daily life. Not just economic or financial policy matters or the rocket and missile technologies, but increasing number of aspects of daily life are being analysed with pinpoint accuracy using unlimited data. For example, a part of the Microsoft search engine Bing, known as Farecast, can advise the customers on buying a particular day's ticket by examining 225 billion flight and price records. These methods can be extended to reservations of hotel rooms, taxis and so on. The micro- and macroeconomic trends of individual as well as social banking can be identified by dipping into the pool of information and identifying the trends.

The trail of clicks left by the internet users is becoming one of the mainstays of the internet economy. Value can be extracted from these trails. This is known as the 'data exhaust'. The Google search engine, for example, is partly guided by the number of clicks on an item to determine the relevance of a particular query.

The satellites have become the key to the functioning of telephones, TV, radio, mobiles etc. Now even the transmission and publication of newspapers takes place via satellites. This is a novel development. The atmosphere is full of electronic texts and images to be used any time anywhere. The electronic text (signals) keep hanging about constantly.

All sorts of TV antennas, dishes, transmitting and receiving gadgets, and particularly the mobiles are fast changing the scene of communications. The technologies are getting obsolete so fast and the new ones emerging so rapidly that it is impossible to keep track of them and to bind them in a book or an article. Only a general picture can be drawn or only a general trend can be traced, in a temporary manner. Hundreds of TV channels have emerged and new ones are constantly emerging.

The mobile has definitely become the *new vehicle of communication and change,* which also affects production and economic-financial transactions, which have become exceedingly fast as never before. The cost of communication and information is falling really fast.

All this does not fit into the traditional or existing concept of 'capitalism'.

The satellite communications have changed the nature of things and commodities and of their use, as also the way they are produced. The use of chips, computers, mobiles and electronics has increased rapidly. We are becoming increasingly dependent on the system of information for the exchange of commodities, their production and information about them. Not only this, the whole production system and social system are more and more dependent on the production and dissemination of information.

The international communication system is giving rise to new methods of production, exchange and distribution. For instance, the information about prices, shares, quality of commodities, exchange, finance, banking and so on has increased as never before. As a result a new system of information-driven human and market relations is coming into being. We can no more pretend that nothing has changed and that it is business and market 'as usual'. We have to note that the market processes have speeded up in an extraordinary manner, which in turn are causing an increase in the speed of all other processes including production, transport and locomotion, thought processes, culture, finance and what not. Therefore, the information revolution is not confined to information alone but rapidly spreads to other areas of social activities such as production, distribution, culture, etc. The process affects the entire socio-economic and political structures and processes.

For example, the information revolution is deeply affecting money-commodity relations and the world market. The present-day world market is as much the product of production processes as of the information revolution. The exchange and the motion of the exchanges has increased so much that a new world market has come into being. The countries have to adjust and adapt themselves to the market forces, which in turn are the product of information at light speed. Unless a country keeps in step with such speeds, it is bound to collapse and get totally cut off and die out. New methods in the world market are being adopted. The faster the transmission of information, the greater is the change in the countries and in the world market and economy. Information via the world market directly affects production systems and production relations.

Thus to keep pace with the increased rate of money-commodity exchanges, the rates of production have also to be increased. That in turn demands an increase and change of production processes and methods. These further demand suitable changes in the relations in market, production and exchange.

Consequently, the communications at electronic or light speeds demands a drastic change in the very nature of means and methods of production, which means replacement of industrial methods of production by new post-industrial methods based upon electronics. The old, industrial methods of production do not fit in with the new electronic methods of communication and information transmission. Consequently, production has also to be put on electronic basis, and this basis is not industrial but post-industrial. If this shift is not brought about, production will disintegrate.

The electronification of production today is a basic task before the society. *All other tasks are secondary.* Production is becoming information-oriented. On the one hand, the existing production system is increasingly using information and its techniques and is thus undergoing many changes; on the other, production itself is increasingly shifting, producing information about production and about everything else. Production itself appears to us as information system. *Its appearance as an image precedes its appearance as a solid 'thing'.* The image, that is information, itself appears as a use value, that of representing, bringing in its wake, the commodity, the real use value. Exchange value appears as non-exchange value before it becomes value and use value.

Production expresses itself as and through its opposite, the information. The process has turned upside down, inside out. Production began to use information just to speed up, to disseminate itself, to control and regulate itself better. But information has quickly gone out of its control and now is controlling production itself. It is a conflict between the tangible and the non-tangible, in which the latter is quickly ahead because of its very high speeds. *Time has become the determining factor of production.* The very production system (mode of production) which used to produce commodities is now producing *huge amounts of information* whose proportion is increasing far more than the production of commodities.

Production is emphasizing information more than production. The production, is becoming part of the information system and is losing its contact with the production system. Iron, steel, machines, tools, textiles, transport, consumer goods and any number of industries are fast getting connected with information systems. Consequently, their machines and tools are changing rapidly and they are being computerized using electronics. They are thus getting connected with international consumers, markets and system of exchange.

Thus the information revolution is quickly changing the entire system and mode of production itself. Thus, it can be stated that:

1. The transition from the industrial to post-industrial age is taking place via the information revolution.
2. Information technology is drastically changing the machine, tool, factory system and mode of production itself.

3. We are no more in the production system; we have begun to *come out of it* and entering an information system and mode of information.

Today, strictly speaking, we are no more part of production-based society, though information-based society has not yet taken proper shape and only some contours or outlines of it can be seen. Therefore, we will have to *re-work* all the basic concepts related with and produced and developed in the industrial society and in the industrial mode of production. We have to determine the place of information in social development and in society itself. We have to place all the concepts created during the industrial revolution and age in the context of information and re-work them, give up old ones and develop new ones. For example we are still to work out the place of 'information' in the socio-economic and political system.

We can definitely state that the primacy of production is being lost to the production of information and to information-driven production and society; information and communication rather than production are becoming the *base of society*.

Therefore, we can state without doubt that the old and existing society has begun to disappear and a new society is emerging rapidly.

References

1. Maurice Estabrooks, *Electronic Technology, Corporate Strategy and World Transformation*, Westport Forum Books, 1995, p. 28.
2. Estabrooks, ibid.
3. Ibid., p. 29.
4. A.I. Kitaigorodsky, *Electrons*, Mir Publishers, Moscow, 1987, pp. 221–22.
5. Estabrooks, op cit., p. 29.
6. From the Internet: Type 'Howard Aiken'. Also see Shallis, pp. 104– 05.

7. Michael Shallis, *The Silicon Idol*, Oxford University Press, 1984, p. 105.
8. Based on Shallis, p. 106.
9. Jeffrey Henderson, *Globalisation of High Technology Production*, Routledge, 1989.
10. See for more details, Henderson, ibid., p. 28.
11. I.P. Gurski, *Elementary Physics: Problems and Solutions*, Mir Publishers, Moscow, 1987, p. 271.
12. See; K.D. Pavate, *The Wonder Chip*, NBT, New Delhi, 2004, p. 41.
13. Pavate, Ibid., p. 42.
14. Maurice Estabrooks, op cit., p. 4.
15. Ibid., p. 49.
16. Ibid.
17. V.G. Pujari, "Information Technology in the Textile Industry", *Information Technology in Everyday Life*, Computer Society of India, Tata-McGraw Hill & Co, New Delhi, 1991, p. 266.
18. I am especially indebted to Shri B.B. Prasad, formerly technical scientist-engineer at the JNU Computer Centre, New Delhi, now retired, for the great help in using the computer system of the Centre. Shri Prasad also explained the technical intricacies of the system.
19. See, for example, R.K. Balandin, *Vladimir Vernadsky*, Mir Publishers, Moscow, 1982, p. 106; *On the Road to the Noosphere*, APN Publishing House, Moscow, 1989, p. 1; also consult, Anil Rajimwale, *Environment versus Development*, Sunrise Publications, New Delhi, 2006, in 2 volumes.
20. Sinan Aral, *The Economist*, February 27, 2010, p. 4 of Data Supplement.
21. Ibid.

5

From Mode of Production to Mode of Information

Post-Industrial and Post-Modern System

As we have seen, the STR is working on the tools, machines and other industrial components, transforming them in a profound manner, and even dissolving them.

These developments form the basis of the post-industrial revolution (PIR). In what sense are we talking about a 'post-industrial' society (PIS)? Before dealing with this concept, let us have a look at some of the features of the industrial society.

The industrial revolution was based on the discovery of steam power and the invention, and social, economic and productive use, of the steam engine and the machines and tools based upon it. That is why, we call it *industrial* revolution. We continue to linger on in this stage or phase of development, but there are clear signs that the stage is taking leave of history. The 'industrial' is ceasing to be industrial in an increasing number of features, which can increasingly be termed *post-industrial*.

Industrial production and the age based upon it was basically geared to creating larger and larger means of production, factories/mills, machines, tools, engines, modes of transport of large size, etc. That was the distinctive feature of the industrial revolution. This trend towards the larger scales gathered speed in the second half of the 19th century and the first half of the 20th.

The trend has today been reversed. Therefore, no question can be posed correctly today unless we recognize that the means of production, the factories, the machines and the tools *are growing smaller*, setting off qualitatively new chains of development towards miniaturization for *the first time* in history.

We have to look briefly around us, and we find the world is becoming smaller in every way. Time, space and matter are collapsing. For the first time, un-natural materials are becoming the means of production and communications. So far, we had used what is given by nature. Even if certain artificial materials were used, it was only to a limited extent. We are still closely aligned with the natural products, creating economies of scales.

It is for the first time that the forces *within the atom* have been released on such vast scales into production, communications and the society as a whole, that they are causing changes in the society. The social development has been overtaken by the technological development. These forces are becoming *the driving force* of society.

The micro forces contain miniature spaces and times, and exceedingly rapid speeds within them. At the same time they are capable of covering vast spaces and overcome time. It is these that the social development is trying to win over and negotiate. In the process, there is a historic shift from the tangible to the intangible in the production and labour processes, in information and services, and in the social development and evolution as a whole. The developments touch the very horizons of the nature of the *Homo sapiens* itself.

Extraordinary events are taking place in the realm of the computer, its monitor, and electronics. The future of society is tied up with these developments. There is a clear dialectics emerging between the software and the hardware and in each of them, and this is the *decisive contradiction* or duality of the modern or rather the post-modern means of production and communication. The conflict between the hardware and the software is *the central contradiction* of the modern and postmodern means of production/information.

And today, *the computer itself is under dissolution.* The computer is the very means which brought about a social revolution in the last four decades or so. It is mainly made of the hardware. But its driving force, the 'spirit', is the software. The software is the language of the machine, a fact of *the greatest significance.* **Never** in the history of society had the means of production and the machines a 'language'. The use of the word 'language' here is not simply representative or token. It is really becoming the human-like language and is fast influencing and taking over the human consciousness and the society. Its decisive and superior quality is its speed, which has a tremendous advantage over human beings. It is now acquiring an *independent existence,* as evidenced by the exceedingly rapid growth of the internet. The human society, as a result, is making a sharp turn in its history, for the first time. In future we are compelled to solve all the basic questions of existence itself.

The *key-board is dissolving rapidly.* It has already become part of the software; so far it had been part of the hardware, holding up the growth of the machine, though not very much and not for too long. *This is the beginning of the dissolution of the machine and of the tools themselves.* The event has far-reaching significance. The event also means that everything, all the hardware, can be converted into software, and they are in fact getting converted into software. The tablet and the iPad are the confirmation of this process, which has already set in, and is gathering speed. *It is a transition from the machine to the non-machine.*

Software, acting as the computer, is likely to become part of our body as a bio-electronic system.

The machine is becoming a system of conveying information. It is itself a pack of information, which can be manipulated. Information is getting an upper hand over material productive processes. Information drives production, which is edged outside the system of information.

This is a clear indication of *the emergence of the mode of information.*

Just Another 'Industrial' Revolution?

It would be a mistake to consider the STR as just another industrial revolution of a higher and more productive type. There is no doubt that the STR is a new industrial and technological revolution. It has increased productive capacities several times. But it is much more than a better productive system. It has not only increased the productive capacities of the society in an unprecedented manner; it has qualitatively changed its nature by adding information as a new factor of production. Information has entered history as a factor not only of production but of the social development itself.

The new industrial revolution in fact is *dissolving the industrial nature* of the industrial revolution, and thus setting up social development on a new basis. That is how grounds are being prepared for a post-industrial evolution of society in multidirectional forms. The STR has called into question the entire history of social development so far.

The STR is changing the relationship between matter and idea, brain and machine, biology and technology, etc fundamentally. Consciousness has become a far more important factor of development. Artificial intelligence has become a reality. For the first time, the functions of the brain ('logical functions' etc) are being handed over to the machine (computer).

The electronically mediated communication is creating a new type of individual and subject, which is decentred and temporary.[1]

We will have the occasion to discuss this further on. It is a micro-electronic revolution based upon the forces inherent to the atom. It uses the forces or signals emitted by the electrons and their movement.

The modern electronic computers, mobiles and other gadgets convert every process, event, action and work into electronic symbols and numbers. These numbers are basically 0 and 1, constituting the binary language of the software of the computer. Everything, whether words and sentences, outlines of drawings, paintings, films, images, music, voice and so on: everything is constituted by the binary language of the electronic signals. Everything has a number base. If we pay a little more attention, we will find that increasing numbers of functions of our lives are convertible into numbers: transport, education, various forms and entries, banking and finance, industrial and other economic and productive processes, information flow, etc.

This is a sign of the mode of production.

STR and Information Revolution Transforming Industrial Spinning Mills

Modern spinning mills are the creation of the industrial revolution. In the pre-industrial era, they were hand-driven, and with the introduction of the steam engine they became machine and mill proper. They became 'industrial'. Later on, oil, electricity and other sources of power were used, which drove the engine, and the engines were improved with suitable innovations.

The mill and machines are industrial because they are driven by a centralized driving system, with a large number of machines arranged in rows and propelled by engines, etc. The worker drives and looks after both the driving system and the machine proper as also after the whole production unit or the shop floor.

It is this mill, particularly the spinning and weaving mills, which are being drastically changed by the STR into 'post'-industrial systems.

In this context, it was interesting to visit a new spinning mill in AP near Guntur.[2] It is using German machines, though they are no more the latest. Newer ones have appeared. Yet there are some interesting features to be noted.

Almost all the 'work' is done automatically, except for a few jobs. The word work here has to be put within quotes for obvious reasons, which need a discussion. The production begins in the hall where the cotton bales are kept, packed and pressed. They are worked upon by a moving machine which takes its threads apart and mixes them. The result material is then sucked up into a pipe and taken to the next room. The machine moves the whole length of the bales to and fro. It is a fascinating sight, as are all the other functions in the factory.

The cotton then is worked upon by a system of carding machines, and transformed into thick and loose threads, which keep getting thinner but more organized through the next system of machines. Then the rolled thick threads are put into a system of a series of spinning spindles, and are gradually worked upon into finer threads. It is fascinating to watch the carded threads being divided into so many thin threads by so many, hundreds, of spinning spindles. They all work automatically, some 600 in one stand, with several of them in one hall. The whole system works automatically, with breaking of threads the only interruptions, which are looked into by the workers moving to and fro. The threads are spun and wrapped onto fast moving bobbins, which are put up on the machines automatically, and once thread is worked out, they fall automatically into open tubes to be taken away to the original place from where they are wrapped afresh by new threads.

This initial stage is called 'bale breaking'.

These threads are worked according to specifications and ultimately at the end of the production process finally wrapped onto bigger spindles as the product of the factory to be sold.

We hardly saw a dozen or so workers in the whole factory at a time.

I also had the opportunity to visit a somewhat older version of a modern spinning mill in Ludhiana.[3] Another one was a mixed type of embroidery mill.

In the first, Guntur, mill, an interesting scene presented itself. It was the first time I saw it. It was the lunch-hour. Some workers were having taking their lunch; others had finished their meal *and had spread some kind of bedding on the floor and were having a nap!* It is a normal practice in that factory and I suppose in many others. The personnel of the management were going around for some work or the other without bothering or the workers without getting bothered. This is the new type of worker, with new habits, freedom and relations with the management. And this is a direct fall-out of the new technology, which provides so much leisurely time for leisurely work. Work is truly being handed over to the machines run by electronics.

The other factory was equally interesting. It basically contained older versions of machines including handlooms and embroidery machines, each running at its own melodious and regular musical manner, though somewhat loudly! The interesting thing was the various stages of their computerization and fitting them with other electronic means like the micro-processors. Some of them had small boards fitted down at the side to register and note stages of the work done, while the worker would accordingly adjust his work. One result of computerization was that the worker did not have to get up to the top of the machine to adjust the jacquards and other objects.

Now, several questions need answers and discussion. We observed the nature of the workers. They appeared no more than *observers* of the ongoing processes, and not exactly 'workers' i.e. they were not exactly doing 'work'. The work was being done *by the machines*. They only saw whether there was any flaw or fault or something missing in the production process and so on. Is this 'work'? If no, then what are they producing? Who is then producing or what is being produced? This is a crucial question. It is quite obvious that the value being put in into the commodity is very small. For example, what value was put into the first process, that of picking and mixing the cotton threads and then transferring it to the next shop? *By the worker, nothing at all.* By the machine, yes some amount. That amount can only be a transfer of the wear and tear to the new commodity.

It is thus clear, and at the same time debatable, that the 'new' commodity has very little new value. Its exchange value is formed mainly by the fixed value transferred, and hardly from the variable value of labour, rather the labour power.

Therefore, the commodity is speeding towards being *value-less*.

Further new and advanced machines have come into operation, which eliminate human labour almost entirely.

So, as explained in the *Grundrisse*, the worker stands beside the production process rather than participating *in it*. The inevitable conclusion is that *the commodity is being created by the machine and not by the human beings*. We simply cannot escape this conclusion. And the workers who stand beside are not workers, since they do not perform any 'work', though they do spend time and even their bodily energies, but not exactly in the course and as part of the production process. The labour process stands *separated* from the production process.

Production is now dominated by the *scientific process* rather than by the labour process.

Mode of Information: Fulcrum of Post-Industrial Society

Till now, human development has been characterised by a *mode of production*, which has driven the society so far. This is a crucial, and the most important, point in our discussion on the post-industrial society or PI production. Now we are in for a massive turn in the course of social development. This turn will be changing everything that we held dear to our life. Till now, the 'mode of production' has been the key concept, the centre of our life, which explained the way we produce, consume and live. Everything in our lives, including philosophy, thought, culture etc is determined by the mode of production, which permeates, dominates and guides the society.

In the scientific theories propounded by Karl Marx, and not only by him but by many others, the concept of mode of production occupies the central and determining position. Its most developed and relatively perfect form is the capitalist mode of production. The theory held its ground so far. It has become part and parcel of our life, thought and economic theories.

Marx was the first to really explain the origin, evolution and development of society, as also its structure in terms of the mode of production. In fact, the concept was his discovery. He presented a simple, yet scientifically profound explanation of the mode of production. It goes something like this.

What distinguishes human beings from animals is the fact that the latter procure their food from nature while human beings *make it*. In order to eat they must first *produce* their food and not get it ready-made from nature. And in order to produce food the humans must *first fashion tools*, which evolve into the means of production. Making tools is precisely the point where society originates. The making and use of tools leads to the emergence of society and its different structures and stages.

By extension the tools become the means of production and productive forces. Human consciousness is the reflection of the creation and use of tools and their extensions. The tools evolve all the time, never for a moment staying at a point, leading all the time to an economy of labour. And this is a *very important point*. Fashioning of tools is a simple but decisive point of departure in the history of biological evolution. Darwin's theory had explained how biological evolution took place and how human beings emerged from the apes biologically.

But the other side of dialectics was left to Frederick Engels to explain. Biological evolution alone does not fully explain the emergence of human beings and does not at all explain the emergence of society. Frederick Engels completed the dialectical other half of the question. It was only then it could be explained how the human being emerged as a biological being and how society was formed. He explains it all in a very brief yet fundamental paper 'Role of Labour in the Transition from Ape to Man'.[4] It is one of the most profound articles or theses ever written, on the same level as Darwin's theory of biological evolution. The biology and physiology of the apes create conditions for the creation of tools, and the use of tools in their turn create conditions for the further development of human consciousness. The process is dialectical, inter-penetrative, and mutual, with periodic reversals of the poles. The biological and the social constitute the two opposite poles of the question, that is of the origin and evolution of human society.

Thus human beings have evolved due to and *within the mode of production, not outside it*. The society developed further, in stages, due to the conflict, contradictions, unity, interplay and mutual penetration of the means of production (forces of production by extension) and the production relations. The whole history has been based upon this basic conflict, all other conflicts accruing from it.

The concept of the mode of production is a crucial tool of the knowledge of society and its development.

Here it would be in order to note the formulation of J.D. Bernal, which we have quoted elsewhere.[5] He says that language was itself a means of production, perhaps the first means.[6] This statement is loaded with so much meaning and potentials that it is necessary to go into detailed analyses. This is what he says:

"Long before such elaboration was possible, human society was evolving language, its most powerful means of cohesion and development. *Language is itself a means of production*, possibly the first of all." The pursuit of game with bare hands or unshaped sticks and stones, needed cooperation of several individuals, and such a cooperation presupposed the use of gestures or words. "This may well have happened long before any instruments had been shaped for their purpose. Early language must have dealt mainly with the getting of food, including the movements of people and the making and using of implements."[7] Bernal also refers to J.B.S. Haldane's views on the pre-human origins of speech. Haldane also thinks that some Paleolithic techniques may have been instinctive, like the making of birds' nests.[8]

Words of a language are necessarily abstract and generalized symbols. "The manipulation of these symbols in the brain together with direct visual *imagination* constitutes *thought*."[9]

Thus language emerged even before the tools, in Bernal's opinion. This may prove an important point when we deal with the mode of information.

Knowledge, Production and Information

It is easier to trace the emergence of knowledge and information in the information age based upon language as the means of production. The technologies of the present era are distinguished from those of the industrial age by their high knowledge content. This content is increasing steadily, in fact rapidly. It has the ability to record the workers' skills and to encode them into the instruments of production using digital technology. His skill is then played back in the absence of human beings. With progressively less machinery and labour, knowledge becomes dominant in the production process.[10]

This is an interesting development from the point of view of the mode of information (post-industrial society). It provides us a clue to the emergence of the post-production mode. The instrument of production is encoded with skill through digital technology. This is possible only in the electronic technology. Therefore, it is an unprecedented and qualitatively different technology, putting human development on a new course.

We may bring in a crucial point made by Shallis at this juncture. He says that when a machine is interfaced to a processor, it is transformed.[11] This digitalized or electronified "tool becomes a system of its own."[12]

Consequently, manufacturing is transformed from a series of productive processes into a system of information flow.[13]

Here we can discern a clear transformation of production of goods into information production or creation. The process is imperceptible and smooth. This is because of the growing importance of knowledge in a qualitative process, leading to a qualitative change into information flow as the dominant process. The whole system and base of the system is changed. The process proceeds beyond the industrial limits and becomes post-production and information dominated.

Information/knowledge threatens the system based upon production and exchange of goods.

Knowledge expresses itself from time to time as technology. Technology is the congealment of experience and information/knowledge.[14]

Mode of Production to Mode of Information

Today, human society has made a radical break with this line of evolution. Now the situation has changed qualitatively and dramatically. Dramatically because nobody expected it and the results were totally unforeseen. *For the first time ever, human beings have begun to develop outside the mode of production and inside the mode of information.* Today, *the mode of information has replaced the mode of production.* A new phase of social development has begun; in fact, in a sense, society has begun developing anew, this time with information as its basis.

Because of this sudden and rapid turn, the concept of the mode of production is proving to be inadequate to explain the present phase of social development. The concept is unable to cover the new trends, and therefore is proving to be more and more limited, and will have to be given up altogether.

The role of information within and outside the factory is on the increase. The world satellite system, internet, e-mail, mobile and such other devices and systems have greatly increased the importance and role of information. Information has become the most important factor in our lives, whether within the factory, offices, education, services, shopping, finance, banking or any other sphere, and in society as a whole including in its motion..

It is now the information which fashions human relations. Work, labour, production, communication, classes, state, government, nation, country, etc. are being created anew by information and its production system. It is a society of images rather than of tangible products.

Society is getting transformed *from production society into information society*.

Factory, the most basic and one of the oldest characteristic of industrial society, is itself being fashioned more and more by information. From industrial factory, it is becoming information factory. It is the speed of the electronic signals which are forcing the factory, tools and production to change.

Factory is now an information flow to and from the machines. Chip-controlled machines can run the system of machines, and in fact the whole factory. The entire industrial process step by step becomes controlled by the chip-run machines.[15] It is an information-dominated and run production, with gradual shift to information production. It goes beyond the industrial limits.

Consequently, the commodities themselves are being transformed, as exemplified, for example, by the bar code, which is synonymous with the time, space and identity of the commodity.

The contradiction is that production took days, weeks and months, while the information about them, or about anything, takes just minutes and seconds. Therefore, production is under pressure to speed up. There is a growing contradiction between production and information, and this propels the society forward. Thus, production is being driven to the limits, and its end as an independent and decisive system is becoming clearer by the moment.

These changes within the factory and in the productive machines are part and parcel of the broader changes that have gripped the world. The satellite system, in conjunction with computers, has created a cover of information around the earth, which is growing rapidly every hour. The earth is enwrapped in unprecedented covers of waves, signals, symbols, images, photos, videos, audios, pages, e-books, journals, and other forms of information. These electronic and electro-magnetic waves are becoming a novel part of the planet earth. This simple yet profound fact is of great and decisive significance for the future of the earth, society, human beings and for human consciousness itself. In fact, it is the waves which are now guiding the social development. *They are creating a new kind of society using information as the vehicle.*

The modern electronic communication is and revolutionizing every economic, social, financial, political, ideological, philosophical, linguistic, subject-object related, etc. process.

The *limits of production* are reaching rapidly. It is becoming clearer that production alone cannot sustain the society. The society must become, with the passing of time, an information processing system, with itself as an *adjunct of information*. It is through processing information that production is being run. Once you process information, you prepare grounds for production of commodities or directly produce commodities. In other words, information straightaway creates commodities. Image gets converted into commodity. This is the revolution, the basis of emergence of *post-industrial, information society*.

Millions of instructions are fed to direct machinery through the semiconductors and computers.[16] The industrial base is thus threatened. Developments in science and technology underline the fact that a clear break with the industrial past has been made. The electronic revolution makes it possible to encode information in electrical pulses rather than in gears and springs.[17]

This is to be quite clearly seen in the growing use of 3–D printing and associated technologies.

The modern communication is speeding up every economic, social, political and cultural process. The latter have to change according to the former. The rate of production, exchange, transport, banking, payment and so on is being accelerated dialectically, that is, in an inter-dependent manner. Speeding up of one sector inevitably leads to the speeding up of another, and so on. And at a certain point along the line of speeding up, the process gets converted into information. Commodity production and money-commodity exchange have acquired unprecedented aspects. It is the hours, minutes and seconds that determine the nature of society, not days, weeks, months or years, *as used to happen* in the industrial age. Today, it is the consumer who is dictating terms increasingly.

The great historic speed up of production, upsetting everything in its path, and more than that, the instant circulation of information upsetting production, is forcing increase in demand, forcing a radical reorganization of the society. This is a novel feature of the post-industrial economy, a natural result of transition to the information-driven society. Every commodity, process and service is getting faster as never before. There is a danger that the existing society will not be able to face this onslaught of high speeds and will disintegrate to regroup or re-emerge as a new entity or unity of entities. Things clearly are going beyond capitalism. We are now living in a post-production, post-capitalist society.

Therefore, a retooling of society and economy is an essential aspect of the present-day human existence. It will be interesting to study the nature and effects of this historic retooling. The new tools are extraordinarily and exotically unprecedented. They emanate as non-tools in the form of electronic and light emissions, performing the same functions as the tangible tools, yet getting dissolved in the process. They in fact dissolve the hitherto existing social structure created over millennia. They include the use of temporary and *momentary* tools like those of the laser beams. Information is relegating the tools to a secondary and momentary position.

It becomes essential under the pressure of growing circulation of information to speed up not only production but also, and more importantly, banking and finance and in fact the entire society. This is a crucial feature of the new emerging world with great implications for the future.

Dissolution of Labour and Production Processes

Among the implications to be examined is the ejection of labour and production processes out of circulation. The capitalist mode of production had come into being when labour power had become a commodity and entered circulation. Now labour power is ceasing to be a commodity and is thus ceasing to be part of the production circuit. The functions of labour and labour power are being discharged by information technologies. Some of these points we have discussed in Chapter 4.

Science, information and technology are becoming the *new productive forces,* which are inseparable from the information forces.

An example of the American AT & T Company will be illustrative. It began the new production cycle in January 1987 and gave up the old relay system, which was slowing down the *market entry rate* of the products. Instead, the simultaneous production method was adopted. Designing, production of various parts and so on acquired simultaneity. Designs were being adapted according to needs at the shop floor itself.[18]

After three production cycles, the time gap between the demand of the consumer and the supply was reduced by 50%. The production cycle got reduced from two years to one year in 1990.

The contact lens making company, Nipro of the US (Clinton town) was connected with computers with another company situated in Jackson Relay with Vistacon. Nipro used 120 moulds to fulfil the orders of the latter. Vistacon managers were in direct contact with shop floors of Nipro. Vistacon produced lenses according to the needs and demands of each individual. Nipro also kept a watch on Vistacon. Consequently, no defect or delay was found in the supply of one billion parts. The two companies together reduced several indices of production including stocks (reduced upto 80%), space (up to 60%), inspection expenses (up to 90%), etc. Annual expenses were reduced by up to 90%.[19]

The collaboration between Gillette and Nipro too led to similar reduction in key areas.

Today, we are passing through a crucial revolution in use process and usage. The revolution is somewhat like the mass production and consumption of the industrial revolution. But there is a difference. Instead of mass production, we can now talk of precise production based upon information. It has been made possible due to the development of parallel computing. There is no limit to the computing capacity of the machine because any number of increasingly more capable chips can be added to the system. The information processing takes place simultaneously along several lines. There is hardly a difference between memory and processor. The two can be brought together. The memory is a distributed one.

For example, waves can be produced or transmitted within the establishment and endless amounts of data can be produced dealing with all sorts of details. Any number of maps, graphs and pictures can be generated. Earlier their computing would have taken weeks and months but now the computers can do the job within hours and even minutes.

This is loaded with meanings for the future.

Value: Reduction Towards Zero. Labour Theory of Value Irrelevant

There is a great increase in the production of values and in their exchange. The knowledge and information about production and its methods have also spread rapidly. Thus, *information itself has become a new productive force.* This pushes the human being, the worker, *outside* the process of production and transforms her/him into an *observer. He is producing use value without contributing value.* This is a great contradiction of the present transition period. '*Commodities*' are being produced without value or with progressively declining value, moving towards zero, whose estimation can no more be done in the old, *industrial* manner. *This renders the labour theory of value irrelevant*, because its objective conditions have disappeared. Endless number of copies of information can be made through floppies, discs, tapes, videos, pen drives, and mobiles, and directly without their intervention. This does not involve any labour power. They are being copied on a mass scale and are being used in various spheres of social and economic life including production, giving rise to a different kind of economy.

Baudrillard has dealt with the 'political economy of the signs', but in a critical manner.[20] Marx had also criticized the political economy in his *Critique of Political Economy*. Obviously, we will increasingly deal with the *political economy* and *economics of the signs and information* and their forms, rather than with the tangible objects. Political economy will come in for extensive and fundamental criticism.

Labour and Science

We want to raise the question that the whole structure of theoretical systems like Marxism and many others were developed upon labour and labour process and their primacy. They are thus based on the derivations of the industrial revolution.

But the problem is that the labour process itself is disappearing, being replaced by science. What are the implications?

Now, today, the way we raise the questions, and the questions themselves, have to change. The questions/problems cannot be based on *industrial* relations, production and industrial/factory revolution. We have to base ourselves on science as part and parcel of our social system. If the labour process has been separated out of the production process and is disappearing, then the new society, though continuing to produce, *is not based upon labour and the labour process*. It is therefore not raised upon labour-capital relations, and therefore new relations come into reckoning. This calls for a reexamination of the whole social relations and of their process of formation.

Problem is that science replaces labour. Therefore, now we should consider the production, distribution and consumption of science instead of labour.[21] Science acts as the economy- and society-fashioning force, as a new factor of social development. The medium of social change is now science, not capital or labour.

The mode of information signals *the end* of Marx's proletariat.[22] The computer dissolves the old relations and replaces them by new ones. The relations and contacts between the worker and the machine come to an end. New workers or employees do not really 'work'; therefore they cannot strictly be called 'worker' or the 'employees', in the industrial sense. They do not work even when they participate in the production process. The worker is *with* the machine, not in it, is not 'working' with it.

The modern, better to say 'postmodern', worker lives and works among and with computers, screens, information and images. He/she is more concerned with the images and visual results that crop up, every minute and second. These results, the effects, the images themselves become causes of social development. Such a worker, and such a society, loses touch with the solids, the tangibles, the 'seen'. The society is that of images/signals, not of objects. He/she unknowingly, imperceptibly transits into the world of images, which he helps multiply, manages and manipulates. It is a world of images and therefore of production of images, and the human being is dragged away from the objects into the world of its colourful shadows.

This is a different world from that of the artisan or the industrial worker, who is surrounded with and concentrated upon the objects around. He works with his entire body: hands, feet, brain, body, and of course with the tools in order to change it/them. He is among them, in a *Cartesian world,* through labour/capital relations, management/worker contacts. This is the picture that emerges when we talk of 'work'.

The world of the computer operator is quite different. He/she works with the screen, which is the dominant field, creates images, looks at information and images, manipulates images and so on. It is through the images that the individual is in contact with the Cartesian, tangible world of things. The computer worker and mobile operator are in an electronic world where the key-board is the key element of contact with the world. Shoshana Zhuboff relates the experiences of a worker who works in a room full of computers; he is in a state of tension initially but gradually learns to 'work' with these machines and learns to be with them.[23]

'Post-Industrial Information Society'

The data and our discussion clearly show that we have left the industrial society behind and have entered the post-industrial society, with information as its basis.

The decisive factor is that science has become a direct productive and information force. Every process is being converted into waves of information, which in turn affect every social activity.

There are certain characteristics of information, not found in the traditional social and productive forces. Information is not lost while in use. On the contrary, it increases during use, ultimately engulfing the entire world.

This aspect is quite inconsistent with and in contradiction with the individual and private property created by the industrial revolution in particular and the human development in general. Information and its use in fact *violates the laws and nature of capitalism* based on private appropriation, thus going beyond the confines and limits of capitalism, particularly developed capitalism.

Information and Consumer

Owing to the information revolution, there is a sea-change in the manner, nature and structure of consumption and of the consumer. It is a crucial aspect of the information revolution. The revolution has a parallel in the production changes during the industrial revolution. Consequently, it is possible to talk of an information economy instead of production-based one. This is an important point influencing the discussion on the post-industrial society and economy. It only means that while the industrial revolution is production-based, the post-industrial one is information-based. The transition has consequences of an unforeseen nature and we may have to confront some of the most momentous changes in the human society itself, redefining many of its defining moments.

Another point to be noted and studied in detail is the replacement of the productive class by a consuming one driving the motion of society.

Such a transition is possible because of the advent of parallel computing. This type of machine has no limits to computing because any number of parallel processors can be added. The information is processed simultaneously. The difference between the memory and the processors is reduced progressively.

Consequently, huge amounts of information can be processed, all together. For example, the processes going on inside the earth surface can be computed in their endless aspects and inter-relationships. Applied to production, the whole factory can be put within an information system. A *parallel factory* comes up in the form of images and information. And this is the key to understand the mode of information.

Worker as Consumer

It would be a mistake to consider workers only as producers. The worker, besides being a worker, has always been a consumer, but highly exploited one. Today the consumer side of the buyer is enhanced as never before. The STR and associated events develop the consumer aspect of the worker while reducing the producer aspect. A sharp conflict sets in between these two aspects of the worker. By becoming an active and multi-sided consumer, the worker exercises deeper influence on production and distribution. The working class in its broadest spectrum is deeply influencing the developments in the society and economy as consumer. As consumer the worker is directly related with information and its processing.

This is an entirely new development, begging deeper analysis.

Post-Industrial Information Society: Concept of 'Mode of Information'

The dialectics between the mode of production and the mode of information constitutes the basic dialectics of the transition period. The term 'mode of information' has been used by Mark Poster.[24] But his usage is somewhat different from the one in the present book.

Here certain clarifications have to be made regarding the use of the term 'mode of information' by Poster. We use the term in a considerably different sense than Poster. The term proves to be an important tool of analysis. It is a crucial methodological contribution by Poster. The present book has been able to use the term as a really effective tool of analysis. In Poster, the term has several limitations, which are the result of avoiding what he calls 'totalization'. In our opinion, this avoidance has prevented Poster from really using the concept to grasp the new that is emerging at the world level. He analyses the de-centring impact of 'electronically mediated communication' on language structure and the nature and role of the subject. This is of tremendous help to understand the role of language in shaping the new social and subjective realities.

Yet, mode of information cannot be reduced to language alone, nor limited to the impact on the subject. It is the mode as the very basis of the entire range of changes that have gripped the contemporary society. The most basic point is that the hitherto existing society has been based upon and shaped by the mode of production. The mode of information cannot be confined to certain events alone. In our opinion, the mode of information in fact is creating a new society and is re-shaping all the basic relations.

To recall, human society has been shaped by production. The humans are the product of tools, means of labour and machines that create the society by producing the sustenance.[25] Human history is built around how products and commodities are made and consumed.

This crucial fact cannot be ignored in any analysis. Today, we are in the midst of a great transition in which production as the base is being superceded by information. We find the replacement of production of tangible materials by that of production of the intangibles, of information about production and products. The very purpose of our activities is the creation of images even in the course of production. This image in turn drives production and all other activities.

Questions may be raised as to the fact that Marx made the mode of production the centre of his analysis. The mode consisted of two dialectical opposites: the productive forces and the resultant relations of production.

The concept of mode of information re-works this dialectics and derives social relations on a fresh basis.

The point is that first of all the mode has changed its nature simply because information has become the centre of economic activities. The relations that result now are from the way information is produced, used and manipulated, and not from production. Therefore, the relations are and will have to be derived from this new mode based upon information. It is mode in the sense that the base is use of information by new means of information, and its dialectics with the new relations that are being fashioned on this basis.

Consumption versus Production: Place of Body

Baudrillard makes some interesting comments on the role and place of the body in the new world of telecommunications. The modern trend is to look upon the body as an independent organism.[26] In contrast, Baidrillard looks upon the body as dependent on mass communications. The relationship between the body and the society has been transformed. "Our bodies are becoming monitoring screens."[27]

Telecommunications have already surpassed the natural limits of the body and have begun shaping it. For example, TV shapes the angle, depth and context to absorb visual information; radio similarly affects our ears; the computer produces or copies the movements our body is used to.

Thus the telecommunications surpass the natural senses of our body. It zooms in into the data hidden inside the ground surface. And so on.

The body is being *left behind* by the telecommunications revolution. According to Baudrillard, consumption has replaced production as the axis of meaning and association.[28] The body is the supervisor of the actions of the machines, as we have seen in so many examples earlier. According to Baudrillard, the body is now functioning as *the terminal* in the communication network. "It is the *main receptacle* of the contemporary experience."[29]

The author criticizes Baudrillard for being inadequate.[30] He says, Baudrillard correctly assesses the distraction factories of the global communication industry that confuses our sense of change. But to treat humans as 'monitoring screens' or 'terminals in mass communications networks' is an unsuitable answer to this confusion. His sociology does not take circulation into account and is ahistorical.[31]

Benjamin's sociology in contrast, in the opinion of the author, allows for reaction, and his discussion of mass reproduction and global circulation of images, bodies and commodities does not negate but demands a political response.

Positive Response in Baudrillard

Now, here two points have to be discussed. It is wrong to suggest, as Rojek has done above, that Baudrillard has not responded to modern day sociology and politics. The point is that the author is trying to confine the statements to certain formulations in sociology. There is an inherent and hidden, may be unintended, response to postmodern and post-industrial technology in Baudrillard. It is extraordinary that one can even talk of *humans as screens and terminals* in today's world, which is true literally as well as symbolically and conceptually. This development need not be fitted into the traditional modernist and humanist concepts of the human being as 'liberated' and 'independent', as the criticism seems to suggest. Sociology has its own limitations, which at present we will leave aside.

The STR and the ICR are undoubtedly converting human beings into screens and terminals and so on through a basic transformation in the software and loss of hardware and through an *identification of electronics with biology*. These two sciences combine to provide qualitatively new directions for human development. After all, it is now a fact that screens and keyboards can be fitted with or created on the clothes we wear and on our skins. This has been possible because the computers can now be converted into software. Thus their functions can be discharged by the human body and skin. The humans are therefore becoming 'screens and terminals'. Human beings are being transformed into strange beings wherein they are becoming *the objects of their own creation*, thus becoming points or substrata of electronic changes. We can no more deny this.

What Baudrillard misses is the integration of the changes taking place in all the fields. But the author, Rojek, too misses the central point, which is the emergence of a postmodern mode of information. The point is that human beings are objectively becoming the object of these developments of postmodern processes, and thus are becoming new kinds of subjects. Such subjects play their role in vastly different ways, ways that are quite distinct from those in the industrial age. Pessimism in Baudrillard and in the author's criticism, accrue from the fact that they both want to confine the human being within the shackles of modernism and industrialism, even while seeking or claiming a postmodern terrain.

The second point that needs explanation is whether such a human being is suitable for a transition to a new society. Pessimism reigns supreme in postmodernism and among the postmodernists precisely because the existing human being is getting disintegrated. But this is something only to be welcomed! Postmodernism refuses to break itself free from enlightenment and humanist 'projects' (whatever they mean). Sociology as a discipline is now inadequate to explain the new postmodern world; it has to change drastically. Otherwise it will only be nostalgic for the past and shedding tears, somewhat like orthodox Marxism!

The terrain itself is a non-terrain. It is the unity of the subject and the object in a way that it is impossible to separate one from the other and to dissect each in detail. Such a human being can only further help the electronic changes along with itself (himself and herself). The self is dissolved and combined with a self that is coming into being independently at molecular and atomic, nuclear scale. Communication becomes the independent driving force of social development, which more and more is the spread of consciousness beyond. Humanness is enveloping the vast exteriors of the earth and its environs.

It is a break with the past and it is one of the hallmarks of a postmodernist society.

Baudrillard seems to be developing a system of signs and language resulting from a surfeit of commodities.[32] We may take Marx's 'fetishism of commodity' as the starting and guiding principle. What Baudrillard constantly seems to derive is the post-modernist, post-industrial image, which at the same time does not strictly accord with the nature of the commodity 'as commodity', but increasingly with the relations of signs generated by them, losing their commodity forms.

The practical objects are all inter-related in a structure, yet they are all the time in flight away from their technical elements. And this flight is towards a 'cultural system'. The objects are all isolated from each other; it is the user who connects or unites them mutually according to needs.[33]

Baudrillard makes an interesting suggestion of the "'spoken' system of objects, that is, the study of the more or less consistent system of meanings that objects institute..."[34] This is among crucial points in the analysis of a post-industrial society. The relations between the objects establish the relation of signs, which then is consumed by the consumer. The spoken system presupposes a plane of objects which is structured on the technology: this place is distinct from both the spoken place as well as the plane of functional account of the objects according to the functions of their constituents.[35]

Here, technology plays an important role in establishing and giving shape to these relations. The information revolution plays a particularly crucial part here.

"The technological plane is an abstraction: in ordinary life we are practically unconscious of the technological reality of objects. Yet this abstraction is profoundly real: it is what governs all radical transformation of our environment." It is even the most concrete aspect of the object, according to Baudrillard. This is because technological development is synonymous with objective structural development. "... what happens to the object in the technological sphere is *essential,* whereas what happens to it in the psychological or sociological sphere of needs and practices is inessential."[36] The discourse of psychology or sociology refers us to the object at a level unrelated to any individual or collective discourse, namely, the level of *technological* language.

In this connection, Baudrillard discusses Gilbert Simondon's account of the petrol engine. Modern engines are 'concrete', whereas earlier ones were abstract. In earlier versions each component was separate, individual, not connected with others and connected only when necessary. Now, through a process of merger, the functions are continuous, successive, inseparable and convergent. This is a technological reflection of a process whereby the object is truly represented as a technological one. It is concrete, and internally consistent and unified.[37]

"Technology gives us a rigorous account of objects in which functional antagonisms are dialectically resolved into a larger structure."[38]

So far as the modern serial object is concerned, a process of the 'liberation' or 'emancipation of the object' sets in. Due to functional development in mass production, *"liberation from the function of the object only, not from the object itself"* takes place.[39] The furniture like tables, chairs, beds, almirahs, etc are stripped down to their barest minimum of functions. Yet they function better. They function as they should function. They are no longer obscured by the moral theatricality of the old furniture. They are liberated from the old ritualistic ceremonial nature, deliberately put in order to emphasize their class and positional relations. They are thus also, to that extent, liberated from the ideology which justifies the unnecessary superfluous functions of the objects. This is a mutual liberation: such liberation in furniture liberates something in the human being too, who by liberating himself/herself liberates the furniture of the superfluous.[40]

"Today at last, these objects emerge absolutely clear about the purpose they serve." They have 'freedom to function', that is they are now functional objects. And "that is practically the *only* freedom they have."[41]

"Similarly, the bourgeois and industrial revolution gradually freed the individual from his involvement with religion, morality and family." The individual is now free to sell his labour power. Both the freedoms have a profound correlation: while the object has become a 'functional' object, the social individual is liberated in the form of the sale of his labour power.[42]

"Now, just so long as the object is liberated only in its function, man is liberated only as user of that object."[43]

The relationship between the objects is through space; when the space is opened up, full of rhythm, and is expanded, relations between the objects are established. The space can be opened but this may lead to destructuring the objects. A balance is somewhere established.[44]

Consumption

According to Baudrillard, objects and material goods are not in fact the object of consumption. They are the object merely of needs and satisfaction of needs. Buying, possessing, enjoying, and spending are not 'consuming'. "Consumption is not a material practice"[45], nor is it a phenomenology of 'affluence'. It is not defined by use of clothes, other materials, images, visuals etc. "...consumption is *the virtual totality of all objects and messages ready-constituted as a more or less coherent discourse.* If it has any meaning at all, consumption means *an activity consisting of the systematic manipulation of signs.*"[46] "Just so long as it is freed once and for all from its current meaning, that of a mechanism for satisfying needs, consumption may indeed be deemed a defining mode of our industrial civilization."[47]

These points need deep study, as they impart new meaning to consumption, which acquires new meaning in the context of the STR and the ICR.

"To become an object of consumption, an object must first become a sign."[48] That means it must become external to a relationship that it now merely signifies.[49] So, first of

all the objects are mediators of a real relationship, e.g. tool or house create certain relations; then they become certain signs, which signify these relations. Thus they are signifiers.

This conversion of the object into signs and a system thereof implies a transformation of human relation into a relation of consumption, according to Baudrillard. It is a process of consumption and of consuming. The object consummates and abolishes this relationship. Before long, the sign replaces the object.[50]

This is a very important, even crucial, point. Though Baudrillard basically confines the process to the cultural and sentimental processes, it actually applies to and helps us understand the nature and results of the information revolution.

The point is that the ICR converts everything, every process, into a signal or a sign, a reflection of what it actually is. But what is actually going on gradually is relegated into the background and is step by step replaced by the image of the thing and the process. What we begin to deal with ('consume') is the reflection. It is in its image/s that the object is consumed, already. It is a unique kind of consumption.

Baudrillard is right in so far as he says that what we consume is not the object itself. The scientific and information revolution converts the object into something that we can consume *even before consumption*. Theoretically and practically, all the industrial and other kinds of tangible processes and objects can be transformed into images on the screen. In fact, new processes and aspects are revealed in the course of this transformation, unknown previously. When a command is given to an industrial process, it is also a variety of consumption. It establishes a particular relationship with the object 'under command', which is then transformed. The relation is 'outside' the actual relation between the object and the subject. The object is transformed into an image for better understanding and use. It is also a new stage of consumption, wherein use of the tangibility is not enough or where the non-tangible form has to be consumed. At the same time, the conversion prepares the object better for consumption. It is a whole dialectics of endless relations.

Thus we become related *with the relation* between subject and object, and not with the object itself. In the process we seek to change the nature of the object and its relation with ourselves. It is thus a new kind of relation, a typically 'post-industrial' one. And this speaks volumes for the future.

In other words, conversion of the object into signals, information and images *is a post-industrial act.* This conversion is the axis of postmodernism and post-industrialism. What we control is the creation of the image, and we are confident that we will be able to produce the tangible thing as and when we think necessary and fit. This is something unprecedented in human history. To be post-industrial means to control the image, the information, to create them, and through them the production, which is just one of the activities and not the main one. The base of society changes, both in structure and development. The images can in fact not be 'consumed'; they can only be disseminated. So, consumption is dissemination, it is during dissemination that consumption takes place. Baudrillard commits a mistake when he falls back into 'culture'. It is not the pre-industrial culture that we are dealing with. It is the particular result of production at a certain point that we come across, and which is characterized by culture of consumption of images.

'Late' Capitalism and Postmodernism

There are theories which relate postmodernism with 'late' capitalism and culture. Prominent among such theorists are Frederic Jameson, Robert Heilbroner, Baudrillard in his own way, and others. Jameson for example calls postmodernism the cultural logic of 'late capitalism'.[51]

It is not clear as to why postmodernism should be termed the logic of capitalism and that too of late capitalism. Jameson says, the Marxists therefore should oppose it.[52]

The above-mentioned authors have not made their concepts clear, and it is very difficult to establish a consistent logic in them. It appears strange that postmodernism should be reduced to 'culture' only and that it should be considered the logic of late capitalism. On what basis should postmodernism be considered a 'cultural' logic? This is nothing but reductionism, that too without technological and economic determinism, to use words in a positive sense. In what way is it a cultural logic *only* and why should it be devoid of any economic base?

The present-day culture, if taken in symbolic and imagery form, is the product of the information revolution, where the images take on mass form. This quantity lends it new quality. Earlier, culture was an organized and defined activity that determined the non-economic aspect of people's lives. Culture was something estimated as distinct from economics and opposed to it.

Problems have been created by industrial and post-industrial revolutions. Among the new features is the 'mass production' of culture. Information about cultural activity is now being mass produced. Besides, certain new kinds of cultural activities are constantly coming up. They are also being mass circulated. The distinguishing feature about this activity is that culture is being beamed deliberately at the masses, with a mass 'appeal', justifying the 'cultural logic' of late capitalism.

In 'Dialectics of Enlightenment', Adorno and Horkheimer examine[53] the socially approved channels for the discharge of the 'discontents of modernity'. An ideological critique exposes the negative and exploitative side of the mass culture, which they term as the 'cultural industry'. Technologically advanced mass culture is also a form of mass deception. But it should not be reduced to deception alone. It has a positive side too. The masses come to know a lot about science, culture, literature, politics, religion, philosophy, economics and so on in considerable detail. They otherwise would not have been able to know so many details in such a short duration.

In the conditions of mass culture, it is through ideology that capitalism is sought to be stabilized. It also means that something that is no more stabilized as capitalism, has transited into post-capitalism, and has to be 'stabilized' through ideology. While mass culture is something to do with the mass who consume culture, cultural industry dishes out something to the masses from the above.

This process hides the real nature of capitalism and its domination of the masses. Consumption seems to take place in our free time but actually is coupled with the time after work, when the exhausted consumer must have something to relax or escape from the day's stress. It is a pre-digested culture, not something which is yet to be digested. According to Adorno, the high and the low of culture are not diametrically opposed but are torn halves of a freedom which at present cannot be united.[54]

There are too many problems with these analyses. They work within the parameter set by the existing history and refuse to go beyond. How can they claim to be postmodernist is a wonder. The views take a pessimistic and even cymical view of things. This is not to say that they are totally wrong. The point about the mass culture being forced upon the people is well taken and is a reality. It is no doubt the play-field of the giant business houses that extract maximum profits from culture and even dish out all kinds of nonsense and absurdities. All this is true.

But it does not at all explain the new tendencies in postmodernism and culture, nor do they define a postmodern culture. They also do not exhaust the immense cultural potentials of the new technology. It is not that what resides in the masses traditionally is in a water-tight separation from what is being 'dished out'. The point is whether the culture has changed qualitatively and whether as human beings we are creating new culture and transmitting it through new electronic or whatever media as part and parcel of our lives. In other words is there a postmodern culture?

There is a drastic need to redefine culture in the context of postmodernism, which these authors have failed to do.

Electronic mediation establishes new relations between human beings, which leads to the question of culture anew. For example the contemporary cultural consumption may not be distinct songs and dances but their mass forms. The mobiles, computers and TVs make it possible to convey and inter-connect instantly. This instant nature of culture is something new and different. While there is a culture of the mobile, there also is the mobile for culture. *The very use of the mobile is itself a cultural act.* Or the use of the laptop may be generating new values at unseen and minute levels because of their production of images and information every moment and on a mass scale. This qualitatively changes the presentation of the question. Now we have to find out whether culture can preserve its existing structure or is being decentred owing to the electronic revolution.

A dispersed culture disperses among the vast humanity and renders it transformed. Such culture is being mass produced by the images. It acts also as a great leveller, cutting across class, gender, caste, community, racial, and national barriers. Something is taking place which never happened in human history.

According to Best and Kellner,[55] techno-culture explains the new turn in culture. According to them, all human cultures have had their technological components but no culture till the 20th century has been so dominated by technology and technological thinking as ours.[56]

This is what we have said just a while ago. Anyway, we will go ahead. According to Best and Kellner, techno-culture arises when culture is defined more by science and technology than by religion, social norms, ethics, etc. Even families and individuals are wired with each other, which overcomes all other influences. These cultural relations become electronically mediated. New technology also leads to new possibilities for creating new culture.

Features of techno-culture:

1. The first feature of techno-culture is that technology more and more pervades human society through new apparatuses, gadgets, machines, etc. The result is that our relation with nature as well as society is mediated. With the development of the consumer society, we are increasingly surrounded, in fact engulfed, by electronic commodities. We have more technological gadgets than ever before. Virtually every activity is mediated. The rhythm of our life today is far different and farther from the natural surroundings.[57]
2. With growing machine use and automation, the tasks of society and individuals are now being executed by machines. Automated systems are now running the world of work. They are even talking to each other,

as is clear from the use of robotics. Micro-technology is taking over our homes and workplace.[58]

3. Techno-culture is distinguished by the domination of techno-consciousness. It is a form of thought governed largely by mathematical and analytic reasoning. It is called *instrumental reasoning* by the Frankfurt School. According to Best and Kellner, within techno-culture, information replaces knowledge; as Marcuse said[59], 'one-dimensional thought' replaces critical and dialectical reasoning. In this and other aspects like emergence of paid instrumental aristocracy, techno-capitalism triumphs.[60]
4. [It is difficult to agree with the second half of the point made by Best and Kellner. The point about one-dimensional thought is difficult to agree to. But it needs to be discussed.]
5. Techno-culture replaces social life with commercially and technologically mediated communities such as in the universities, malls, etc.[61]
6. Techno-culture also invades nature and biology.

Mainframe and PC: Impact on Culture

Best and Kellner[62] provide an interesting debate on the work of Turkle on this issue. Turkle interprets the transition from big computers to PCs as corresponding with the shift from big machine and bureaucracy to innovative computer work and a new type of subjectivity and culture. Giant IBM mainframes are suited to centralization and hierarchy and are thus 'modern'. They are figures for modernity. Such computers are related with mechanical machine type of work and science, and are universalist, rationalist, top-down, with a cult of experts, and masculine, that is rooted in hard masculine science, logical and abstract.[63]

On the other hand, the PCs *are more compatible with postmodern logic* and aesthetics. Postmodern PC technologies are soft and feminine, more graphic, more maneuverable. Modern PCs are user-friendly, requiring only a click or two, without going behind into the technical details. Simple clicks help you to navigate the cyberspace.

Modernity and Post-Modernity

Among the ideas that permeate the world of postmodernism is that of 'post-modernity'. Gianni Vattimo is among the leading theorists of post-modernity.[64] According to the translator's introduction to the book, "The idea of 'post-modernity' lies at the centre of contemporary intellectual debate in the West."[65] The field deals with painting, aesthetics, ballet, theatre, cinema, literature and philosophy. It is observed that the Western ways of seeing, knowing and representing them have irreversibly changed, but it is not clear as to what exactly this means and in what direction.[66]

The translator's introduction raises a question whether these changes represent an impact of STR/ICR, influence of mass media and de-industrialization in the West and their impact upon culture and society; or do they constitute the logic itself of modernity? Vattimo seeks to develop a philosophical base for understanding the closure of modernity and its consequences for the arts and sciences.[67]

His concern for philosophical tradition is accompanied by the awareness of the failure of philosophy to tackle the problems of alienation caused by the technological civilization. The 'desert' is growing in all the fields, as the introduction by the translator says. He hopes that this enquiry will help to fill the empty space.

The problem with this book is that it is based on a nihilistic outlook, and it is difficult to say what it can offer by way of solutions. If the attitude to technology is negative, and the problems are traced to 'alienation' caused by it, then one is afraid the very base of 'post-modernity' is lost sight of. Further on we are told that "*The End of Modernity* must be set against the backdrops of the tradition of European nihilism to which it belongs."[68] So the aspect of nihilism is confirmed. In this context, the question arises as to whether post-modernity comes after modernity and what is the linkage between the two.

The translator of Vattimo's book Jon Snyder suggests that modernity and post-modernity are concurrent in the work.[69].

A Discussion on Modernism and Postmodernism

This means that there is clear confusion about the concepts. We clearly differ with the meaning/s of the terms used such as modernity and post-modernity. It is obvious for us that modernity and modernism are the product of the industrial age. What we mean by the modern is basically a negation of the feudal mode of production by the industrial/ capitalist, accompanied by the corresponding changes in the way of life, social attitudes, culture, thought, democracy, philosophy, trends towards urbanization and so on. It is also obvious that modernism is ultimately based upon large-scale production and production base of such a nature. Modern market and means of communications, in particular the railways, outline the contours of modern life.

Modern thought is a way of looking at things and thinking, which place things in a certain relationship. The basis of this relationship is the modern industrial relation between the subject and the object.

So, this more or less, constitutes the modern, modernism and modernity for us.

Now, the problem for us as far as the relation between modernism and postmodernism is concerned is basically the impact of the electronics revolution and of what goes by the name of STR and ICR on modernism. What impact has the STR etc on modernism and on the modernist society? That involves the impact upon and changes in production methods, ways of looking at things, thought and philosophy, subject-object relationship and so on and so forth.

In other words, the problems are deeply concerned with the phase of transition that the world society is going through. We consider that postmodernism is the logical result of modernism or of 'the modern' due to the impact of the STR. The structures of objective life and thought process created during the industrial age are being dissociated, changed, modified, made obsolete, new thought, philosophy, subject-object relationship, mode of production, means of production, information and circulation are coming into being, which do not tally with the laws, existence, objects, ways of creating objects, subject-object relations etc of the modern period and structure. The subject itself is undergoing drastic changes. Electronics is creating new linguistic forms and structures, the subject is decentred, production is decentralized, means and tools of production are getting smaller and smaller, tools are even disappearing, and hardware is dissolving, ceding primacy to the software, and so on.

Therefore, we have to analyse the emergence of a new postmodern, post-industrial society based upon the mode of information, and not on the mode of production.

References

1. See Mark Poster, *Mode of Information: Poststructuralism and social Context*, Polity Press, 1990.
2. The visit took place in 2013.
3. This visit took place in 2014.
4. Frederick Engels, *Role of Labour in Transition from Ape to Man.*
5. See Chapter 10 of this book.

6. J.D. Bernal, *Science in History* (in 4 volumes), Penguin, 1969, Volume 1, p. 72.
7. J.D. Bernal, ibid.
8. Bernal, ibid., see Notes for pp. 41 and 72.
9. Ibid., p. 73, emphasis in the original.
10. Jim Davis and Michael Stack, "Knowledge in Production", *Race and Class*, 34, 3 (1992), pp. 1–2.
11. Michael Shallis, *The Silicon Idol: The Micro-Revolution and its Social Implications*, Oxford University Press, 1984, p. 47.
12. Shallis, p. 47.
13. Shallis, pp. 47–48.
14. See also, Davis and Shack, p. 3.
15. Shallis, p. 48.
16. See also, Davis and Shack, p. 4.
17. Davis and Stack, p. 7.
18. John Hanley, "AT & T's Speedier Product Cycles", *World Link*, Geneva, Nos. 3–4, 1990.
19. *Tom Peters Seminar*, Vintage, 1994, pp. 255–56.
20. Mark Poster, *Mode of Information*, p. 57.
21. Mark Poster, p. 52.
22. Ibid., p. 129.
23. Ibid.
24. Ibid., p. 5.
25. See, Frederick Engels, *Role of Labour in Transition from Ape to Man.*
26. Chris Rojek, "Baudrillard and Politics", as Chapter 6, in, eds. Chris Rojek and Bryan S Turner, *Forget Baudrillard?*, Routledge, 1993, p. 112.
27. Rojek and Turner, p. 113.
28. Ibid., p. 113.
29. Ibid., 113, emphasis added.
30. Ibid., p. 120.
31. Ibid., p. 120.
32. See, Jean Baudrillard, *The System of Objects*, Navayana Publications, New Delhi, p. 6.
33. See, Jean Baudrillard, ibid.
34. Ibid., p. 2.
35. Ibid., pp. 2–3.
36. Ibid., p. 3, emphasis in the original.
37. See, ibid., pp. 3–4.
38. Ibid., p. 5.
39. Ibid., p. 16; emphasis in the original.
40. Ibid., p. 16.

41. Ibid., emphasis in the original.
42. See, ibid., p. 16, footnote no. 3.
43. Ibid., p. 17, emphasis in the original.
44. See, ibid.
45. Ibid., p. 218.
46. Ibid., p. 218; emphasis in the original.
47. 39. Ibid., p. 217.
48. Ibid., p. 218, emphasis in the original.
49. Ibid.
50. See ibid., pp. 218–19.
51. See, Fredric Jameson, *Postmodernism, or, the Logic of Late Capitalism,* Duke University Press, 1991; also see, Jon Simons (ed.), *From Kant to Levi-Strauss: The Background to Contemporary Critical Theory,* Edinburgh University Press, 2002.
52. Jon Simons (ed.), *From Kant to Levi-Strauss: The Background to Contemporary Critical Theory,* Edinburgh University Press, 2002, p. 115.
53. Simons, p. 140.
54. Ibid., p. 141.
55. Steven Best and Douglas Kellner, *The Postmodern Adventure: Science, Technology, and Cultural Studies at the Third Millennium,* The Guilford Publications, New York, 2001, p. 215.
56. Best and Kellner, ibid., p. 215.
57. Ibid.
58. Ibid., p. 216.
59. Herbert Marcuse, *One Dimensional Man: Studies in the ideology of the advanced industrial society,* Boston: Beacon, 1964.
60. Best and Kellner, 216.
61. Ibid., p. 217.
62. Ibid.
63. Ibid., p. 218.
64. See, for example, Gianni Vattimo, *The End of Modernity: Nihilism and Hermeneutics in Postmodern Culture,* [tr and intro by Jon R. Snyder], The John Hopkins University Press, Baltimore, 1988.
65. Vattimo, p. vi.
66. Ibid.
67. Ibid., p. vi-vii.
68. Ibid., p. x.
69. See Vattimo, ibid., translator's note.

6

Are We Living in Capitalist Society?
Some Questions of Transition to Post-Industrial Society

The crucial question in the discussion on post-industrial society is: are we living in a capitalist society any more? The normal answer would be, yes, we are in a capitalist society, we undoubtedly are part and parcel of the capitalist society, we live in capitalism. When we look around we find the whole system functioning according to capitalist laws and with capitalist features. Both supporters and opponents will confirm it. Besides, we are living in a normal society, a society where everything is according to human nature and habits acquired through the ages. We even forget that it is any particular society, and for common people the particular stage and nature of social development does not matter much. They are living in a society, and that is all that matters. What the common people will want is better amenities and facilities. It does not matter whether the society is capitalist or whatever.

More penetrative and conscious people, academics, leaders, analysts are more concerned with the problem of it being a 'capitalist' society or not, etc. A substantial amount of literature is being manufactured on various aspects of capitalist society as a separate field of study. Others like the activists and leaders are busy either improving it or overthrowing it altogether.

Yet, on a deeper penetration, we come across certain interesting developments. There have emerged in the recent decades and years, features of the present society, which do not exactly fit in with the concept of capitalism, both in popular perception and in the strict theoretical sense. If we look around carefully, we find momentous changes in the society in the last few decades, which we generally choose to ignore. We are experiencing many unprecedented and fundamental changes. Phones, communications, transport, TV, mobiles, computers, chips and many other changes have caught hold of our lives. They continue to change our lives *fundamentally* in the last few decades alone.

These changes are too rapid for us. They are producing conflicts between the slow-motion economic, cultural, political, family, civilizational, social etc life derived from the industrial revolution, and the extremely rapid-motion electronic revolution causing breathtaking transformations in the means of production, information transmission and way of life. This is *the basic contradiction* of the present transition. Though science and technology are developing rapidly ahead, the society is very slow in changing old ideas, habits and practices. The two do not often match each other.

There is even resurgence of revivalism, and very strong at that, including through the electronic media, etc. It is strange to find even computer specialists and others offering water to the distant sun! or women observing 'karva chauth' for the welfare of their husbands, by looking at the moon through the net. They include women working in the electronic field! While women are progressing in every field, and claim advance in many sectors, and it is true to a considerable extent, they are still to fight off the extremely traditional and obsolete strait-jackets of traditions. Why should educated women not fight off the outdated and extremely sectarian closed-minded ideas? They and the men must start doing so. It is strange to see information on science and technology and on astrology and position of stars side by side on the same page of newspapers.

There are any number of conflicts and contradictions, which are but natural. The STR is yet to unleash a corresponding cultural and social and theoretical and ideological reform movement.

STR and New Ideas: Extraordinary Times

But this is at present not our main point. The point is that we are witness to many new developments not fitting the traditional and existing society.

We are living in extraordinary times, a time of unprecedented transition, much higher and deeper than in the industrial age. There is an extraordinary growth, in fact an outburst, of the development of means of production, which is changing into means of information and communication. Never before did the productive forces develop so much so fast. They are just smashing and driving away all the existing social structures. It is an unprecedented development.

It imparts crucial responsibilities on us. The most important one is to recognize the fact that we are part and parcel of the historic social transition based on a novel type of technological revolution. This central axis or contradiction determines every other event.

Consequently, we are on the verge of a new, historic age, a new society post- everything that existed so far and continues to exist.

There is rapid urbanization, growth of high-rise buildings, swift transport, fast trains, fly-over, air services, industrial and electronic development, etc. The urban and the whole social scene are changing. Unprecedented urbanization and a rapid loss of rural and agricultural areas are going apace. The nature of society is therefore changing. *For the first time it is urban and not rural.*

The market is bursting at the seams. This quantitative explosion certainly has qualitative implications. Except from time to time, most of the goods are available which cannot be consumed. The society is being overloaded with consumer goods. Consequently, the consumer is becoming the main factor in the *social* market, on occasions dictating terms. The struggle for market and for its expansion and democratization is growing. Thus the market mechanism has become important as never before.

The prices of goods in the latest sectors like electronics are falling rapidly. *This does not accord with the nature of capitalism.* The fall in prices of electronic goods is due to the space between the electrons and in the atom. Thus for the first time a *non-economic factor* has entered economics, and the factor is *not working according* to the capitalist laws.

Rise in prices has been the trend of the society in general and capitalism in particular. The general trend of the price of electronics is to fall, and here lies a key to the problem under consideration.

Since labour is going out of production, the commodity is losing value. Consequently, their prices are *a survival of the past,* and it is doubtful how far capitalism will be able to stick to the past to maintain the prices. Profit continues to be the motive force of capitalist production. But how far can capital gain profit out of non-creation of value? This is a serious new question.

The labour process has separated out of the production process and is dissolving. Therefore, commodity production is under a serious threat.

Capitalism must get profit, therefore must change models of commodities, to the extent of being artificial and ridiculous. It is trying to prevent further development and improvement of commodities, but they being products of electronics, are going rapidly *out of the capitalist orbit*. The smaller the object, the more difficult it is to gain *profit* out of it and more difficult to own it. The institution of property is already being shaken and dispersed. The process is almost reaching the border-line where it will become a means of personal use and even production at personal level. 3–D printing technology seems to confirm this conclusion.

The small and the minuscule are unsuitable as the source of profit. History of production shows that *production has always been carried with tangible objects*. This has been so even under such a productive system as capitalism, which abounds in endless number of commodities. In fact, commodity production today can be equated with the capitalist mode of production.

But the entry of electronic production is a new factor and for the first time production is being carried on with sub-atomic forces and a variety of rays and at the same time, very small, even microscopic objects are being manufactured. This in no way accords with the capitalist mode of production.

If commodities can be manufactured by remote 3–D printers and copiers, the laws of commodity production break down. Production is becoming individual oriented, as distinct from petty commodity production. It is nearing the production of use values only, while the exchange value is being siphoned off.

We find people today much better dressed and with better living. They are no more the beggar-like people with torn clothes found a few decades earlier. Capitalism has certainly created a mass of effective productive forces, which has spread all over the society. Credit should go to the scientific and technological revolution, which is a product of the capitalist mode of production.

The life-expectancy has grown and general well-being can be seen. This is not to cover up or conceal the contradictions, crises and anti-people aspects of capitalism.

The crises of industrial capitalism are those of its growth, not of its collapse. The present phase of transition from capitalism and industrialism to post-capitalism and post-industrialism contains serious crises of explosion of productive forces, of their transition, of the novelty of the information revolution. The society is nearer the aim of meeting the basic needs of the people. The people have become more consumer-oriented, in addition to being the usual consumers of basic necessities like food, clothing, housing, etc. Today, for the first time, people focus on having things like mobiles, TVs, computers, etc. Mobiles are becoming more interesting every day, reflecting the vast tectonic shifts in the social formation. It reflects a collapse of space, time, labour processes, cultural activities, and what not. It threatens to become the basic means of production, something which capitalism will find it difficult to negotiate.

Capitalism and New Productive Forces

Is capitalism capable of handling the new technological forces? The fact is that it is under capitalism that the greatest ever burst of productive forces has taken place. As we have seen, there has been an explosion of new technologies, methods of production and information, and extraordinary events in the field of education, health, transport, ways of living, etc. The role of market forces, the operation of supply and demand, the flexibility in the system to adjust and to overcome crises, etc. have all helped science and technology to become the new forces in social and economic fields.

Capitalism is a vast field with a wide variety of ownership and property. While growing monopolization and financialization certainly exist, the extraordinary growth of tiny, small, medium and non-monopoly sectors must not be ignored. The growth of monopolies has certainly led to a concentration and centralization, but has not resulted in throwing out the small-scale production and distribution. In fact the latter has grown. This fact must not be lost sight of.

In certain senses the smaller scale of economic and social activity has benefited more from the STR than other sections of the society. Use of sub-atomic and quantum levels of energy, of science as the productive force, and the operation of the electronics has spread the productive and informative capacities to the remotest corners and almost to every individual. This is mass scale capitalism. That is one reason why capitalism still has tremendous potentials for growth.

Mass and individual level productive and information forces take capitalism almost to its own limits, where the border-line between capitalism and non-capitalism or post-capitalism gets blurred. There is no 'individual' capitalism: it is either pre-capitalism or post-capitalism. This is exactly what is happening with capitalism. The capitalist ownership and property is breaking up into individual private 'ownership', which is highly volatile. In fact, the individual capitalism (ownership, property, production etc) brings the means of production to every individual. In that case it is 'not-capitalism'.

Introduction of information (that is science) into production removes the main basis on which capitalism is created. Information being anti-production is, by implication, also anti-capitalism. It is not possible for the laws of classical capitalism to survive for long in 'information capitalism'.

The material conditions of a post-industrial order are strengthened, which simultaneously have a tendency towards post-capitalism.

At the same time, the mobile is the most effective means of information today. It is for information that its use is spreading so rapidly. This is a *non-capitalist* aspect of society.

The technology is becoming children-oriented and women-oriented, particularly the former. The children therefore lay the basis of future societies. Instead of being this society and that, the change has become one continuous process. Human consciousness enters the very domains of the atom, particle and the wave. Thus consciousness becomes one with the mode of information, something that contradicts the laws of 'capitalist' development.

What do we see around us? The poor may not have proper food, but they *must* have mobiles. Why? This is something that has never happened before. Human beings do not live by bread alone: that has been a saying, not very old. And it is true, cleared after much debate. Why capitalism is unable to tackle new means of production and communication after having developed them most and even while continuing to do so? This is because capitalism must *gradually dissolve itself* in the course of creation and use of continuous new means based on electronics, light energy, nanotechnology and so on.

Capitalism is a system based on development of large and larger scales of means of production. Capitalism means large-scale factories and machines. Otherwise, it will turn into the petty production system of workshops, small factories, artisans and so on, and it cannot be that. Otherwise the steam engine will be useless. Industrial capitalism is basically a product of steam engines and of the large-scale production created as a result. How technology is so closely related with the development of society and means/forces of production!

Today, capitalism is facing a sort of *identity crisis*. Suddenly, the trend towards large-scale production has been reversed, *so has been the trend towards capitalism.* This raises several basic questions, answers to which help us understand the present and future societies. The productivity now is so high that the society can afford to shift production to secondary positions. We see everybody using electronic gadgets, which connect to the world of information and which also have a potential for production. The individual has a greater manoeuvrability and control over the processes, even if a limited one.

The production is becoming smaller on scales, creating problems for giant, centralized and large-scale establishments, as had happened with the IBM in the transition from big to mini-computers. So, it is a transition to small-scale production *which threatens to break up the large-scale means of production and every kind of centralized control.* A transition is being made from big industrial production to smaller level and individual level production, weakening the base of capitalism.

At the same time, capitalism itself is spreading in breadth. It is making it possible for the means of production and information to reach every individual, as also the commodities and things. Capitalism has caused the biggest ever commodity explosion and market expansion, which augurs well for the masses and for the future. A basic turn in social development has taken place. Goods and consumption have become mass urbanized force. Therefore, it is not capitalism in the classical sense.

Post-Industrial 'Machines'

It is interesting to note that even the common man is

increasingly using 'post-industrial' machines or gadgets. From now onwards it will become increasingly difficult to use the word 'machine' in the traditional established sense, established mainly by the habits of the industrial revolution. The new human beings are more and more using the 'touch-screen', which is *not a machine* in the strict sense. Use of the 'remote' is becoming common now: in AC, cars, and most important, in the TV. Transferring photos and videos from mobile to mobile and computers is now a common occurrence. Without realizing it, the people and their children are using a tool which is not a tool, working upon or commanding the objects of use set *at a distance*, something extraordinary, magical and seemingly 'non-material' or 'non-tangible'.

Mobiles and computers are sets or gadgets of manipulating and producing information, using it to create objects and further information, to set processes in motion.

How do we evaluate the human beings using tools of remote control? Obviously this is going to be a common occurrence in a future not so distant. It is a new subject-object relationship. To control TV is to control the world, at least for the children, for they start their life with TV and mobiles as their companions and part and parcel of life, as their parents are. They have a whole world to themselves.

Is it capitalism or capitalist society? Why this question? It is because capitalism emerged and evolved on the basis of tangible tools and machines, and established a clear-cut relation between the subject and the object of work. The concept of 'work' and 'labour' are the defining moments, the clear-cut lines defining a whole society and the individual. Exploitation and extraction of surplus value was a clear-cut process. It seems that the process of dissolution of surplus value has begun at the individual level.

Prices are rising generally, of the basic items of life. Yet they are going towards a minimum. There is a simultaneous fast growing trend in the opposite direction, of fast falling prices. It is difficult to apply capitalist laws of economics to these trends. Economics as a discipline fails to explain this new phenomenon.

The public transport is becoming a widespread and common phenomenon all over the world. Does it signify growth or decline of capitalism? It can by no means be termed a decline. It is a rapid growth of rapid transport, a phenomenon acquiring independent existence, independent of capitalist nature of things. Is this transport system capitalist or post-capitalist? It is an interesting question.

The new generations successively are going to be born into conditions far removed from classical and 'existing' capitalism. What then is classical capitalism? And how is present capitalism going to be different from the present one? For example what will the generations two to four decades hence be using and behaving like? How will software users using keyboards and screens on their clothes and bodies react? How will a society using nanotechnology and super-conductivity be like using tools, gadgets, means, transport, information tools and methods? These no more belong to the world of fantasy or sci-fi but have the real possibility of development; science and technology are developing and becoming productive and information in that direction.

The question boils down to this: whether there can be a capitalist society based upon nano-tech and super-conductivity and software minus hardware and so on. It is interesting to note that they are already spreading. They threaten the very basis of the industrial society. And the industrial society today is basically a capitalist society. Can nanotechnology generate surplus value? Are they meant for surplus at all or just for immediate usage? It is not easy to answer, yet bare outlines of the future are emerging.

The new generations are going to live in an environment of the human-computer and brain-computer interface, virtual reality and software operations as a reflection of the dissolution of machines. There is going to be a merger of biology and technology. So they will be part of *a machine-less world,* in a sense. These developments are of vital implications for the future.

The loss of machines, for example, begs answers to several questions. It will be for the first time that we can be talking about humans and society without machines. It is interesting to note that the machines will be dissolving into the physical bodies of the human beings, creating a convergence and dissolution of the biological and the physical. A tool-less, machine-less event is a new beginning for society and history. Humans will obviously be fulfilling many of their needs without recourse to production as a social system. Production will be an *individual system* depending entirely upon the *person-oriented tools* and production. In fact production through software is neither production nor creation of commodities. This futuristic scenario is very much rooted in the present. It raises the vision of creation of use values only, without recourse to the production of exchange value and thus of commodities.

Thus at least in part, the production of exchange values will cease to take place. At least in part, and in growing part, it will be the use values that we will produce, rather create, and this will begin a process of the dissolution of commodity production. The laws of industrial, capitalist, commodity production are getting suspended one after another. The industrial laws cannot survive the electronic and sub-atomic world. It is the laws of the sub-atomic world, expressed as the electronics revolution and its processes, in the transformation of science as the productive force, that step by step dominate the production and communication system. Science becoming the productive force means first and foremost all the scientific laws becoming productive laws. At the same time it also means a quick transmission of information about production. Obviously the processes are beyond the control of existing capitalism. The productive forces have outgrown the capitalist confines and capitalist order of things, which can no more take care of the new productive and information forces.

Science goes beyond the confines and control of capitalism with the use of electronics in particular and micro-physics etc in general.

Does it mean that capitalism has become a fetter and that it is no more able to develop the productive forces? It is too hasty conclude thus. Capitalism is a system of several dimensions and industrial characteristics. They provide favourable structural environment for it. It is not eternal. Capitalism has been responsible for the greatest ever and most rapid development of productive forces.

These very productive forces now find capitalist system is not enough for their growth, and therefore, certain laws are being suspended, new ones being developed and several new features are being evolved which do not accord with industrial capitalism.

When we talk of capitalism, we mean basically industrial capitalism. There has not been any other type except the industrial one. Commercial capitalism is not capitalism in strict sense of the term. Therefore, the question arises as to whether capitalism is as such when it loses its industrial character.

Thus there are simultaneously two realities, inter-penetrating and overlapping. One is the continued existence of capitalism, and the other is the tendency to go beyond its confines. These two in fact form a unified whole in which the latter tendency is gaining ground. Capitalism is not something limited and confined to a kind of 'society'; it is in fact society itself. Therefore, a mechanical separation of 'capitalism' from society will create methodological problems for us, as is generally the case. Often capitalism is looked upon as something definite and distinct, different from society, different from what is common and general for the observer. It is not looked upon as a natural social order at a certain point of time in history.

This is a big theoretical and practical problem, which actually obscures much of the reality under the cloud of preconceived notions and ideological predeterminations. This is true of both the supporters and the opponents of capitalism.

Actually, things are quite different. The observer of 'capitalism' cannot put himself/herself outside the 'frame' of capitalism and then draw certain conclusions, as happens quite often. What we should realize is that capitalism is a normal and natural society, just like any other. It is society, and we can interchange the two words. If we do this, we will in a better position to analyse the trends in social development without binding ourselves to 'capitalism', as supporters or opponents.

If we replace the word 'capitalism' with the 'present society', the things will be much easier, because then we will be free from the prejudices associated with capitalism. Then we will be looking for trends in social development and identifying new phenomena. Capitalism then will be part of society and not vice versa. Capitalism is more of a trend in social development. It has varied potentials, some of which are exhausted, others are not.

The productive forces that the present society have developed have helped the growth of capitalism and now the trend is going beyond the dominant capitalism. Thus the new levels of productive forces both help capitalism, and yet prepare grounds for the suspension of capitalist laws and ultimately of capitalism itself. These forces do not always accord with the nature and structure of capitalism.

The new forces of production and information have a tendency to go beyond the limits of capitalism.

The productive forces have transformed themselves into forces of information with the help of science, which gets converted into technology. What is new and distinguishing is that science and its application becomes part of our individual and social life, an inalienable part.

Satellites, Space Technology and Space Station

One great event totally ignored amidst earthly contradictions and conflicts is the operation of International Space Station or the ISS. It is one of the greatest historic events of mankind.

The space era began with the launch of the first satellite, the Sputnik, in 1957 by the Soviet Union. Since then the human beings have crossed many important milestones along the outward journey into space. Another major landmark was the landing of man on the moon by the US in 1969. Neil Armstrong was the first human being to set foot on the surface of the moon.

One of the major transformations due to our travel into outer space has been philosophical. We are able for the first time in our history *to look at ourselves from outer space.* This is an unprecedented event, wherein we separate ourselves from ourselves; we transcend ourselves, and look back at the planet earth with its society as a unity. We thus look at a different society from that which we live in. We look at a society which looks holistic from space, free of its class, community, national, local and other contradictions, at least with contradictions drastically reduced. We thus are able to visualize, our future. The earth looks a beautiful blue-green and white planet, and thus encourages us to free it from all the social and natural contradictions. We are virtually being requested to free the planet from all the pollution, degradation and ecological toxicity.

It is a philosophical statement as well. It is a philosophical and scientific view.

The greater the advance in technology and science, the deeper we are able to go into space, and the better we are able to look at ourselves. The landing of human beings on the moon and the proposed plans to land on Mars are developments in that direction. We are evolving for the first time as extra-planetary beings, as residents of the planet earth, one of the planets of the solar system and the galaxy. We are developing a different outlook and identity, something quite different from that on the earth, something unique.

The satellite system, Internet and computer network, make it possible to have a more objective, rational and unified look at human beings. It is extraordinary that we thus develop conceptually.

We are able to look at ourselves on the screen in the room itself. We are beamed back to ourselves from space. Our objectivity and the subjectivity, either in space or on the screen, are united at the higher levels.

The ISS is a unique human achievement, which has not received the attention it deserves. It is a giant station by any standards, orbiting the earth for the last several years. Many astronauts and cosmonauts have been travelling to and from the station, which are from different countries. They stay out in the space in the ISS for several months and conduct various scientific experiments. And then they return, to give way to other scientist-cosmonauts.

The ISS is expanding, with new wings being added from time to time. Many scientists work simultaneously and live there out in space. Thus a unique space community and concept of 'space community' is taking shape.

These developments indicate the trends towards the future.

According to an interesting report, a robot is replacing a faulty camera on the Canadian robotic arm of the ISS. This is the first time that the job is being done by a robot. The Canadian robot called 'Dextre', was in the middle of a week-long repair job.[1] Together, Dextre, Canadarm@ and the base make up the ISS's robotic Mobile Service System, making the first ever robotic self-repair in space. Thus the number of space walks is reduced.[2]

Our Attitude to Post-Industrial Society

We cannot explain post-industrial society with the help of the *categories of the industrial* society.

It is clear from the discussions in various chapters that labour process is separating out of the production process and getting dissolved. If labour power is **not** included in the price of the commodity, how then is its price determined? It is clear that the value of the commodity is determined by the inherent energy in the electronic processes, instead of by labour power and labour time. Since the electronic power adds almost no value to the commodity, there is no relation now of the price with the value of the commodity. Instead of being the reflection of value, the price now reflects the whole of social-economic and production process based upon STR. Therefore, all the categories of economics have lost their meaning.

Since the labour base of production is disappearing, *all the classes are threatened* and their structures breaking up.

The classes are losing their close class connection with big industrial production and plants/factories.

Machines, factories, plants, complexes are now getting decentralized, dissociated and dissolved.

Class is a special relation of the group or community of human beings to large-scale means of production. The peasantry is not class in a strict sense of the term; small-scale producers constitute class only imperfectly. Classes were made perfect by capitalism and industrial production. The working class and the capitalist class are the most perfect classes, with fully developed features.

The post-industrial is in relation to the industrial. The former is differentiated from the latter on the basis of several factors and aspects. But the most important is the differentiation along industrial/post-industrial lines. It is a historic event, a major turning point in social development. It is interesting to note that we are giving up every major feature of life created in the industrial era; to be precise, we are giving up every industrial method, way and tool. That is how we are transiting to the post-industrial era.

The post-industrial means the dissolution of the industrial and emergence of features which are beyond the industrial. The STR is dissolving, decentring, dissociating, and decentralizing the factories, mills, machines, tools, etc. Their size and scale are getting smaller and reduced. They are being converted into the software.

Post-industrialization means the dissolution of the commodity, at least its beginning. It is the core of the event. We are covered in a growing layer of the Internet, the external consciousness, the layer of information. So, our development is now guided, more and more, by information and knowledge. Knowledge today is basically scientific, and thus science becomes a productive and information force. Science and technology have *overtaken* social development, and thus for the first time have taken the lead in fashioning and shaping human beings. Human endeavour in the form of science, generalization and abstraction determine the domination of consciousness over productive forces; thus it is a consciousness-led motion of society. The creative consciousness is released as a force tapping all the endless human capacities.

It is by no means idealism, it is pure materialism, but materialism which traces emergence and emanation of consciousness from concrete and objective material forces. We identify the electronic and information base of reality and trace the emergence of ideas from such a base. The material stratum of emergence and dispersal of ideas has changed drastically in the last few decades. In the field of human practice, science and technology have made it possible to work with the forces at the level of particles and waves. It has directly and fundamentally affected social structures.

These material forces, at the service of science, and as science, trace their origins in the very roots of the objective terrain. The emanation of the idea can be traced to the forces constituted by waves, particles, energy packets and energy conversions. An idea is, in popular explanation, nothing but the oscillation and disturbance in the form of waves and particles. Idea are being concretized. The quantum sciences, the very discovery of the quantum in 1900, put ideas in the category of material products. Earlier it was speculation; now it is concretization of a material process. Science never leads to idealism, it always leads to materialism.

Yet, matter is no more something tangible, solid and concrete. It is constituted, at the sub-atomic levels, of endless particulate forces, waves and clouds of waves, energy transformations and conversions and exchanges, instant creation and conversions as endless series. Matter is not that of the natural, tangible, solid world, where one could point out the objectivity with ease and could trace the concrete stage of creation, emergence and disappearance. In this sense, matter takes on certain features of 'idea' (not to be confused with its becoming idea itself). One can get confused with the confusing of ideas with matter at this stage of scientific and social development.

Let us be very clear about it. Certain scientists, thinkers and philosophers are getting confused and are being carried away to mysticism. Nothing is far from the truth. Science and mysticism cannot go together.

The image we see on TV, computer screen, mobile, or anywhere is not an idea, but a *representation* and reflection of material objects and processes, occurring extremely fast. The image is also the representation of ideas. Such a representation is made possible due to certain arrangements of particles, waves and rays, certain ways of their projection on the screen. Only, it is not in solid form, a form we are used to in our social development down the ages. It is a world of images and 'consciousness' in the form of representations we talked about. Material reality and our consciousness are reproduced in the form of information, signs and images.

The border-line between matter and an idea is blurred at a certain level and at a certain stage. The experiments conducted in the human/computer interface and brain/computer interface is a pointer to this development. Our brain interacts and merges with the computer processes, with the software, because of the nearness, even commonness between the waves and particles and the processes of our brain, producing consciousness (ideas, that is, disturbances of waves and particles). Our brain has much in common with the software, which really is an *artificial brain* or its beginning.

We can move the images or visual representations on the screen simply with the movement of our eyes or even with simple thoughts. This reduces thought to material process, wherein the former is deconstructed into individual processes of material nature at the quantum levels. So, for writing, our brain does not have to take the prolonged path via hands, etc., using corresponding brain parts, but simply and directly can interact with the computer screen as part and parcel of the brain. While the brain establishes coordination with the computer system, it at the same time does not need the rest of the biological system or the body. There is unity of software and the brain processes at the sub-atomic levels.

This is an *extraordinary event* in human history.

Then there are certain features, which undeniably constitute the qualities of a 'post-capitalist' order of things. Among them the dissolution of classes and the use of 3–D manufacture. They and others have clearly freed themselves of the capitalist features and laws and have become post-capitalist and post-industrial. The dissolution of classes or its beginning does not fit in with capitalism. Classes acquire the highest development under capitalism, which is nothing without classes and their unity and conflict. Technology has reached a point where the decentralization of production and the trend towards smaller size of machines make it impossible for the classes to keep themselves intact.

The emergence of 3–D manufacture is an event of great historical import. It contains seeds of 'communist' production and distribution. Potentially, each person can produce the necessary 'use values' and can be the owner of the means of 'production', if the word is to be used. Production will become so easy that everybody can produce and consume and/or even exchange easily the necessary things in the manner of the initial barter system.

It is an extraordinary event and we need to watch as the future events unfold.

Post-capitalism is a conceptual tool that helps us identify and trace the emerging trends in social development.

References

1. *The Times of India,* May 28, 2014.
2. Ibid.

7

Bell, Richta, and a Discussion on Post-Industrial Society

It is interesting to know that Daniel Bell first came across the term 'post-indust :al' in a book published in 1917. The book advocated an order of things which were 'post-industrial' in place of the decentralized small-scale production.

The original formulation of the concept of post-industrial society (PIS) was presented by Daniel Bell in 1962 in a discussion in Boston presided over by Robert Heilbroner. The paper remained long unpublished. In 1965 he received a grant for a year enabling him to work on the idea further. The concept of the PIS became one of the base ideas of the 'Commission on the Year 2000' of the American Academy of Arts and Sciences. Many of the papers and ideas were collected as five volumes of working papers and a book *Towards the Year 2000* published in 1967. Since then Bell continued to work further on the concept of the PIS. Many other authors and scholars too have contributed to the working of the concept, even though some of them may not have used the term itself. In June 1970, Bell and Dahrendorf organized a small seminar in Zurich to discuss the theory of the PIS.[1]

Thus Daniel Bell was the first to formulate the concept of the post-industrial society (PIS). In his celebrated work on PIS, published in 1973 and in 1974[2], Bell has identified its main features. In fact, approaches to it were being made a few years earlier. That was the time when the Western society was making a big qualitative transition away from industrial structure and towards the services.

Bell is widely acknowledged as the main authority on the concept of post-industrial society (PIS). His book and the concept is still the reference point in any discussion. Considering the concept was advanced in the early 1970s, it is of great importance. It provides many starting points for further elabouration today. We have mentioned some of the salient features of his concept at the end of this chapter.

Among the authors he has discussed is Radovan Richta, and some others too. This is very interesting, particularly in regard to the interest taken in tracing certain features of the future PIS.

Richta on the Emerging Post-Industrial Society (PIS)

Growing debates took place in the post-Second World War period among the academics all over the world, especially in the West, on 'future society'. Out of these debates emerged the faint outlines of the PIS.

Debates on the concrete features of future society naturally also took place in the socialist countries, veered around future socialism. It is interesting to note that the debates spilled over into the domains of the post-industrial society.

The period after the death of Stalin in 1953, especially in the mid-1950s and 60s, was one of extraordinary intellectual and political ferment.[3] Traditional concepts and dogmas were being given up and there was a readiness to discuss new tendencies, trends and aspects in the industrial society.

Among the debates on the future society was the one of the Czech and Hungarian academicians.[4] One of the most important documents to come out in the early 1960s was the remarkable study by Radovan Richta and his associates in the Czechoslovak Academy of Science. The study is titled 'Civilization at the Crossroads: Social and Human Implications of the Scientific and Technological Revolution', which appeared in 1967.

Interestingly, the study begins by making an analytical contrast between the industrial and the scientific and technological revolutions.[5] The result of this change is conversion not only of labour but all the productive forces into a continuous, mechanized production process, in which man now stands "alongside" the production process whereas earlier "he was its chief agent". "In effect, not labour power (and the working class) but science (and knowledge classes) is the "decisive factor" in the growth of the productive forces of the society."[6]

This is a notable statement made by an academician of a socialist country. He clearly broke out of the dogmatic and rigid interpretation of Marxism and tried to grasp the new developments needing an improvement in the Marxist theory. Richta noted the shift of the worker from being *in* the production process to being *outside and beside* it. The observation is similar to the one made by Marx in *Grundrisse.* It is not known whether Richta had studied the work, but the observation is crucial to the understanding of the PIS.

Richta says that in place of simple and fragmented work, which was the basis of production so far, enters *science.* The application of science takes the forms of technology, skills, organization, etc. Earlier, science used to be separate from industry but now it is becoming part of the sphere of production in "small doses". The sphere not long ago used to comprise only a few hundreds of thousands of people; now it includes millions, who are mainly specialists, scientists, associated workers and so on. Richta says: "By the next century (that is by the 21st century—AR), 20 per cent of total labour force will be employed in science and research."[7] Next, Richta makes another important observation, about *the signs of the emergence* of the post-industrial society. He says there are signs of a *new type of growth*.

His observations on the post-industrial society are the following: Science is becoming the leading variable in the economy "and the *vital dimension* in the growth of civilization".[8] There is "a new dynamic stemming from continuing structural changes in the productive forces."[9] What are the changes? Richta says, the amount of means of production and manpower is becoming less important than their changing quality and degree of utilization.[10] This is a very important point. The quality of the productive forces is changing rapidly, reflecting a shift in their nature. It is not just a quantitative change under the STR but a qualitative one.

The *acceleration* in growth of the forces of production is linked *intensively* and qualitatively with the scientific and technological development.

"At a certain stage in the course of the technological revolution", all the laws of social development appear in a new light. This is primarily true of the relationship between *science, technology and production*. This is as vital as the relation between the department I and department II of the mode of industrial production. In the context of the STR, "growth of productive forces follows a law of higher priority, that is, the *precedence of science over technology and of technology over industry*."[11]

It means, as Bell explains, Richta *identifies the post-industrial society with a scientific and technological society* ('post-industrial **or** scientific and technological society").[12]

He, Richta, identifies a disparity between STR and industrialization, and that is the "relative *decline* in the amount of labour absorbed by industry..."[13] We may interpret this as motion away from industrial production towards post-production. Within the industry, there is a *shift* from the traditional branches to the progressive ones. Absolute validity cannot be given to the process and structure of industrialization.[14]

The motion away from production results in several changes in the industrial system. The society begins to be centred or dependent on non-production.

The consequence of this motion is that in the course of time, the volume of 'services' due to the STR will grow to more than half and will keep growing. This will lead us to a 'post-industrial' or 'tertiary' or 'service' civilization etc.[15] Number and percentage of technical and professional personnel *outside* the immediate production is growing rapidly. The rate of growth of these sections of workers is many times faster than the growth of industrial and related workers.

These points provide keys to the concept of the 'post-industrial society'.

Richta's Confusion Over Laws of Social Development

According to Richta, as a consequence of the STR, the older Marxist concept of 'laws of social development' is no longer valid. Making debatable contentions, he says that the laws by which society develops are not predestined and follow no set schemes. They flow from history, from the motion of the society itself. They change with every turn in this 'essential substratum'.[16] He characterizes the STR as the profound intervention in the civilization base of human life. This intervention must "impinge on the *elementary laws of history*". "In many respects the course of civilization acquires a new logic and time scale."[17]

Here Richta contradicts himself. He says the laws of society are 'not predestined' and at the same time they 'flow from history'. He is right in saying that they flow from history, which only means they are built into history. He also talks of 'elementary laws of history', which can be taken as another term for the objective laws. If they are a product of history, they are objective in nature, to be modified and used only by human intervention.

Richta himself admits intervention of the STR into the elementary laws of history.[18] The point is that the STR itself is the result and further continuation of the natural and social objective laws. STR renders certain laws superfluous and introduces certain others, such as based on the quantum forces and the electronics.

Richta makes important observations on the time cycles of the traditional societies and their modification by the STR.

The rhythm and time cycle of life in civilizations were based on the rural activities. Down the ages, the rhythm of production was set in with the natural cycles, as in agricultural societies. In the industrial civilization, the period of capital turnover was the starting point for all the surmises about the future. The 5–year or 7–year planning in socialism was usually based on the turnover period of social labour.[19]

Once science begins to determine productive activities, these traditional determinations become irrelevant.

Science has a different character from other modes of activities including labour. It is this feature that sets apart a society based upon science from that based upon industry. Science owes this feature to its exceptional power of *generalization*. In contrast to other processes, science is not consumed but is improved upon in the course of its use. In the process, it costs nothing. Besides, science has a peculiar exponential feature of growth. The more we know, the more we can find out. In this regard, science differs fundamentally from all other industrial activities.[20]

The point made here about the quality of generalization in science is quite significant. Among others, it means that, in contrast to concrete objects in the course of production, science can overcome problems through generalization, thus encompassing various hurdles. Science as a productive has the quality of enhancing and spreading solutions through presenting and creating new solutions.

Richta made these points at the initial stages of the STR, and therefore are very important and in some ways ahead of the times.

On this basis, Daniel Bell identifies three problems. They are of importance to the discussion of the post-industrial society. One, since STR is not led by the working class, what will be its role in the future society? Two, the new society will emphasize the professional and technical class. Three, highly trained research, scientific and technical staff will constitute the new ruling class of the future.

In contrast to the earlier technological and productive forces' development, the STR has to be universal, rapid and independent and with the simultaneous and universal participation of the people, at least the majority of them.

At the start of the STR, the actual practice of management passes into the hands of trained managerial elite in many capitalist countries. Under state monopoly, these elite acquire certain independence in relation to traditional capitalist groupings.

Importance of Richta's Views

Richta provides certain approaches to the understanding

of the concept of PIS. Some crucial elements of his theses could be identified as important in this regard:

1. Science enters production and replaces labour.
2. Labor stands 'alongside' the production process.
3. Not labour power but science is the main factor in the new productive force.
4. Specialists, scientists and professionals replace the workers.
5. The major proportion of the labour force is being employed in science and research.
6. Science is the vital dimension of human civilization.
7. Growth of the productive forces is intrinsically related with science and technology.
8. Laws of social development are modified or changed. For example, the 'law of precedence' begins to operate, such as the precedence of science over technology and of technology over industry.
9. There is a relative decline of labour in the industry.
10. Volume of services is growing, leading to post-industrial or tertiary or service sectors.
11. Science differs from all other industrial activities in that it grows rather than decreases in the course of its use. It does not cost anything. Science is a generalization, rather than a particular use.
12. The professionals will be the new ruling class.

Richta made a great contribution to develop the concept of PIS.

Bell on Post-Industrial Society (PIS)

As we have noted, with Radovan Richta the discussion on the STR also leads him to what may be called the 'post-socialist' society.[21] The future of socialism is being treated as if it is post-industrial. With many features accruing from the impact of STR, post-socialism is similar to post-capitalism. Thus both the socialist and the capitalist societies are industrial, with many similar features.

This point was also made by the present author in a seminar on Gramsci's birth centenary held in New Delhi in 1993.[22] It was stated that from the industrial point of view, both the capitalist and socialist societies were similar, though not from the point of view of relations of production. When both societies enter the stage of STR, changes in the means, production and information structure are the same. Therefore, the concept of the PIS covers both the order of relations.

The term 'post' here denotes the transition from the industrial to the post-industrial order of things. According to Bell in the PIS, the controlling agency is not technology but the political managers. In all this, according to Bell, we face anew a puzzling kind of problem: that of the *retreat of theory*. In this specification, theory means the model of determinate social structure dealing with past, present and future of the structure, with certain predictable concepts.[23] Bell takes recourse to the paradigm shift of Thomas Kuhn to build up multiple starting points in several directions.[24]

At the same time, in the very next sub-section Bell emphasizes the importance of theoretical knowledge. This seriously contradicts the earlier statement on the 'retreat of theory'. It shows an incomplete and dissociated approach of Bell to the concept of PIS. According to Bell, the concept of 'post-industrial society' emphasizes the centrality of theoretical knowledge, which is the *axis around which* the new society will be organized. He is seemingly correct; yet his interpretation of the place of theory is not really 'central'. In fact his interpretation of the 'axis' itself is without an axis. This axis is just one of the many axes around which the new order is emerging. Thus the new society has no central axis, contrary to Bell's starting point.

He opposed the concept of convergence between the capitalist and the socialist societies. They do not have a common "axis" of development. Interestingly, Bell does not agree with the Marxist concept of deriving the entire society from a single basic feature, such as the mode of production. The social, cultural and such other activities have multiple sources.[25]

Without going into further details, we may express *our difference with this approach.* It is a fragmented approach in which the basic unity of concept is ignored. Marx treated the mode of production as the source from which other activities are derived. He was explaining the origins of society, the unity and conflict between the productive and production relations, emergence of various institutions, activities and the social structures from this basic source. He was also explaining the source of social development. Thus he provided a dialectical methodology.

It is this methodology that we are following in this book when dealing with the concept of the post-industrial structure or society. We look upon the post-industrial society/formation as the logical development of the industrial society, acted upon by the STR. Bell makes the mistake of not treating the industrial society as based upon the concept of the social system. This he states in the course of contradicting Jean Floud.[26] He says: "I do not believe that societies are organic or so integrated as to be analysable as a single system."[27] Then how do you interpret the society and its development?

In what way does a post-industrial society differ from the industrial society? That is how Bell poses the question. He says that Prof. Tominaga is correct in a historical sense. The industrial society is a continuation of the trends unfolding out of the industrial society.[28] Even in Saint Simon and Marx, respectively, the role of engineers and science in social transformation were pointed out.

Bell divides societies into pre-industrial, industrial and post-industrial ones for *analytical* purposes.[29] There are structural problems in each kind of society. In industrial society the chief economic problem is that of capital and the related monetary questions. [30]

In the PIS the chief problem is the organization of science.[31] The PIS is not a picture of a complete social order; it is an attempt to describe the axial change in the social structure. But it has no specific determination in terms of basis and superstructure, as per Bell. The various societies (countries) entering the post-industrial phase will have different political and cultural configurations.[32] The problem of the relation of science to public policy will have to be solved by these societies.

The term PIS is used to describe the extraordinary changes in the structure of world society, not wholly displacing the agrarian and industrial worlds, yet transforming them in essential ways. The PIS represents the principles of innovation, new modes of social organization and new classes of society.[33]

Human services, primarily health and education, are the major expansion in the contemporary society. They are today the major means of increasing the productivity. Bell says that "I have broken this area into a further distinction (after the pre-industrial 'primary' and the industrial 'secondary' of tertiary (transportation), quaternary (trade and finance), and quinary (health, education, etc)."[34] But the novel and central feature of the PIS "is the codification of theoretical knowledge and the new relation of science to technology."[35] Only in the 20th century has such a codification taken place.

Bell writes in the Foreword to the 1999 edition of his book on the post-industrial society[36] that the following major changes have taken place in the American society in the last 25 years:

1. From manufacturing to services: Today (that is in 1999) only 15% of the American force is in manufacturing compared to 26% some 25 years ago. In terms of numbers it is 18.8 million against 126 million.
2. Occupational changes: extraordinary rise in the professional and technical employment and the relative fall in skilled and semi-skilled workers.
3. Property and education: Inheritance of family farm, family business and family occupation etc was the sign of social status earlier. Today, education has become the basis of occupation, promotion and social status.
4. Finance capital and human capital: Some three decades ago, capital was regarded as finance capital amassed as money or land. Today human capital has become more important and the concept of social capital has taken shape.
5. Intellectual technologies like algorithms, software, linguistics, programming, simulations etc are running the 'high technologies'.
6. Infrastructure of the industrial society was transportation. That of the PIS is communications.
7. Industrial society is based on the labour theory of value. Development of industry proceeds through labour-saving devices. Capital is substituted for labour. In PIS the knowledge theory of value operates. It is the source of invention and innovation. It is a value-added process and there are increasing returns to scale. It is capital saving.

In what ways do these and other points help trace *the transition* from industrial to post-industrial society? Or how can we state, on what basis, that certain trends are emerging pointing to the movement towards the PIS? These will be crucial points for our discussion.

If we go through the points made by Daniel Bell and Radovan Richta, we come across several crucial aspects. Some of the important ones have been mentioned above and elsewhere. Added to other features, they provide a fairly comprehensive picture of what may be identified as the post-industrial tendency in social development.

One point is that the "post-industrial society is based on services." "What counts is not raw muscle power, or energy, but information."[37] It clearly means the post-industrial society is *not* an industrial society. Bell further qualifies it by pointing out that whereas in the industrial society, it is the quantity of goods for living standard that matters, in the PIS it is the quality of all the major necessities of life like health, education, recreation, and art etc. If "an industrial society is defined as a goods-producing society—if manufacture is central in shaping the character of its labour force--then the United States *is no longer an industrial society*."[38]

The change-over to PIS is signified by change in sector distribution and more by pattern of occupation, by the kind of work people do. Most of them are white collar workers, professionals and technical employees. This is the central occupational category of the PIS.

The "government has become the single largest employer in the society".[39] Society thus acquires another post-industrial feature.

According to Daniel Bell, the theory of PIS first and foremost deals with the transition in the social structure. In it, science, technology, services and intellectual technology play the dominant role. Emergence of services as the leading or the main sector is a distinguishing feature.[40]

While the industrial society is organized around the axis of production and machinery,[41] the post-industrial is mainly organized around the services and related fields such as theoretical knowledge.[42] The emergence of the PIS is mainly due to the change in the structure of the society.[43]

Thus PIS is negation of the basic features of the industrial society.

References

1. See, Daniel Bell, Preface, *The Coming of Post-Industrial Society: A venture in social forecasting*, Arnold-Heinemann Publications (India) Pvt. Ltd., 1974.
2. Daniel Bell, *The Coming of Post-industrial Society*, 1974.
3. Daniel Bell, ibid., p. 106.
4. See, Bell, ibid., Chapter on 'From Industrial to Post-Industrial Society', pp. 105–112.
5. Ibid., p. 107.
6. Richta quoted in Bell, ibid., p. 107.
7. Ibid.
8. Ibid., emphasis in the original.
9. Ibid.
10. Ibid.
11. Ibid; emphasis in the original.
12. Ibid.
13. Ibid., p. 108.
14. Ibid.
15. Ibid.
16. Ibid.
17. Ibid.
18. Ibid.
19. Ibid.
20. Ibid., p. 109.
21. Ibid., p. 112.
22. See, Anil Rajimwale, in *Science and People*, Special Number on Gramsci Centenary, New Delhi, 1993.
23. Bell, op. cit.
24. Ibid., p. 112.

25. Ibid., pp. 112–13.
26. See, ibid., p. 114.
27. Ibid.
28. Ibid., p. 115.
29. Ibid., p. 116.
30. Ibid.
31. Ibid.
32. Ibid.
33. Daniel Bell, *The Coming of Post-Industrial Society*, New York, Basic Books, 1999, x-xi, xiv, xv-xvii; from internet, Amazon, WorldCat.
34. Ibid.
35. Ibid.
36. *Foreword*, Ibid.
37. Bell, *The Coming of Post-Industrial Society*, 1974, p. 127.
38. Ibid., p. 133, emphasis added.
39. Ibid., p. 157.
40. Ibid., Introduction, Section on 'The Dimension of Post-Industrial Society'.
41. Preface, ibid., p. x.
42. Introduction, ibid., pp. 14, 18.
43. Preface, ibid., p. x.

8

Fourth Technological Revolution
Dissolution of the Tool and the Machine

The dissolution of the machine is the key to the post-industrial revolution. There are several events and trends pointing to the event. The dissolution of the machine leads to the dissolution, change and emergence of other crucial processes, to the post-machine processes.

New developments need urgent attention, as they are leading the technological and scientific revolution to new levels. These very rapid and deep-going developments may be included collectively under the term 'fourth technological revolution' (FTR) because the STR has also been called the 'third' technological revolution.

Before proceeding ahead, let us point out that Jeremy Rifkin titles his latest book as *The Third Industrial Revolution*.[1]

A number of news items keep appearing in the newspapers on new developments in science and technology. Besides, more serious scientific journals are full of the latest developments. They all point to the emergence of new levels of scientific and technological revolution. They also indicate, undeniably, to the emergence of a new society radically different from the existing one, at least to its beginnings.

Among the developments, some are quite startling. Paper and cloth computers, complete with screens and keyboards, are now common. A news item appeared in March 2014, in *The Times of India* about creation or assembly of a toy gun with the help of electronic printer, provided with some assembling or raw materials. At a computer command, the printer assembles the toy. This is an extraordinary development with great implications for the future.

Experiments in quantum computers are being reported. These computers will have computing and processing powers several times the present ones.

Another amazing event has taken place in the field of nanotechnology. A one-minute movie of a young man kicking a football has been made at nano-scale. The development is fraught with futuristic possibilities.

With the discoveries of new planets and stars, almost by the hour, we have begun to live in a world of real celestial bodies, getting identified with them. With the discoveries and their ever higher numbers our consciousness is gaining a *universal character*. The Permanent International Space Station (ISS) and the Hubble telescope, as also the numerous satellites, are contributing to the enhancement of knowledge every passing moment. This growth is unprecedented.

According to a latest discovery, a new particle has been found, which exists for 2.5 billionth of a second! It is said to have 'water-like' properties. It is supposed to help solve many mysteries of the quantum world.

Google Glass

The glass connects to the Internet through smart-phone, hooking up with the phone via Bluetooth. The Google glass uses a prism to project images directly into the eyes. What we see looks like images on a large TV screen. You can just order it and it will carry it out. For example if you order saying: 'take a picture", pressing a button simultaneously. And there appears a picture of say sunrise or sunset. At the same time the details of the picture taken can also be had through the Google.

It can also show you the way when riding your vehicle. The eye-movement is equivalent of the finger movement on the touch-screen or the mouse. A prism projects the image.

The Google glass has CPU and GPS, speaker phone, battery, touch-pad interface, camera, prism and some other crucial elements.[2] Everything ready for the future!

The chief characteristic of the fourth technological revolution appears to be the *rapid loss of hardware* and *transfer of sensory activities* to the appliances/equipment.

Software and End of Machine

First of all, what is a machine? As we have stated elsewhere, in Chapter 2 (Dialectics of Machine Development), the machine has three component parts: the tool/s, main body holding the tools, and a motive power and arrangement to drive the machine.

The electronics revolution is distinguished by the fact that it acts upon the various elements of the machine, machinery and factory, transforming and ***dissolving*** them. It is an unprecedented development in the history of society and of the means of production. *Each of the components/ elements is being worked upon by the STR.*

To put it simply, we may state: The tool is becoming intangible in nature through the use of laser beams and such other means. The main body of the machine is getting smaller and more compact, and sometimes its functions are being taken over by the electronic system or the software, fully or partially. The motive force, that is steam power in the earliest stages of the industrial revolution, has now been replaced by diesel and electricity. This has led to the motive arrangement becoming sleeker and smaller and also distributive. The developments have automatically and dialectically led to a transformation in the machine system, which has acquired a tendency to become smaller, sleeker and increasingly compact. Many functions of the solid tangible parts are being taken over by the temporary emanations of waves, rays and particle sprays.

In the meantime, technological changes have resulted in the inventions like cells and batteries, which make it possible for the machines to become smaller and economical. Batteries have led the revolution in the energy transmitting systems. Now energy need not be carried over long distances and through massive mechanisms. The energy can be split up and produced and carried by 'hand-held' systems. This prepares the ground for the collapse of the machine system. The system becomes portable, to be taken anywhere, any time.

In totality, the machine acquires the tendency to become smaller, sleeker and more economical. It thus prepares the ground for the collapse of the industry and the industrial revolution.

It is at this point that the computer intervenes. It has the aspects of both the machine and non-machine or post-machine. A 'non-machine' evolves only after the machine, and begins a process of post-industrial revolution. The computer is undoubtedly a *universal* machine, which transmits commands and instructions to the established machines. Never before, has a production and communication system spread so fast and so rapidly. It guides machines, mills, factories and system of machines, however big and complicated, and in fact the entire society. It is a 'machine' run by information, and this distinguishes it from the traditional machine. It is a machine which increasingly converts the existing machine into information signals.

A machine can never 'run' by information; it can only be run by a motive force. The moment it is run by information, it ceases to be a machine. Its dissolution begins.

With the passing of time, the computer is *ceasing to be a machine.* It is the dialectics of hardware and software, that of *the machine and the anti-machine/non-machine/post-machine,* that constitutes the computer. The computer therefore is not a machine in the usual sense. It has many features *antithetical* to what we call the 'machine'.

The computer is nothing but the dialectics of hardware and software. Hardware is the system of hard, solid, tangible parts of the machine. Initially, the computer was almost all hardware, which simply transmitted signals of electrons etc. Gradually, a system of electronic signals evolved which is now called the 'language' of the computer or the software. It now dominates the hardware and constitutes the computer itself.

Thus from being a mechanism to transmit signals, the computer has now become, through stages, an intelligent system of command emanation. The hardware is now a hurdle in the path of the evolution of the signals and the language. In order to remove the hurdle, the hurdle itself should be converted or translated into software. This is the best way to dissolve the hardware. It is *dissolution as well as retention, the same thing at the same moment, yet opposite*! It is a living dialectics. The signal making has become an independent activity, facilitating conversion of all the tangible processes into the electronic processes. It is the conversion of the reality into the images that creates and drives the social existence. Software creates a separate world of information and signals. Information can be created only by waves and signals, and not by hardware for any length of time. Information (software) now assumes an independent existence, creates its own mode and begins directing the world of production.

Gradually, as the STR and the electronics revolution proceed, the software becomes a more prominent aspect of the computer. Today, it has become the dominant aspect of the computer and mobile. Hardware is getting reduced in proportion as the software increases.

Today, a stage has arrived where hardware itself is being converted into the software, as for example, in case of the keyboard.

There is technologically no need for hardware and hence for the machine, tool and the industry.

The STR works upon both hardware and software. Software is not the result of the industrial revolution. STR is the only force that can undo the creation of the industrial revolution; it is also the only force that can rescue and develop the software further into the post-industrial phase. *Unless the dissolution of the hardware takes place fully, no new society can emerge.*

Software is an intruder, an attachment of the information system on the hardware. In fact, the software was developed to facilitate the functioning of the hardware, that is, the machine. Through the software, the human beings began to transfer the mental capacities to the machine, and thus to free themselves of fast and complicated mental jobs. The development of software is thus a constant attempt to free ourselves of mental labour.

But software has unexpected results for the machinery and for society. Initially helping the hardware, the former displaces the latter from one sphere after another. The software has this characteristic that it can even *act as hardware* in all the functions.

The conflict between hardware and software in fact is a conflict between the industrial system and the system dissolving the industrial, a conflict between the industrial and the post-industrial. By consequence, it a dialectics *between the old society based upon hard tools/ machines and the new one based upon software.*

These are two different starting points for the societies. The society based upon the software, information and broader consciousness exemplified by the Internet signifies a new beginning for the human history, society and consciousness. It is a crucial development, which needs to be understood properly.

We are on the threshold of an entirely new beginning. The software signifies not only an end to the tool. Therefore, the hitherto existing history ends and a new one begins. It is the beginning of society *without the machine.*

How do we then conceptualize the evolution of the human society here onwards? How is history going to be created in the absence of the tools? What is the basis of the material society?

It is clear that it is information which is the determining factor of social development from now onwards. The material conditions of production, tools and machines are now part and parcel of and secondary to the information-driven processes. Thus the software leads a society based upon information. It is information as such which now propels production. It is development minus the machine. Software replaces the machine and the tool.

What was the society based upon so far, particularly the industrial (capitalist) one? It was *based upon hardware* almost entirely, on hard materials that constituted the base for the machines and the tools. It is around this hard material that the whole society and its history is built up. Therefore, there was and is a predominance of physical work, with an intermediate field of shift from the physical to the mental. Use of physical force is a survival of, a throwback to, the ancient societies, in particular to the hunting life. Intelligence down the ages has become increasingly integrated with production and labour processes.

In the course of the industrial revolution, the physical capacities are handed over to the machine, and mental capacities 'man'/oversee the tool and the machine. Mental powers and intelligence do not run the machines and the tools in actual operations; they (the former) only intervene from time to time. A tool is operated by the machine as directed by the human intelligence. Tool is an extension of human intelligence and work, *as if* the humans were working.

Yet, the unity and conflict (dialectics) of the tool and the machine need a motive force. This motive force is provided by the industrial revolution in the form of steam power and its result the steam engine. Therefore, it is a key to the motion of the means of production, society and history. The industrial revolution works out methods to replace humans physically from the production process, though not mentally. Even physical participation is considerable. The concept and practice of automation was also a product of the industrial revolution. It was this automation that freed the human mind from production and thus entirely took the human being out of the production process. That is the beginning of the new society and new mode of production. It constituted the basis for Marx's *Grundrisse* and many other works.

It is at this juncture that the electronics revolution, and more particularly, the scientific and technological revolution (STR), steps in onto the stage of world history. It begins a radical transformation of the society in all its aspects. STR is a multi-sided event, which begins to impact all the basic aspects of the society. Science becomes the chief productive force, bringing about change in all fields.

The use of science has unleashed processes inside the atom onto the society. This is the source of radical transformations in the productive base of society and of the domination of information.

Science makes it possible to render the natural forces into the very productive and economic forces.

At a certain stage technology becomes the application of the science of electronics. Electrons become the new productive force threatening the very existence of the state and all other giant social structures. The beams and signals of information begin a re-arrangement of social structures.

3-D Technology

According to the newspaper reports, a robot can be 'created' out of a paper sheet in no time! The corner of the paper has a switch and a motor; on command, it gets switched on, and after a few minutes, a robot rises out of the paper and begins to walk! Straight out of science fiction!

Actually, the material in the paper sheet acts as the raw material for this transformation; the switching on leads to triggering a process of re-arranging the materials and soon they constitute themselves as a robot.

The recent developments in science and technology have raised the visions of a fourth technological revolution. The fourth is different from the third one in many respects. The third technological revolution was based upon electronics and computers. The fourth technological revolution is based on nanotechnology, molecular and atomic computers, 3D printing, collapse and multi-dimensionality of the mobile and such other inventions. The revolution is spreading really very fast. Growing richness of the mobile is a key event.

New trends have emerged in science and technology. Enabling the making of objects at a distance through 3-D technology augurs a new era and has great and unforeseen implications. Creation of 3-D robots is another new development with immense possibilities.

Nano technology, collapse of time and space into the mobile and such other developments are pointers to the future. The mobile has reached the point where it combines an increasing number of functions in one small apparatus. It has become the symbol of the future. The individual has truly become powerful, for the first time. An individual can discharge several functions at a time or at short intervals. The software represents the congealing of labour as never before.

This collapse into the small gadgets constitutes the basis of the new, the fourth stage of the technological revolution. Now 'anything' is possible, anything can be created, or destroyed. The things have moved beyond the pre-fixed, the imaginable, 'orderly' processes.

Anything can be created out of anything. A wall can become a truck, a truck a car, furniture, house, stationary system becoming one with speed, paper into a robot, and so on.

You can see all the things or images thereof in 3–dimensional spaces. One can just think and get things written on the screen, can create three dimensional figures on screen just by looking or thinking, can write words and articles if you only think, This is a great leap, really and conceptually. All our existing concepts are scattered, they simply collapse and vanish.

The fourth technological revolution is characterized by the transfer of most of the mental functions to the machines and acquiring of autonomy and independence by the automated systems. This is evidenced by growing independence of the robot, which is taking over an increasing number of functions from human beings.

Download of Brain: Indication of Future Society

Already experiments are being conducted on transfer of the functions of the brain to the computer. Now journals and papers carry the news of downloading of the entire brain contents into the software of the computer. The brain can thus be 'emptied' entirely and refilled with fresh information. This is an unprecedented development in the field of science and technology, the very horizon of the human evolution.

Human evolution has been brain-centred, with the growth of the brain serving as the factor of superiority among all the living beings. The brain has grown as a result of the development of the means and forces of production, primarily due to the development of the tools.

The brain/computer interface and the downloading of the human brain show the growing merger of the contents of the brain and consciousness, and the software. This is a historic event and a drastic turn in evolution, almost a fresh start in human development.

What does the brain/computer interface signify? It has tremendous *philosophical* implications. For *the first time in history*, our brain is making *direct contact* with the software, with the screen. The two have found their common level and are getting merged.

The brain can now move things, images and ideas at will. The brain can think directly, not via the body. It can operate in tandem with software.. Earlier, commands used to travel via hands, eyes, and other body parts. Now the brain and thoughts (consciousness) can interact directly with the screen. The dividing line between matter and idea gets blurred. Ideas are being dissected down to their constituent material sources. For the brain the other body parts are only media to convey the command waves. If they could be dispensed with, then the brain could establish direct relation with the electronic processes displayed on the screen. Brain waves unite with the waves and particles in the quantum world. Software simply becomes the extension of the brain (thoughts). Thoughts can write, move things, command direct to the computer processes. Our *thoughts do not necessarily need the entire body; they can even dispense with part of the brain and reside elsewhere in a different receptacle.* This is corroborated by the experiments on the 'downloading' of the brain.

Reports are now regularly appearing in the newspapers, detailing experiments in human/electronics interaction, with unexpected and unprecedented possibilities for us. Most of them we can't even imagine. We can 'unsee' or 'see' a particular object among a crowd of objects, simply by wearing a particular kind of glasses which make the object 'disappear'! This is simply science-fiction put into practice. It has many applications in future, where one can interact with the object in the most diverse ways.

According to some other reports, developments in the direction of eye-directed motion of objects are taking place. One can fly a plane with just looking at the board or panel or computer screen. Similarly one can direct a car by looking at it or its electronic panels. One can just think and letters and commands will appear on the screen and will direct the computers.

The central point of these developments is the interaction between thought and the object or our brain and the object. Electronics has reached point where it is in direct interaction with our brain and thought-process. Our thought and brain processes are being dissected and dissociated into their constituent parts and processes. Electronic and brain processes are finding common grounds and are becoming similar.

If objects can be resolved to particle/wave level, they can be manipulated directly by the brain; if brain waves and ideas can establish a common level with objects, they can easily grasp and manipulate the objective world.

These developments have tremendous social and philosophical implications for the future. The question naturally arises: are we moving towards a just or more equitable society? Can we use these events to create a better distribution? It seems that the developments are becoming individual-oriented and are progressively enhancing the role of the individual. That means the problems can be better solved at this level.

Manipulation of the object has tremendous potential to solve our basic problems. Some of the problems can at least be solved by people without the help of the state or the government or the top structures.

The developments described or indicated above and events like them create conditions where one can work and produce 'at will'. This is going to impact the production and work process deeply.

These developments also raise the question whether we moving out of the capitalist-industrial mode of production. Obviously we are. The brain/computer interface is directly hitting the very base of the capitalist-industrial production.

Microscope to Nanoscope

Nobel laureates Eric Betzig, Stefan W. Hell and William E. Moerner have found a way of bypassing the presumed scientific limitation of 0.2 micrometers (half the wavelength of light) for observation under microscope because an optical microscope cannot yield a resolution better than this.

Living organisms were studied for the first time in the 17th century using an optical microscope. But it had a major limitation: there was a physical restriction to the size of structures to be observed or resolved. According to Ernst Abbe (1873) the microscope resolution is limited by the wavelength of light, i.e. 0.2 micrometers. These three laureates have found ways to overcome or bypass this limitation.

Stefan Hell developed the method of stimulated microscopy or STED in 1994. A light pulse excites all the fluorescent molecules, while another light pulse quenches all fluorescence from all the molecules except those of nanometer size volume. Only this volume is then registered. By sweeping along the sample and continuously measuring light levels, it is possible to get a proper image.

The smaller the fluorescence in a single moment, the higher the resolution of the final image. Thus there is no limit to the resolution of the optical microscope.

Another method is the single molecule microscopy. Betzig and Moerner worked in this field independently of each other. In this method, first a weak light pulse activates the molecules, leading to fluorescence of many or a single molecule. The images are processed using the probability theory to render them much sharper. All images are superimposed. The position of each glowing protein is registered very precisely.

Thus the size of the object under observation is no longer a limit at 0.2 micrometers because nanoscales of objects are illuminated and observed. This is a great breakthrough in optical microscopic observation. Nanotechnology has entered the arena of observation.

Blue LED

Another field which attracted the Nobel Prize is the

invention of blue LEDs for inventing blue light emitting diodes. The Nobel went to Isamu Akasaki, Hiroshi Aramo and Shuji Nakamura.

Incandescent bulbs lit 20th century; the 21st century will be lit by LED lamps, noted the statement of the Royal Swedish Academy of Sciences.

The blue LED constitutes the third, after red and green, of the coloured LEDs that can produce white light in an environment-friendly and energy-efficient manner. The work on deepening the p-n junction of the semiconductors led to greater emission of light including blue light.

If the amount of light flux produced per unit of power supplied is 16 for a tungsten bulb and 70 for a fluorescent bulb, it is 300 for a LED supplied source.

This development has tremendous implications for the future.

IT Sector and Real Estate

The IT sector contributes about 6% of India's GDP, providing employment to about 2 million people. Due to the rapid growth of technical education, with proliferation of engineering colleges everywhere, the technical personnel have grown very fast in numbers and quality. Among others, they have contributed tremendously to e-business and other fields. E-retail brands like Infibeam, Flipkart, Amazon, Jabong, have emerged in the last few years.

The IT boom has been one of the most important catalysts driving the real estate business upwards. There has been large-scale displacement and migration of population including those involved in the IT boom. They have created fresh demands for real estate, housing and residential areas. Further growth of the IT sector is likely to push the development of real estate.

Business Portals

Infibeam is one of the leading online shopping portals in India. Its online e-commerce platform is Buildabazaar.com, a self-service one, where the users can create their e-commerce store, upload their product catalogue, customize their website, and sell their products. This website is offered as a 'software as a service' (SaaS) platform for creating online retailing stores and travel booking sites.

The platform was launched in May 2011, and has reached from 1000 stores in December 2011 to 18000 in February 2013. Major retailers in India have created online stores using Buildabazaar.com. The total value of transactions on the platform is claimed to be over 500 crore of rupees.

Internet Domain

Computers and websites are identified by a unique set of numbers known as the Internet Protocol (IP) address. Since monitoring IP addresses is a difficult job, the domain name system was created for each IP address.

The Internet or the cyberspace is like the universe. It has grown from a minuscule size of matter to hundreds of billions of galaxies, each having hundreds of billions of stars.

The cyberspace had only 6 domains in 1986; today it has 265 million names registered worldwide.

STR, Tool, Machine and Computerization

The contemporary STR is working upon the basic components of the industrial revolution, transforming them, as we have discussed above. A huge historical shift, as a result, is being caused in the further direction and nature of social development.

History has always worked upon the tools and means of production, and consequently upon the forces of production. The dialectics of society and history causes the tools to be an element which is always in motion, never ceasing to develop even for a moment. Momentous changes in the tools have produced great histories.

Tools and means of production have always been the objects of social development as also the creators of ever new facets of productive history, the creator of successive phases of social motion.

But the present-day STR is qualitatively different from the earlier revolutions in the methods and means of production. One reason is that it is occurring before our very eyes in a very short period of time, within a generation or two or four, within decades so to say. Its impact can be evaluated and felt as never before. Therefore we can 'see' social motion and history being made, so to say.

The distinguishing feature of the present revolution is that science is directly involved, becoming a productive force itself and through conversion into technology. There is a most rapid conversion of science into technology as never before. The distance between science and technology has reduced in an unprecedented manner, and this is a great historic event.

The conversion of science into productive force and into technology acts upon various points of the productive forces created during the entire history of social development, in particular during the industrial revolution. It is easier in fact to act upon the tools and machines produced by the industrial revolution because they are the nearest to science and technology, as for example the steam engine.

The products of the industrial revolution are driven by mechanical, physical and chemical laws. The STR is driven by electronic and quantum laws and by other forces within the atom. An interaction of the two creates a dissolution of the industrial and emergence of the post-industrial order of things. The electronic and quantum forces are too fast, they get converted too rapidly, for the industrial forces to sustain.

In one case science acts on the forces of nature. It needs a whole involved series of social structure to put them at productive use. In the other case, that of the STR, the forces not found in nature, the 'unnatural' processes, those residing in the atom, are unleashed. They dissolve the industrial structures rapidly, simultaneously creating post-industrial and non-industrial structures to handle the new forces. *The industrial world collapses.*

Science by unleashing forces not found naturally, works rapidly and deeply upon the various points of productive capacities developed by the industrial revolution.

Dialectics of Transition from Machine Tools to Computerized System

We have already dealt with the emergence of the tool and its attachment with the machine in the industrial revolution. In the last three or four decades, we are witnessing several intermediate stages of the combination of the tool and machine with information, replacement of the functions of the tool by those of information, and growing domination of information over the production process. The process goes a considerable way as the post-industrial process of change.

Here we will trace certain transitional steps, which will clarify the transition to the post-industrial order.

During the industrial revolution, changes in the product or the object was the main purpose of production; during STR the production of information, symbols and images is the main objective of production and every process.[3]

The operator today is shifting away from the machine; the industrial revolution brought about a unity of the two. Now he/she is working with images rather than with the solid objects. The machine is not run and guided by the operator but by the information system attached to the machine. Software is a new element in production. According to Lojkine, software is a new instrument or means of work.[4] It is an 'indirect' work, an extension of our brain, according to him.[5]

Here we beg to differ and want to clarify that software is not a new tool or instrument. It no doubt takes over functions of the tool. But the most important point is that the software dissolves the tool and the machine. This is *the greatest revolution* carried out by the software. This is part of the fourth technological revolution.

This is an important point, a key hint to the nature of new developments.

This at once changes the nature and definition of work. What is 'indirect' work? It would be interesting to debate the point. Either there is work or no work. Indirect work obviously involves supervision of production processes via the use of electronic means. This 'indirect' work is actually the production process without the labour process, in which the operator/overseer 'indirectly' participates as an onlooker and regulator with the help of the automatic logical systems.

Such a 'work' needs the aid of logical systems or of handing over of logical functions to the inanimate 'machine' systems. This aspect is actually dissolution of 'work' itself, and has far-reaching consequences. If work is dissolved or disappears, how is the human being placed and what is the nature of the production process?

Jean Lojkine is not a supporter of capitalism in any way. In fact, he says that the capitalist managements are not allowing a labour-less factory to emerge. Besides, according to him, the technological revolution is only a means to increase relative surplus value.

The industrial revolution established the connection between the worker and the object (job) through the use of new tools. This is reflected in the process of manufacture and industrial production. In the computer automation, a relation is established between the worker and the images produced by the computers on the screens.

It is to be noted that the post-industrial processes are characterized by *the replacement of things by images*: instead of creating tangible things and forms (commodities), the production process first creates images, which then are converted into things. So image and image-transmission is essential to the production process. Electronics first enters the scene as an appendage of production, then gradually becomes the main motive force, and then replaces it altogether as the main process, with production becoming secondary and accidental.

Lojkine in his illuminating work on the relation between industrial and computer revolutions and the impact on the tool, draws three crucial conclusions. There are beginnings of computer integration of the production cycle as a whole, from product design to after-sales service through CAD and CAM. This could prove to be a revolution even more fundamental than one brought about by automation.[6]

Here we may observe that the earlier automation was that of the production as such, while the present one is an automation based on the intrusion of information, leading to a fundamental realignment of the relations of structures within the production and a domination of information over production, negating production itself. So *computer automation negates production* as such.

The second point Lojkine makes is about impacts of the new forms of automation (computer-driven automation) on direct and indirect labour, productive and unproductive labour, division of labour and its organization, etc. there was considerable upheaval due to the transition from the earlier 'hyper-mechanization', as he calls it, to the new forms of automation. Hyper-mechanization is continuous functioning of a series of manufacturing lines, presses or robot welders.[7]

The third point he makes is that the new technological base seems to validate the theory that the material forces of production are propelled by their own dynamics. At the same time, there are extremely complex and dialectical relations between material and human productive forces and between forces and relations of social production. Neo-Taylorism still dominated considerably.[8]

Studies of new factories and establishments by Jean Lojkine bring out the fact that automation and computerization have forced step-by-step changes in management relations, forms and structure.

Percentage of capacity utilization takes precedence over direct labour utilized. Machine utilization becomes more important.[9]

There is objectification of the manual labour in the form of the machine tool in the industrial revolution,[10] while in computer automation, there is objectification of the cerebral functions.[11]

In the industrial revolution and machine control, the relationship between the 'individual and matter' is defined via the machine tool as an in immediate direct relation between the human and the manufacturing process. In the machine tool, the worker's function emerges as an extension of the mechanical process. On the other hand, in the automation process, the objectification of the direct work as a whole leads to the new forms of indirect forms.[12]

Thus electronics first appears as an accessory function in the integration of the machines, becomes a revolutionary technological element in information and communication.[13]

On the transition from the automation revolution to the computer revolution, Lojkine makes important points. He confirms our concept of the transition to the post-industrial order. Industrial revolution means W-M-P, that is, worker-machine-product. Automation means W-A-M-P, where A represents the information processing machine. Lojkine quotes Alain Chenu to the effect that 'A' represents the "machine that processes information automatically and has a better memory and speed of calculation than the human brain."[14] Data processing takes precedence over product transformation.[15] In data processing, instruments of work handling products (machine tools) are replaced by instruments of work handling symbols. In that sense, the "computer revolution places a new instrument of work in the forefront, i.e. software" as also extension of indirect work and cerebral activities.[16]

It is a relationship between people and extension of their symbolic cerebral activities. "This means that the activity of conception is no longer separated from the activity of production..."[17] As Lojkine points out, CAD/CAM (computer-aided design/computer-aided manufacture) revolution does not in itself abolish the difference between direct and indirect work and between intellectual and material work. The trends go beyond the divisions between biotechnology, automation and computerized communication.[18] CAD and CAM prepare material grounds for computer automation.

Lojkine sums up that the computer revolution is linking up of 'decentralized intelligence'.[19]

Lojkine is surprisingly against the very concept of society being post-production and post-industrial.

According to him, it is an *idealist* interpretation of the computer revolution.[20] Yet he equally surprisingly states that the computer revolution is the inter-relationship between the individuals at mental levels, of their abstract activities, particularly between their memories.[21]

Through computerization, the numerically controlled lathe machines are guided by computers. All the motions of the machine are tracked and production and stocks are traced. CAM and CAD systems are examples. In computer-controlled numerical guidance the various stages are converted into numerical codes. The transition from one process to another is more flexible and easily recorded. Computer program controls various stages. Thus the guidance and control are transferred from human beings to the computerized machines.

Computerization of the control systems in the mode of production directly affects the machine tools, which now become more flexible. In their existing form and nature, machines and tools are becoming a hurdle in their electronification. They are at present not suited or fully and properly suited to the ongoing electronics and computer revolution. This similar with the raw materials. Therefore they have to adjust themselves in every way to the ongoing spread of information technology. Now their limits are coming to the fore, and thus limits of industrial production are becoming clearer.

Microprocessors have the advantage of size and speed over the industrial materials and processes. Dialectics sets in between the two aspects, which is resolved through greater spread of electronic technology. The tools are being transformed very rapidly as also the machines.

For example, the nature, shape and size of the bobbins are being changed and being made 'smarter', so to say. They must be ready for far greater RPMs, must detach easily from their stands to allow new ones to take their place. Since the thread holders, the stands, and endless other parts and tools must act in time, they have to be shaped accordingly. A unified process from carding to weaving has emerged, with a series of new tools. They provide necessary instructions (commands) to the parts, tools and areas of the machines and adapt them accordingly. The tools have to adapt and change in course of time.

Due to the growing use of computerized control of production processes, the labour process is gradually disappearing. Hazeltine AG Company introduced in Europe the first six-stand cold rolling mill built by the Siemens. All the indexes of the steel sheets passing through the stands are recorded and controlled by computers. Every stand sends its data and figures for various parameters. When the Engelhard Industry introduced computers way back in the decade of the 1970s itself, the measurement of thickness of rolled steel sheets per second had increased by 20%.[22]

The use of computers has brought about fundamental changes in the oxygen furnaces. Earlier, the operators, engineers and scientists had to keep track of temperature levels, the composition of gas and steel mix at the point of the blow, the various chemical and physical indexes and their constant changes. Now computers have totally taken over this job, and eliminated the changes regarding oxygen and nitrogen. Earlier at least 7 minutes used to be used up for every change of temperature or structural improvement. Now this much time is saved as also so much of oxygen.[23]

What did the computers do? They discharged the following crucial tasks: computing temperature of hot metal, scrap and lime, so that proper temperature and chemical mix is prepared; decide oxygen flow; automatic dynamic control; prepare the path of heat and temperature; etc.[24] In the biggest blast furnace in Europe of August Thompson/

AEG the carbon/iron proportion at the time of coke charge is fully operated by the computers.

The Italcedar Company of Genoa runs a steel complex situated in three places simultaneously. The information system run by the computers control everything, from production to noting and meeting the orders placed by the consumers. It prepares the whole scheme of production and distribution, and every work-piece is recorded in all its details on the screen. The sensor machines in the Chase, Brass and Copper Company keeps information and track of every detail of the motion, position, shape, size etc of raw materials, wastes, mixed metals, furnaces, every single piece of solids, etc.[25]

There are many kinds of automatic production systems, among them flow line and batch manufacturing. In the flow-line system something is produced on a large-scale. For automatic observation and control, "distributed computer technology" is used. For cars, two-wheelers, TV, microprocessors, airplanes, etc highly specialized equipment is used.[26]

Batch production is more flexible: instead of manufacturing the same type of product in large numbers, they are produced according to demands including individual demands. As a result, one single product may differ from another. Consequently, the machine runs on a particular program and the nature and structure of the machine is quite different. Manufacturing is done in batches of certain numbers according to need. Alvin Toffler has done extensive work in this field.[27]

Flexible Manufacturing System or FSM is rapidly spreading all over the world. It involves an automatic use of things and processes controlled and directed ('commands') by the software. With the growing use of FSM, the use of raw materials, various accessories, parts, time space, etc are getting drastically reduced. In the manufacture of caterpillars, 8.5 hours were consumed earlier; later it got reduced to only 0.3 hours.[28]

Any amount of data is available on the effects of the use of robots. Even in our country now, robots are being used in Maruti and some other units on a limited scale. Their use world-wide have brought about drastic changes in the nature and scene of manufacture.

According to slightly older data, in the Yamazaki Machinery Works Ltd in Japan, while earlier there were 215 workers, only 13 remained after the use of robots. The production time was reduced from three months to three days only. In the Fuji Complex in Japan, in a plant there were 30 machining centres run by the computers aided by robots. Production increased five times. The traditional plant would produce ten times more capital and labour for the same amount of production.[29]

Greater use of program logic *is converting the industrial processes into computing processes.* This is a crucial transition. The industrial processes must be converted into non- and post-industrial processes to increase their productivity. But this brings fundamental changes in its wake. Human beings make a shift from tangible productive activities to the image manipulation, an altogether unprecedented and unexpected result of computerization. Production by increasing itself in a quantitative manner, shifts itself out of itself, to the margins of the production system, thus making a qualitative shift.

Now the entire industrial plant can be controlled by the information flow, and only a pair of wires is enough to control the entire process. Special sensors or the 'transducers' attached to the microprocessors can know the exact state of any process at any place at any time. The plant gets connected as one from the shop floor to the management room and even the owner's place in one single system. Thus the new programs are needed which make the system far more flexible.

Microprocessors and transducers keep track of the stocks and the space occupied by them; the energy and electricity consumed or required, the quality, shape and size of the constituents of the stock and so on. Things become consequently very precise. This is a great revolution indeed.

In Ontario Steel Mills, the computer reduces the speed of the ingot precisely when it needs heating so that it does not slip on the rolling table.

The Chevrolet Car Company of the US produced for example 40 000 disk brakes every day. Each of them had a sensor attached. The data concentrators were connected with hundreds of machine tools which were guided and directed. The central computer control received the information about all this and about speed, time, RPMs, etc within 0.1 seconds.

The Ford Motors used to produce 26,000 gears every day in the 1970s. Then microprocessors were attached to increasing numbers of the machine tools, 264 machine forms, 143 product shiftings, etc. In other words, the jobs were transferred to the computers, like computer cold heading, hot water rinse, automatic gauzing, finish rolling, gear checking, etc.[30]

Hundreds, even thousands of chips kept a 'watch' over the processes. The machines and the tools are given automatic instructions to shift to the next step and so on. Defective tools are taken care of.

Textiles are a very good example of the computerization of production. The use of microprocessors has increased in the textiles tremendously in the last few decades. In the winding machine, the space between two slubs, cone winding, the thickness and other aspects of the thread and such other ones are covered by the processors. In wafting and warping processes, the endless indexes like breaking of the thread, 'beam run out' speed, and most of the other processes are displayed on the screens via on the spot microprocessors. Stock position is taken account of. The state of every loom and machine in the weaving and spinning departments are connected with the central computer screens via the chips.

Even in dying processes, the photo-spectrometers are connected to the computers, which adjust and/or convey colour positions. Colour chemicals are thus saved and deing made precise.

These are some of the examples of the preparation of ground for the fourth technological revolution in the course of the third technological revolution. The connecting points between the two become at once clear to us.

Use of Robots

Today the use of robots has become a common fact. It has virtually replaced human beings in many places as the main factor of production and has taken over many functions. The robot is being used to pick up and use the tools, shift objects from one place to another, to paint and fit in nuts and bolts, and to do endless other jobs previously done by the workers. It is fitted with sensors, cameras, infra-red sensors and other sensory means, and is connected with computers and TV system.

The use of robots is a problem or field that needs proper study and generalization. Today, the robot has become an important constituent of the shop floor, with far-reaching implications.

It is one of the extraordinary developments of modern science and technology in production.

Information, Fourth Technological Revolution and Post-Industrial Tendencies

The discussion makes it clear that information has become a crucial factor of production, both in productive and economic senses. It is as important as money, capital, raw materials, machine, finished products, tools, etc. Rather it has become even more important than all of them. It represents the information and knowledge of the workers, technicians, engineers, managers, etc., and operates even in their absence. The production process proceeds even in the absence of the producers. The proportion of labour is getting reduced in the production. The proportion of the tools and the machines is also getting reduced and the proportion of information is increasing.

Knowledge and information have in fact become the most important factors of production, increasingly converting it into information processing. This lays the basis for the fourth technological revolution.

What is 'Information'?

How do we identify and define information; and how do we then trace its role in production and in information-run economy and society in general?

Information covers the signals, information produced at various points of production, knowledge of reflection, images, etc of the endless production and communication processes going on in a complex, office, factory, etc. On a broader scale information reflects the processes and motions.

Information is a living, very active and effective factor that propels human beings and society.

It becomes increasingly effective with the increase in its speeds. Here the information revolution has played the most important role. It has made it possible to use information in small or big doses or bits back into, for example, the production process. So we produce information and then we use it to propel production and labour processes, among others.

The STR is making it possible to store information and use this stored information or bits and parts of it to drive certain processes needed by us. We are using it, we having to use it, in circulation, production, banking, finance, exchange, communications, and endless other areas. There is a veritable explosion of information on the planet earth, an avalanche in which our society is getting enveloped. Society is almost getting choked with information. The very existence of human beings and society is threatened by the information explosion caused by the information revolution. So much so that we are moving towards a situation when *anything is possible at any time through any means, and we can create anything from anything anywhere anytime!*

Earlier, production could not be carried on without machine, capital and labour; now it cannot be carried on without information. The skill of the labourer is converted into information which is then stored in various forms such as tapes, disk, floppy, mobile, recordings, pen-drive, microprocessor, computer, etc. It is in this form that it is fed back into production.

Besides, information changes the form of structure or organization of production. This applies to any part or entire series of components of production, from shop floor to managerial activities, workers' interventions, designs of tools and machines, which is very important, composition and formula and state of chemicals, nature of bio-techniques, genetic and DNA structures, and so on and so forth.

For example, when information is used to drive the shop floor, the space and time references of the worker and operator changes. They now have to work with the information received *about* rather than the job itself. This is a fundamental and momentous change. The person concerned goes out of the production process and into the processing of the information. The tool/machine combination then must be adapted to using information and knowledge and thus become more 'scientific'. They must also become specific to information rather than to production.

The worker/operator works 'from a distance' that is he/she distances from the work itself. It is a process of the worker distancing himself/herself from its own self, from being a worker. His/her job is to act as the worker, but the intervention of information apparatuses and of information itself begins a process of conversion the worker into a non-worker. This is a historic shift.

The basic reason is the speed of information which penetrates everything and goes far ahead of the worker in the supervision of the machines and thus of the production itself. It is precisely at this point that the labour process separates/crystallizes out of the production process. Time becomes a crucial component in production.

It should be noted here that at the shop floor and elsewhere in the factory, there is virtually no expenditure in the production and distribution of information. We can observe the processes and their indexes on the screen without any expenditure. The information can be shared by more than one person at one or more screens without any expenditure. The information machine or information-driven machine is *different qualitatively* from the industrial machine and tool.

There is a major difference between information collection and processing by human beings and what is conducted by the computerized automatic system. The computer is extremely fast and can perform and compute in virtually no time.

Human beings are forced to change and restructure themselves according to the extremely rapid changes in the software.

In the traditional assembly lines, changes are very slow. Besides, the jobs of the workers are clearly divided into separate pieces of the labour and productive processes. The industrial machine and factory system, and consequently production system, is relatively stable.

This is not so with the computerized information-driven production. It changes all the time, every moment, leading to a destabilization of the individual and human relations. The intervals between the events are being rapidly reduced.

It is interesting to note that the microprocessors, computers and the mobiles are behaving more like the human intellect, like 'artificial intelligence'. *To this artificial intelligence* the humans are fast transferring their functions with *accelerating* rapidity. In the process, ever faster electronic systems are being created to catch up with the needs of processing.

This historic process is destabilizing and destroying all the historic and existing structures of production, creating new ones. Human activities are now entering the sphere of production through information. The dialectical abstract and concrete electronic signals emerge forth as tangible, solid objects as well as higher logical forms.

The labor process is rendered just a superfluous event, particularly in the services. Alvin Toffler[31] has described at great length the third wave of production, comparing it with the 'second wave'. In the industrial age, we beat the metal sheets into thinner ones, use hammers, roll it, drive holes and pieces out, scrape out, and so on.

But it is different with the micro-electronics revolution. We penetrate the metal down to their molecules and atoms, and thus change them and manipulate them. We send information using, not gears, springs, wheels etc or even telephones. Information emanates from electronic signals. Repeated use does not affect the chips much.

The aim of labour is increasingly the production of information and knowledge.

This point is very important: labour is rendered a superfluous and a surface event.

The purpose of production now is 'production' of knowledge, and this provides a new dimension to the social development. Such a production is the negation of production, anti-production.

Already in new branches, the expenditure on software constitutes an overwhelming majority of the total investment. While in the US in 1920, those working in the educational sector constituted only 9% of the total, today it has crossed three-fourths to one-fifth and even more.[32] Today, production has already lost its primacy in every field in the US and other advanced countries.

In the entire history of humankind, the development of the electronic digital computer has been *the greatest event*. This tool is a *logical* tool, and it can create a new tool all the time, a tool that often acts independent of human thought. There never has been a 'logical tool'. It is thus the very negation of tool as well as of the human consciousness as part of the brain; this consciousness is now finding independent existence and application, becoming a challenge to the human brain and consciousness. Software uses logic and computation of the human being but also increasingly copies it. This is exemplified by the 'massively parallel computation'. Computers and robots are rapidly replacing human beings and their labour. *Thus capital does not need living labour anymore.*

By controlling and directing the machines and tools, the computers and electronic automatic logical systems, do away with the industrial revolution and begin a new revolution unlike the previous one, in fact the *very opposite* of that.

The electronic 'industries' are radically different from the traditional industries. Knowledge/information assumes a special form of the labour-power, negating it completely. It puts a question mark over labour power. Electronic systems, gadgets, tools, machines and equipment amplify and change information and thus bring about a drastic change in the values or things we use. In human society, the exchange of information has a crucial place, and the information revolution not only enhances this role but renders it dominant. The human relations of the previous times as expressed through information and experience exchange are now replaced and reflected, expressed in the form of electronically generated information. Mark Poster has done extensive work on the electronically mediated language and communication, which according to him, gives rise to a new mode of information. (See Poster, Mode of Information)

Thus electronics give final form to human interaction at the level of information, as expressed in electronic communications. Thus electronics becomes the very essence of human relations and human communications.

Electronic communications produce a different kind of social layering and strata tuned to the generation and exchange and working of information. *A new society thus is being created.*

Collapse and Reorganization of Labour Process

Worldwide realignment, reorganization and collapse of the labour process is taking place, posing new problems for the social structure itself.

The semiconductor industry is today the most important one, which is simultaneously making a transition to the post-industrial system. It is an interesting development. It is a sign of the growing importance of information in production, engulfing the whole of production and thus radically transforming it. The semiconductor technology has become so advanced that today the whole range of products, tools, machines and parts thereof are manufactured by the automatic microprocessor-driven production systems. The entire production processes and assembly lines are being automated or already have been automated. Automatic assembly can now be used for the small-batch production runs associated with customized semiconductors. This is development of great significance. Units like the Fairchild, Motorola, national semiconductor units etc have already converted to electronic automation.[33]

Consequently the production and labour processes the world over are being reorganized and refashioned. The process basically began in the 1980s and has today accelerated to a point where they now enter the fourth technological stage.

Japanese and many other Western companies have adopted *kanban*' or 'just-in-time' manufacturing system. It is a method of batch production requiring highly synchronized and continuous deliveries of materials, saving overhead and storage space and cost. US companies like General Motors, National Semiconductor and other ones of different countries have been using the system. *Kanban* holds the same importance as Taylorism and Fordism in the earlier phases of industrial capitalism.[34]

Mode of Information: Core of Post-Industrial Society

Till now we have been analysing and explaining the existence and evolution of society in terms of the mode of production. The concept of the mode of production is the key to the nature, structure and stage of a society.

In Marx's theory, in particular in his *Capital*, the concept of the mode of production is central to the capitalist production processes. The concept of the mode of production is also the basis of the materialist conception of history. Not only in Marxism but several other systems too, and unconsciously in many authors and their works, the conception is used as a method to understand the society and its history.

Till now, production has been the source of motion of society. We cannot think of society without production and production-based distribution. It continues to be crucial for human existence. The concept of the mode of production helped us understand and explain human existence and culture, civilization, ideas and ways of life. It has become an important source of knowledge and information regarding society. The entire industrial economics and political economy is based on the way production is carried on.

But because of the ongoing microelectronic revolution, a fundamental change has taken place in this situation. The role of information, knowledge and means of information has become dominant, and production is rendered secondary. The mode of production is now failing to cover society. Processes are emerging which do not fully fit in with industrial features, which contain the features of both the industrial and the post-industrial production or which have become fully post-industrial and information-based.

When we say a process does not fit in with the industrial nature and framework, it clearly means that the process has gone beyond the latter. In the industrial process, information is used by production. In the post-industrial process information uses and transforms production. By helping production, information in fact helps or forces it to shed its production form and to get converted into information. So there are two forms of existence of production: one is production itself, the other is information-based production. The latter is not production proper; it is only a by-product. The relations are inside out. They are opposite poles, where production conforms to information. We are brought into production as an outsider with information on our side, but on our side as the director of both production and information. So it is *inorganic intelligence,* the non-human information production system, that directs us on what to do as regards production. We can only dictate our needs, but only *according to the laws of information production.*

So, production is no more production of material goods but production of information, which then may be used in several branches of social production including material production.

A refashioning of production, and therefore of the whole society, is underway.

The terrain of the whole society is shifting from production to information. It is being rendered a different socio-order. The satellite system has transformed the individuals and their conscious organizations into part and parcel of society. The satellite system and Internet have become the growing consciousness of society that engulfs us and deeply transforms us.

The extremely fast electronic waves and beams are cutting across the whole existing social order, social and economic structures, as well as through the political and even ideological formations. This is simply unprecedented.

The limits of production at the social scales are becoming clearer. The electro-magnetic warp around the earth is also around society and our consciousness, and leads to the inevitable conclusion that we are now being led by our own consciousness. This simple fact is decisive for the future. The waves of communication and information are creating a new society. Modern electronic communications are rapidly creating ever new structures of social and technological nature simultaneously, to which we should adjust and adapt. The system and speed of production, exchange, banking, finance and so on are accelerating and in turn they accelerate the creation of new structures.

Consequently, the pressures on the existing structures are increasing every moment, the pressure to speed up, to change, to innovate and so on. The production and communications of the post-industrial age cannot be compatible with those in production and circulation, banking etc of the industrial era.

This is reflected in the conflict between industrial and post-industrial structures. Information/communication and production are in mutual conflict, posing historic problems.

While industrial processes are tuned to days and hours, the electronic ones take place in hours, minutes and seconds. This is a conflict. Today, the consumer needs everything better and well-displayed. So the industrial production has to change. Better and faster is the 'philosophy'. Better tools and machines, which should be self-acting and run on software, drive the processes towards quality. Money-commodity exchanges and financial transactions are taking on new forms. Money-commodity and money exchanges need to be rapidly computerized and electronified. Otherwise they will be relics of the past.

If the world is going along satellite communications, counting notes manually will only destroy the finance and economy. The bank will have to use the electronic system and the factory electronic hammer or other means to produce iron and steel sheets. Only then the motions in different sectors of economy will be in mutual correspondence, which is what the latest technologies demand.

Information has many features which differ from the traditional social, economic and technological means. It is not reduced during expenditure; it rather increases. So its *use value is unlimited*. Thus a new factor is added to the social development.

Electronic information does not fit in with industrial and capitalist structures and economy based upon private property. It is out of that system. Not only this; information/ communication in electronic form threatens the private property relations.

Information *about* production has led to better quality and higher and more precise production. A series of commodities are being produced which now do not contain any value; their number is increasing. They cannot be evaluated through industrial methods. The labour theory of value is under the scanner, and needs to be re-evaluated. Baudrillard not only criticizes political economy but also the political economy of the signs and images. (Poster 57) Today the problem is not so much of production as of equitable distribution and consumption.

Today the dividing line between the computer and worker is disappearing. The computer is not just a solid machine; more than that, it is a software program. Not only do we run it, it in turn runs us. It has a program, it is a 'living' machine with a language of its own. From the philosophical viewpoint the dividing line between the machine and the human being is being blurred.

Information, Computers, Work and Time

The world is being transformed, redefined and re-emerging in terms of information. In the course of the information explosion, technology is processing information and things are being turned into information. With continuously reducing size and cost every machine is being rendered flexible to the extent that it can churn out information of an unlimited nature. This is in contrast to the earlier machines that only provided limited information, which were mainly stored by humans or were strictly directed and limited by them. Information earlier was an adjunct to the machine and the 'thing'. Now it has been 'liberated' and drastically modifies the machine itself to its dissolution.

The chip-controlled machine tool processes information into its realization. "All manufacturing and service operations can be turned primarily into information systems."[35]

One can get an idea of the historical build up of information in some data. A journal from the 1930s may occupy 2 or 3 inches of space for one year's copies. In the 1970s they occupied some 15–20 inches for one year of publication.[36] Information appears in various forms like volumes, books, journals, newspapers, government and private reports, and so on. They all contain 'information'. Now they can all be transformed into computer or software/digital form.

Information played an important role even in the industrial age. We have mentioned the forms of printed matter above. There was the telephone, telegraph and other methods. Gradually a medium like the radio came into being, which along with the telephone, laid the basis for the subsequent stages of communication. One of the sources of concentration of power into the hands of the industrialists and the capitalists was the separation and control of information. It was separated from production and then used to control production and associated processes. Ultimately, information is liberated from the human biological limits.

It is interesting that the emergence of humans has been linked to the property of the mammalian brain to store more information than can their genes. Thus human beings emerge as information processing animals. Invention of writing, and then of printing, enables humans to store more information in libraries than could be stored in their brains. Microtechnology today allows intelligence to be stored and amplified in external electronic form, external to the humans themselves.

These changes progressively require less time, and in the electronic phase, far less than ever, and most unexpectedly. The new means of data storage and retrieval and for information processing is transforming the whole society. This helps us to put forward the concept of the post-industrial society as the one to explain the changes. While industrialization meant primacy of products or things, post-industrial organization means primacy of information. Information is the essential resource of the new society. Industries are being turned into information processing centres, a key basis for the post-industrial order of things. It is a revolution. Even according to old data, transmission of data from 1974 to 1984 in Europe increased twelve–fold. More than half the gross national product of the US comes from the information industry.[37] Shallis mentions Daniel Bell adopting a similar approach by outlining *four stages* towards information society: speech, writing, printing and telecommunications, each of which is an abstraction of the previous one.[38]

The introduction of microchips, robots and computerized automation in manufacturing is changing the scenario of industry. Industries like watch-making have been wiped out almost completely and new industries and branches of production are coming into being. By the 1980s, the proportion of electronic digital watches had increased to about 60% of the world market.[39] Automation has proceeded in the automobile industry at a steady pace. In many branches, it is fully automated and highly robotized. In the 1980s itself, the Fiat Robogate factory was fully robotized and produced cars completely untouched by human hand. It was designed to weld one car body every minute. A central computer controlled the handling of components, their transport within the factory such as to the assembly and welding robots, quality control etc. The system could handle more than one car model simultaneously.[40]

"Money is symbolic of human labour, even when it has been reduced to moving electrons in some computer circuit. If money is generated by machine labour and then distributed to the non-working population to buy the goods the machines make, then the net result is that the machines will be working for nothing, the goods will be effectively given away. As only a proportion of the money people spend will be on goods, that means the goods will not only be given away with money attached, they will have a negative price."[41] That will be an absurd proposition, as money cannot be created out of 'nothing'. This point will have to be answered in the context of the electronic revolution.

Towards the end of his chapter on 'Computer and Work', Shallis states: "The computer not only alters the structure and extent of employment, it also redefines the nature of work. Although the computer releases people from mindless, repetitive and mechanical work, it does not offer any substitute."[42]

The first part Shallis's statement gives the impression of being exciting and futuristic, and one waits to find something new and novel, throwing light on new work or dissolution of work etc. But the second part, and further, is disappointing: he says the *computer does not offer any substitute*. This statement is a damp squib after some profound and enlightening analyses we come across. The author does not take his line of argumentation further and suddenly breaks off. He says further on that work becomes not the fruits of human labour but the output of the machine.[43] As he goes further, the pessimism grows. He says: "Modern industrial society, of which computers are the current leading technological expression, has already destroyed the dignity of most forms of work. The computer extends and enhances that process."[44]

All this does not fit in with the general tenor of the narration of the book. The author further laments the destruction of people's skills, the creativity, the favouring of a handful of privileged people to the exclusion of all others, and so on. Service for and cooperation is taken away, is the complaint.

Part of the criticism and complaint is justified and real but it cannot be generalized. There are several other negative aspects of impacts of the electronic technology but these are only one side of the picture. The point is that the problems are not new, and they need to be tackled at social, economic and political levels. It has not been indicated that the problems are peculiar to the STR or are its distinct result.

Besides, one should be tracing the new impacts on nature and structure of work, and this involves an analysis of labour and production processes, redefinition of work, place and role of work, and an objective dispassionate analysis of new features of these processes. These unfortunately are not able to emanate due to the obsession of the writer with subjective enlargement of negative aspects and a failure to discover the new structure and nature of work. For if work/labour is getting re-oriented or re-figured, these phenomena have a far-reaching implication.

Along with money management, time management became more important, and the industrial organizations changed their strategies and organization accordingly. Towards the end of the last century, the companies were already undergoing suitable changes in this field. They were adopting 'flexible fast-cycle' manufacturing methods. Not only, production cycle but the total cycle of a firm had to be shortened to compete in time sense. There was much scope for reduction of the cycle. In the 1990s, less than 10% of the elapsed time cycle was actually spent on value addition in products and services. The remaining 90% was spent unproductively. The cycles have progressively brought down the time cycles since.[45] The case study of the AT&T regarding reduction of the time cycle is interesting. The efforts to reduce the time cycle began in January 1987 and the teams were able to reduce the total cycle by more than half after only three cycles. The old non-linear relay system was given up in favour of the simultaneous and parallel system of management. Engineers, managers and employees were given greater autonomy.[46]

While studying the STR, we should be unfolding the qualitatively new features in scientific and social evolution. STR is a break in social development, it is qualitatively different from the industrial revolution, and it is an unprecedented and the greatest revolution that the human society has experienced.

Making of the Fourth Technological Revolution

Digital Manufacturing: Use of 3-D Printing

Just as the third industrial revolution (TIR) allows millions to produce their own energy, a new digital manufacturing revolution opens up similar possibilities in the field of manufacturing and production of durable goods. In the new era, potentially everybody can be one's own manufacturer as well as power producer. This is the world of 'distributed manufacturing'.[47]

This manufacturing of the future is that of 3-D printing. It is no more a science fiction but a reality. Suppose you push the print button on the computer and send a digital file to an inkjet printer. With 3-D printing, the machine produces three-dimensional objects. With the help of the computer-aided design (CAD) the software commands the printer to build successive layers of products using powder, molten plastic, metals, etc. to build scaffolding. The printer can produce many or multiple copies just like the xerox machine, and all sorts of goods like auto to aircraft parts, jewellery, mobile phones, cells, medicines, toys and what not can be 'printed' (manufactured in 3-D manner).

This has been called 'additive manufacturing' in contrast to 'subtractive manufacturing'. The latter involves cutting down and joining together various materials. According to analysts, millions of customers will easily download digitally manufactured, customized products and 'print them out' even in their houses.

3-D entrepreneurs are particularly enthusiastic about additive manufacturing. It is because the process requires *as little as 10% of the raw materials* used in traditional manufacturing and also uses much less energy than the conventional factory production. The 3-D manufacturing will greatly reduce the logistics cost. It is a giant step in the direction of energy saving with far-reaching implications.

Similarly additive manufacturing has the potential to drastically reduce the production costs and thus to create hundreds of thousands of *mini-manufacturing units* of predominantly small size as also of medium size, and they can effectively challenge and compete with big business.

According to a newspaper report,[48] 3-D printers have an extremely broad application. They can be used to print replacement auto parts, and such other objects, perhaps even the entire vehicle.

Recent researches have shown that they can be used to produce food for astronauts and to build crucial components for satellites and spacecrafts.

In 3-D printing, material is taken to a surface and layer after layer of material is put upon one another in a controlled manner so that an object is created. Simple materials like plastic and metals are used. Now even food can be produced. The idea of food producing is especially useful to the astronauts. Raw ingredients could be used to create different kinds of food for the 9–month space journey to Mars. Space rocks and other materials could be used to create printers and other equipment.

3-D could also be used for world-wide food production.

Microsoft is reported to make 3-D printers in the next instalments of the Windows, which will be automatically loading driver software that will ease the 3-D printer set up at home.

According to Shanen Boettchaer in a company blog post, they want to make it so simple that anyone can set up their own table top factory. "Making a 3-D object on your PC will be as writing a document in Word and sending it to print." Microsoft estimates that some 70 per cent of 3-D printing is already performed on machine running Windows. 3-D statues and imageries can be produced from 3-D photos of the individuals. The firm hopes that the designs created in 3-D drawing applications will be seamlessly submitted as 3-D print jobs because the driver software will understand 3-D file formats as easily as it understands 2-D printing formats.[49]

Making Robot Arm Move with Mind

Researcher Andrew Schwartz of University of Pittsburgh points out that the "technology, which interprets brain signals to guide a robot arm, has enormous potentials..."[50] A patient paralyzed neck down was experimented upon on a mind-controlled prosthetic hand.

The scientists developed micro-electrode arrays that connect brain cells to electronic circuitry. The circuitry consists of square grids just 16 sq mm with 96 points penetrating the brain's surface by 1/16th of an inch. They scanned the lady patient's (name Scheuermann) brain to determine exactly where to put the electrodes. In February 2015 they implanted the device into her left motor cortex. This is the part of the brain that controls the movement of the right arm and hand.

These implants were linked to a robotic limb capable of joint and wrist movement like a human hand. The patient was able to use the prosthetic arm after training just with her mind. She took part in a 13–week long training programme. She could perform a number of movements and jobs with the help of the prosthetic arm, including picking up objects.

Brain-machine interface works by *converting brain signals to computer signals*. Further development of the artificial arm can multiply its functions at direct command of the brain. They can use a fully implanted wireless system in their home without anybody's help. The patient can even eat chocolate using the arm.

DNA for Future Computers

Scientists have found a way to 'switch' DNA structure using copper salts and Enthylenediamine tetraacetic acid. It is an advance that could pave the way for computers built from DNA and not from silicon. The acid causes the DNA to fold into an 'i-motif'. It can be switched a second time into a hair-pin structure using positively-charged copper. This discovery is a great boost for nanotechnology. It could create logic gates for DNA-based computing. Logic gates are elementary building blocks of digital circuits in computers.[51]

References

1. Jeremy Rifkin, *The Third Industrial Revolution*, Palgrave Macmillan, 2011.
2. *The Hindustan Times*, March 7, 2014.
3. See, Jean Lojkine, "From the Industrial Revolution to the Computer Revolution", in, *Capital and Class*, Sage Publications, 01/1986, 29 (1) p. 125).
4. Ibid.
5. Ibid.
6. Ibid., p. 111.
7. Ibid., p. 111.
8. Ibid., p. 112.
9. Ibid., pp. 112–13.
10. Ibid., p. 120.
11. Ibid., p. 122.
12. Ibid., p. 123.
13. Ibid., pp. 123–24.
14. Ibid., p. 125.
15. Ibid.
16. Ibid., p. 125.
17. Ibid., p. 126.
18. Ibid., ibid.
19. Ibid., ibid.
20. Ibid 126.
21. Ibid.
22. U. Rembold and R. Dillmann, eds. *Computer Aided Design and Manufacture*, Springer, 1986, pp. 423–39.

23. Ibid., pp. 423–39.
24. Ibid., pp. 423–39.
25. Ibid., p. 436.
26. *Perspectives in Science and Technology,* Volume 1, Department of Science and Technology, Government of India, 1990, pp. 355–56 (PST).
27. See Alvin Toffler, *Power Shift,* Bantam, New York, 1980.
28. See PST.
29. PST.
30. U. Rembold and R. Dillmann, op. cit., p. 461.
31. Toffler, *Third Wave.*
32. See, Jim Davis and Michael Stack, "Knowledge in Production", *Race and Class,* 34, 3 (1992), p. 2.
33. Jeffrey Henderson, *Globalisation of High Technology Production,* Routledge, London and New York, 1989, p. 143.
34. Henderson, Ibid., pp. 143–44.
35. Michael Shallis, *The Silicon Idol: The Micro-Revolution and its Social Implications,* Oxford University Press, 1984, p. 112.
36. Ibid.
37. Based on Michael Shallis, *The Silicon Idol,* pp. 113–14.
38. Shallis, ibid p. 114.
39. Ibid., p. 117.
40. Ibid.
41. Ibid., p. 126.
42. Ibid., p. 131.
43. Ibid.
44. Ibid., p. 132.
45. John Lindquist, "The Global Impact of Fast Time Cycles", *World Link,* Geneva, March-April, 1990, Number 3–4.
46. John Hanley, "AT&T's Speedier Product Cycles", *World Link,* Geneva, March-April 1990, Number 3–4.
47. Rifkin, p. 117.
48. See, *The Indian Horizon* (daily), New Delhi and Hyderabad, May 6, 2015.
49. *The Indian Horizon,* New Delhi, May 6, 2015.
50. *The Indian Horizon,* Science & Technology Pullout, April 22, 2015.
51. *The Times of India,* August 20, 2015.

9

Renewable Energy and Technological Revolution

Society at Crossroads

Another field that proves the industrial revolution is at the crossroads is nature and crisis of energy. Contemporary industrial life has been marked by oil and other fossil fuel energies. They are now on the way out, though this fact can be discerned only in faint outlines. Consequently, the technologies based upon them are getting obsolete. The industrial infrastructure can be seen to be ageing and stuttering. The smoke-belching scenes have of course disappeared long ago along with the towns and industries associated with them. Coal is no more the driving force of the industry. It has largely been replaced by oil. But now oil too is going to be history.

"By the 1980s the evidence was mounting that the fossil-fuel driven Industrial Revolution was peaking..."[1] The carbon-era is coming to an end. The great economic revolutions take place with the convergence of communication technologies with energy systems.

According to Rifkin, by the 1990s a new kind of convergence was taking place. The internet technology and renewable energies were about to merge to create the TIR or the third industrial revolution.[2] Hundreds of millions of people will produce their own green energy in their homes, offices and factories and share it as 'energy internet'.[3]

Thus there is a real possibility of the 'democratization of energy',[4] which will bring about fundamental re-ordering of human relationships.

Third Industrial Revolution (TIR)

In the words of Rifkin the third industrial revolution (TIR) is the last of the great industrial revolutions, laying grounds for what he calls the 'emerging collabourative age'.[5] Its completion will signal the end of the 200-year-old era marked by commerce, industry, entrepreneurial markets and mass workforce. Simultaneously it will begin a new era of collabourative behaviour, social networking, and professional and technical workforce. The centralized business operations of the first and second industrial revolutions will be replaced by and subsumed under the distributed business practices of the TIR. The traditional and hierarchical structures of economic and political power will make way for lateral power spread across the society.[6]

Rifkin makes certain very important statements regarding the next fifty years or so. By the middle of this century more and more commerce will be overseen by intelligent technology. Thus freed humans will be engaged in the creation of social capital which work not for profit and thus create a new kind of civil society. Such a society will become the dominant feature of the century. The next period of human history will see new driving forces of history. We can arrive at a sustainable post-carbon era by the middle of this century.[7]

Oil and End of the Second Industrial Revolution

In 2001 oil was selling at $ 24 a barrel. Exactly seven years later, in 2008, it was selling at 147. It was unbelievable and nobody could imagine it would reach this. But Rifkin was among the very few or perhaps the only one who forecast the oil crisis and the price going beyond $50.[8] Nobody thought things would happen in their lifetime. But they did happen.

Virtually every activity in our life is dependent on oil: food, medicines, fertilizers, cement, plastics, clothes made of petro-chemical synthetic products, power, heat, light etc, are all dependent on oil. Their prices began to increase rapidly, and affected all the aspects and sectors of our society, political, economic, social, personal, cultural etc. "We have built an entire civilization on the exhumed carbon deposits of the Carboniferous Period."[9]

According to the studies of Rifkin, by July 2008 we have reached the outer limits of our global economic growth. Prices are rising uncontrollably, there is allround recession and crisis, and there is growing unrest. We have reached the peak of globalization[10], in a sense. The second industrial revolution is coming to an end as also the oil era. There is a risk of a collapse of civilization. Global peak of per capita oil production has been reached, not to be confused with the global peak of oil production.[11]

Hubbert Bell Curve

'Global peak oil production' is a term used by the petro-geologists to denote the point when the global oil production reaches the highest point on the Hubbert oil curve. It occurs when half of the ultimately recoverable oil reserves are used up. After that, the production begins to drop.[12]

M. King Hubbert was a geophysicist with Shell Oil Company in 1956. He forecasted the peak of oil production in 48 US states between 1965 and 1970. He was ridiculed by his colleagues who did not believe that the biggest oil producer of the world would lose oil production. But he was proved right. The oil production in the US reached its peak in 1970 and then began to fall.

The geologists observe that the global oil production will peak sometime between 2010 and 2035, depending on one's approach and views. The international Energy Agency (IEA) in its 2010 World Energy Outlook report stated that the global peak production of crude oil probably occurred in 2006 at 70 million barrels per day. It was a stunning announcement, sending alarms all over the world, particularly in the US business circles.

According to the IEA, to keep oil production flat, and avoid a great fall in the world economy, a staggering $8 trillion were required over the next 25 years. The economies of India and China in the meantime achieved very high growth rates, 9.6 and 14.2% respectively in 2007. In other words, one-third of the human race was brought into the oil era. Prices rose and a world crisis ensued.

According to the IEA the oil imports for mostly rich countries of the OECD rose from $200 billion at the beginning of the year to $790 billion at the year-end. The import bill of the EU in 2010 rose by $70 billion. The US oil bill went up by $72 billion.[13] The economic columnist of the *Financial Times* wrote an essay on the historic convergence in 'output per head' in China, India and the Western countries. Between the 1970s and 2009 the ratio of Chinese output per head to that of the US rose from 3% to 19%, and in India it rose from 3 to 7%.[14]

Ben Bernanke, chairman of US Federal Reserve Board, pointed out in November 2010 that the real aggregate output in the emerging economies was 41% higher than at the beginning of 2005. China's output was higher by 70% and India's 55%.[15]

All this is likely to push the oil prices further and affect the entire world economy in terms of output, consumption, prices and so on, leading to a downward trend. For the past several decades, we have been consuming three-and-a-half barrels of oil for every barrel found.[16] This fact contains the future direction of our energy development.

Second Industrial Revolution and Its Stages

The second industrial revolution (SIR) went through two stages. A 'juvenile' SIR infrastructure was laid down between 1900 and 1929. After the Second World War (WW II), a high concentration growth of highway network took place in the US since 1956, which began the second stage. The network of roads led to the growth of construction, townships and real estate economy, which continued till the 1990s, when the ICT or the information and communication technology got grafted on the older technologies. The IT sector and the Internet did not in themselves constitute a new industrial revolution.[17] For this to happen, the communication technology must converge with a new energy regime. This has always happened with every economic revolution in history. New communications never stand alone; they manage the flow of activities made possible by the new energy systems.

New communications are fundamentally different from the first generation electricity communications. Telephone, radio and TV are centralized forms of communications designed to manage an economy organized around centralized fossil fuel energies and centralized business. The new second generation electricity communications on the other hand are suited to distributed forms of energies. Lateral kind of business activity is suited to such an energy system.

In the 1990s the ICT was grafted upon the second industrial revolution, which was centralized in nature. It was unnatural. While the ICT enhanced productivity, it was limited by the centralized nature of the energy distributive system.

In the absence of a proper new communication-energy mix, the economy began to live off the accumulated wealth created during the decades following the Second World War. It is exemplified by easy credits and the credit card system. Average family savings in the 1990s was around 8%; by 2007 many Americans were spending more than they made during the 1990s and the first decade of the present century. The bankruptcies had risen enormously and spread to millions.

Mortgage banking industry grew into sub-prime mortgages, requiring little or no money. The housing construction boom became the biggest ever, ending up in the biggest bubble ever.[18]

It was this bubble that burst in 2007–08.

Three Industrial Revolutions

Two hundred years of burning coal, oil and natural gas to propel industry has led to a release of massive amounts of carbon into the atmosphere. The emissions continue to increase frighteningly. The spent energy, 'the entropy bill', blocks the sun's radiant heat from escaping the earth, leading to an extraordinary increase in the earth's temperatures.

The earth has warmed up since 1700. The main reason has been the industrial revolution and the beginning of the industrial activities. The global warming has accelerated since 1870. The carbon dioxide content has increased rapidly.[19] At the heart of the climate change debate lies the issue of CO_2 produced by human activities.[20] Consequently, there has been a tremendous rise in the world temperatures, which has been at the centre of debate at the recent world climate conference at Paris in 2015.

The introduction of steam power technology into printing changed the medium into a primary communication tool to manage the *first industrial revolution*. The steam printing press with rollers and later rotary and linotype led to mass circulation of newspapers, magazines and periodicals as well as books. There was mass literacy for the first time. The advent of educated people helped the society to run an economy based on coal, steam and ways.

In the first decade of the 20th century, electrical communication converged with oil-powered internal combustion engines to produce the *second industrial revolution*. Electrification of industries led to the creation of mass produced goods and in particular to the emergence of the giant automobile industry. Automobiles replaced buggies and horses. The oil industry emerged, thousands of miles of wires for communications were laid down and telephone, radio and TV became the means of communication.

Today, a convergence of internet communication technology and the renewable energies is giving rise to a new kind of industrial revolution, the TIR. Millions of people in the 21st century will be generating their own 'green' energy in their homes, rooms, offices, factories, etc. sharing it with other people laterally like the information on the internet.

This is the essence of the *third industrial revolution*.[21]

The documents and debates of the world climate conference held in Paris in 2015 (COP 20) discussed many aspects of rising global temperatures and ways to mitigate the problem. Among them is the reduction in the use of the fossil fuels and shift to renewable energies.[22]

Five Pillars of TIR

According to Rifkin, the third industrial revolution will

have as much impact as the first IR had in the 19th century and the second IR had in the 20th century.

He describes five features of the TIR. Like every other communication and infrastructure revolution in history, the TIR also has its own structure. The five features are mainly as follows:

1) Shift to renewable energy, 2) micro-power plants to act as the building block of the energy system in every continent, with the blocks collecting energies on site, 3) hydrogen and other storage to be built into every building and throughout the infrastructure, 4) Internet technology to be used to build energy—sharing intergrid on a continent, 5) transport fleet to be transformed into electric plug-in and fuel cell vehicles.[23]

The European Union (EU) is expected to draw one-third of its electricity from green resources by 2020. The grid has to be digitalized and should be able to integrate and handle intelligently tens of thousands of local grids, even units. The entire infrastructure has to be changed to handle this transition. The EU will have to spend at least one trillion euros between 2010 and 2020. Millions of buildings in the EU have to be converted into mini-power plants. They can harness renewable energy on the site and send the surplus back to the grid. Without that the plug-ins and millions of vehicles waiting in line cannot be charged.

Thirty per cent of the new energy will come from green energy resources by the end of the second decade of this century.

The price of new green energies is falling rapidly. The cost of PV or photo-voltaic electricity is expected to fall at 8 % per year. "The growing differential between the rising costs of the old fossil fuel energies and the declining cost of the renewable energies is setting the stage for an upheaval of the global economy and the emergence of a new economic paradigm for the 21st century."[24] Solar and wind installations are doubling every two years, following the trajectories of the PCs, etc.[25]

According to scientists, one hour of sunlight is enough to power the global economy for one full year. In the EU, it is estimated that 40% of the roofs and 15% of building facades are suitable for PV application. If the entire EU roof surface is covered with PV, it will generate 40% of the EU electricity demand. The EU being far ahead has installed 78% of all the installed capacity of the world in 2009.

The future of Europe and the world depends largely on green power. The task is to collect solar, wind, hydro, geothermal heat, biomass and other energy sources. The question also is how to do it. Fossil fuels and uranium are 'elite' fuels, found in certain regions of the world only. Renewable energy is found everywhere.

There are an estimated 190 million buildings in European countries.[26] Twenty seven of these countries belong to the EU. Each of these buildings is a potential mini-power plant. They can absorb renewable energy on the spot and transform it into electricity, etc. The renewable energy source can be sun on the roof and some walls, wind coming up certain walls, sewage being disposed from the buildings, geothermal heat beneath the buildings, etc.

Thus the TIR transforms the existing buildings, which already are dwellings, into potential power houses. It is estimated by the scientists and planners that some two decades from now, millions of all kinds of buildings including the malls, hotels, offices, industrial and technology parks, housing complexes and such others will be converted into mini-power plants. This in turn may cause new construction booms.

These developments are leading to the idea of creating the *energy Internet* or smart grid as the new superhighway to carry the electrons. The power grid will be transformed into an info-energy net, which will help millions of people to produce, distribute and re-distribute their own energy. The surpluses could then be feasibly re-distributed. It will share both information as well as energy constantly. For example, the energy levels and the flow of its distribution can be adjusted according to continuous changes in weather conditions. Several other functions can be discharged by the system. The grid can regulate, for example, the electricity used by appliances. If there is a load on the grid, the software can direct a washing machine in a home to skip one rinse cycle per load to save energy.[27]

The US government has recently allocated funds to develop the smart grid across the country.

The smart grid will be the backbone of the new economy, which will create and use a new kind of internet. It has been suggested that this new network will be 100 or even 1000 times larger than the Internet.

The green energy and the new kind of grid have already changed the balance of power from *centralized* fossil fuels and uranium energies to the *distributed* renewable energies. Advanced software has been created that allows establishments to connect millions of computers of all kinds, increasing their power beyond any supercomputers.

'Homemade' Electricity in Germany

Of about 600 terrawatt hours Germany consumes each year, 50TWh or about 8% of the total are self-produced. The trend of setting up solar panels on rooftops of homes and gas plants in factories is becoming clearer. The share in industry is around 20%.

Homemade power in Germany is not taxed, while the conventional electricity is. It is also not subject to duties for the wider 'energy transition'.

Klausmeier, a small entrepreneur and family hotel owner in Freiburg, Germany, fitted his hotel ten years ago with a gas-fuelled power and heat cogeneration unit in his 45-room establishment. According to him, the homemade power generation has three advantages: cost savings, energy efficiency and climate protection. A growing number of schools, hospitals, industrial plants, home owners, offices, small businesses, etc. are fast adopting home-power and green fuels.

According to a survey conducted in 2013 of some 2400 companies, nearly half of them either have already made the transition or are in the process of making it.[28]

Micro-algae based bio-fuel has the potential to considerably solve the world fuel problem. Studies show that this fuel source produces much higher levels of energy than other comparative life forms.[29]

Algae yields about 2500 gallons of biofuel per acre per year. In comparison, soybeans produce 48 gallons and corn 18 gallons. Besides, these crops need arable land which has to be taken out of cultivation. Micro-algae, on the other hand, can be produced on non-productive land unsuitable for agriculture. If proper use of land is made, at least 30% of the energy needs of geographically large countries can be met through micro-algae.

Change from Fossil Fuel to Green Energy: Shifting Politics

Fossil fuels like coal, oil, natural gases etc are elite energies because they are found in only select areas. They require massive economic, military and political investments, wherein national and international geopolitical shifting interests are to be taken into account.

By nature these fossil fuels need and create highly centralized and concentrated economic interests in the form of, say giant oil monopolies and cartels. They need enormous command control which is highly centralized and top-down. They require massive concentration of capital to move oil and other fuels from underground to the ultimate user. The ability to concentrate capital is the essence of modern capitalism. This centralized energy infrastructure determines the development of industrial capitalism in the rest of the economy and politics of the advanced capitalist countries.

The development of railways led to emergence of a large number of educated staff managing the system. It also led to the invention of the telegraph. Railways required a literate workforce. Written orders down the line were required, and this determined the nature of employees. Without print it was not possible. Besides, coal and steel industries got attached with the railways.

The railways made full use of the telegraph to communicate and coordinate the running of the rail traffic, passenger as well as goods. During the 19th century, the rail traffic generally was single line. Later the introduction of double lines needed the telegraph even more. In the US and Britain, telegraph lines began to be set up along the rail lines (railways or rail tracks).

The combination of railways, coal and steel industries further centralized the management of industries. "The shrinking of distances and the annihilation of time, resulting from the convergence of coal- and steam-powered technology with print communications, sped up commercial activity at every stage of the supply chain... "[30]

Frederick Taylor became the first management expert, and the management became scientific method, with its being recast with the persona of the worker. They were turned into living machines with the production and labour process being turned into the piecemeal system of numerous divisions, each assigned to different workers. The work of each worker was fully planned by at least one day in advance, each man receiving complete written instructions on detailed tasks and the means to do it.

Schools became a microcosm of the industry and the factories. One room schools gave way to giant, centralized schools, almost resembling factories. They were given assignments, instructions and methods to carry them out efficiently and with speed. They became isolated autonomous units with complete bar on information sharing which became punishable. They were graded on an objective basis and judged on merit and efficiency.

Now the third industrial revolution with its decentralized lateral power is challenging this system on a distributed and collabourative basis.

John D. Rockefeller founded Standard Oil Company in 1868, and 11 years later it controlled 90% of refining capacities. Many other companies came onto the scene and they tried to monopolize all the integrated operations from the beginning to the end including laying of pipelines.

By the 1930s 26 oil companies owned 2/3 of capital, 60% of drilling, 90% of pipelines, 70% of refining, and 80% of marketing. By 1951 oil had overtaken coal as the leading energy source in the US. The automobile and telephone industries followed the pattern.

The oil industry has been characterized by gigantism and centralization. Powerful monopoly trends can be seen in this industry. Harnessing, refining and other processes require huge amounts of capital. It has therefore vertical, top down, centralized command. Oil business is one of the largest enterprises and the most costly in every manner ever conceived in the history of mankind.

The oil industry was followed by the automobile industry, and dozens of car companies were formed in the

US and Europe in the first two decades of the 20th century. Later their number got further reduced. In the US only three big companies dominated the industry.

The telephone companies were even fewer at the beginning.

All the industries that emerge from the oil industry similarly need big capital, are of giant size and operation, require huge amounts of capital and are centrally organized. Three of the four largest companies of the world today are oil companies: Royal Dutch Shell, Exxon Mobil and BP. Below them are some five hundred international companies representing every sector and industry. They have combined revenue of 22.5 trillion dollars, that is, equivalent to 1/3 of world GDP of 62 trillion dollars. Thus they are dependent on fossil fuels for their very survival.

The president of General Motors once said that what is good for GM is good for the country. But the reality is that the automobile and the internal combustion engine are designed to turn oil into power and mobility. Oil is the prime mover of economy in the 20th century. The British politician Ernest Bevin said: "The kingdom of heaven may be run on righteousness, but the kingdom of earth runs on oil."[31]

This is one of the results of the first and second industrial revolutions.

The CEOs of the American companies earned 42 times more than the average worker in 1980; the figure went up to 531 times in 2001. Between 1980 and 2005 the wealthiest 1% earned 80% of the income in the US. By 2007 the wealthiest Americans earned 23.5% of the nation's pre-tax incomes, up from 9% in 1976. At the other pole there was growing poverty and disparity. The top of the population in the 'carbon era' have gained far more from the industrial revolution, leading to a top-down organization of the society.

First-Second versus Third Industrial Revolution

According to Rifkin[32], the third industrial revolution is organized around what he calls the 'distributed' renewable energies found everywhere and mostly free: sun, wind, water, biomass, geothermal, oceanic etc. They are dispersed energies and can be collected and worked locally. They lead to collabourative, rather than hierarchical, command relations. Also they lead to greater sharing and distribution.

"The partial shift from markets to networks brings with it a different business orientation. The adversarial relationship between sellers and buyers is replaced by a collabourative relationship between suppliers and users."[33]

Self-interest is replaced with shared interest, according to Rifkin.[34] Adding value does not expend but adds to the total activity as appreciation of contribution.

In industry after industry, networks are competing with market and open-source commons with proprietary relations.[35] He gives the example of Microsoft versus Linux competition. Microsoft is a traditional market-based company, having strict control over its intellectual property. It was unprepared for Linux. The Linux community is made up of thousands of software-programmers, who collabourate mutually to enhance the software code used by the millions. These improvements are kept in public domain and are available without charge to everyone in the Linux network. Global companies like Google, IBM, the US Postal Service, etc have joined the Linux open-source network, becoming its part.

Similarly with Wikipedia. Twenty years ago, nobody could anticipate it. Major encyclopedia companies like Britannica, Columbia and Encarta were unable to anticipate it. They traditionally used to pay academics to write scholarly articles for their expensive hard-bound sets of the knowledge of the world. Today, hundreds of thousands of professional and amateur scholars from all over the world collabourate with one another to prepare scholarly articles on every conceivable topic without pay and make it available to everybody on the planet. The English version of it has 3.5 million entries, almost 30 times the size of *Encylopedia Britannica*. Tens of thousands of people cross-check and improve the contents including providing references, an amazing fact. It is kept competitive with the traditional encyclopedia. Wikipedia is the eighth most visited site on the internet, and attracts 13% of internet visitors every day.

Here, the author, Rifkin, makes a qualitative leap in the concept of the third industrial revolution. It is an important formulation based upon dialectical tracing of the shift from fossil fuel energy to renewable energy.

Nothing is more typical of the industrial way of life than highly capitalized, giant, centralized factories with heavy machines, with the blue-collar workers running them, producing mass scale products on the assembly lines. Just as the TIR economy allows millions of people to produce their own energy, a new digital manufacturing revolution opens up similar possibilities in the field of durable goods. This is the world of 'distributed manufacturing', with 3–D printing as the centre.

We have already dealt with this aspect in the chapter on STR, Tools and Machines.

It is clear that this is not just the TIR, but going well beyond it acquires post-industrial features. How do we look upon 3–D printing manufacture? It has limitless potentials for the future society. It is fully in consonance with the technologies like the 3–D manufacture. The TIR itself becomes post-industrial with the increasing domination of the miniaturized electronic equipments. Therefore, while the solar battery operated energy sources may be of the 'third' industrial kind, the means of production generated by the STR is of the post-industrial kind. There is a certain convergence between the two, and at a certain stage the TIR too may break-up into a post-industrial system, bringing it more in accordance with the post-industrial production.

The TIR is the verge of a new revolution in energy generation and distribution, removing shackles on further development of the means of production, the energy sources and distribution. The building power houses remove any hurdles in the path of the convergence between electronic production and information system and the sources of power. Such a convergence will secure the post-industrial revolution on a firm basis. Decentralization is the key process here, and with it, the centralizing monopolistic trends are controlled and countered.

Old Energy Lobby

Big energy companies have always been the most powerful lobby in the US. Three out of every four lobbyists representing oil and gas interests, were previously the members of the Congress and served in various capacities to regulate and formulate policies and their implementation. It is a situation of 'revolving door' where the same person could enter the oil business and also represent its interests in the Congress after retirement and so on.

Senators and Congressmen on various committees are rewarded with campaign contributions for their work for the industry and for preparing appropriate legislation. After retirement or leaving their offices they are awarded lobbying positions within the industry.

What is the return for the industry? Their return on investments was massive. Between 2002 and 2008 federal energy subsidies to the fossil fuel industries totalled $

72 billion while the subsidies for the renewable energy sector was just $ 29 m. The energy lobby pours billions of dollars into the publicity, public campaigns, financial accounts, educational institutions etc for the politicians to make them toe the line of interest of the oil industry. They fund favourable research and run campaigns at the grassroots to convince the voters that the future of the country lies in big oil.

Sowing Doubts on Environment

Much of the efforts of the big oil is concentrated on sowing doubts in the minds of the people about the realities of the climate change. In the short period of 2009–10 oil, coal and utility industries spent $ 500 million to lobby the government against the passage of the climate-change legislation.[36] The anti-climate change lobby has been deeply influencing the Tea Party movement to believe that there has been no climate change. It has deeply and adversely affected the activists of the movement. Only 14% of them consider it to be an issue while 50% of the general public believes it is very much the problem. Various anti-environment issue groups have been set up and financed to run such campaigns.

A large number and percentage of the candidates of the main parties are as a result against legislations on climate change and global warming.

There is a strong fossil fuel lobby in the US. It has strongly opposed the introduction of renewable energy into the field of electricity for decades. In a few cases where the oil companies did enter the renewable energy field, they have channellized production and feeding of electricity into the centralized unidirectional grid.

Industrial Age to Collaborative Age

Does the use of the word 'industrial' not conjure up the visions of smoke-belching factories, long assembly lines of mechanical workers mindlessly attaching small parts to a product, and conveyor belts and other attachments to the machine system making loud noises within the factory, etc? Have we not left all that behind when we got attached to the Internet and the computer networks?

The answer may be both yes and no. The TIR is the last stage of the great industrial revolution and "the first stage of the emerging collabourative era rolled together."[37] The industrial era emphasizes discipline, hard work, top-down flow of authority, importance of finance capital, operations of the market, private property relations, etc. On the other hand, the collabourative era underlines creative endeavour, person-to-person relations, social capital, common activity, access to global network, etc.

The TIR is likely to peak around 2050 and to even out in the second half of the 21st century. There are already signs that give us a glimpse of the world beyond the industrial era and into the collabourative era.

Third and Fourth Industrial Revolutions: Rifkin Contradicts Schwab

The World Economic Forum met in Davos in January 2016 to discuss this year's theme of the conference: "The fourth industrial revolution". The theme was presented in a paper by the German economist Klaus Schwab. He argued that we are on the cusp of a fourth industrial revolution that will fundamentally change the way we work and live. According to Schwab, the first industrial revolution represented steam-powered and mechanized production. The second introduced electric power and mass production.

The third industrial revolution introduced digitalization of technology. Now a fourth one is going on based on the third. It is characterized by the fusion of technologies, which is blurring the dividing lines between physical, digital and biological spheres.[38]

But Jeremy Rifkin contradicts the claim. He observes that the Davos Conference has misfired on the theme. He does not disagree with the impact and importance of the technological revolution. But he questions Prof. Schwab's contention that it represents a fourth industrial revolution. According to him, digitalization is already a characteristic of the third industrial revolution. Then why a fourth revolution? There is already an interconnectivity and network building in this phase. He says that Prof. Schwab realizes he is on a weak ground. Therefore, he shifts his attention away from what technology does, and concentrates on its effects. The arguments for the fourth industrial revolution fail to build up, according to Rifkin.[39]

Fourth Industrial Revolution and Fourth Technological Revolution

In our opinion, the above-mentioned two concepts have to be differentiated from each other. It is surprising that terms like third 'industrial revolution and fourth 'industrial' revolution are being used. The chief distinguishing feature of the technological change in the last four decades or so has been the replacement of industrial (or phase) revolution by a post-industrial revolution (phase). We have already argued the case in this book. Therefore, generally speaking the use of the term 'industrial' should be given up.

It is better to use the term 'technological' instead of industrial revolution. As for the fourth instead of third technological revolution, key changes have taken place, indicating the onset of a fourth stage in technological transformation. Among the changes, one may mention 3–D technology, collapse of key functions into the mobile, things moving fast towards use of molecular and atomic motions to drive computers, dominance of software over hardware, dissolution of tools and machines, and so on.

We certainly have entered a fourth stage of technological revolution.

References

1. Jeremy Rifkin, *The Third Industrial Revolution,* Palgrave Macmillan, 2011, p. 1.
2. Ibid., p. 2.
3. Ibid.
4. Ibid.
5. Ibid., p. 5.
6. See ibid.
7. Ibid., pp. 5–6.
8. Ibid., p. 13.
9. Ibid., p. 13.
10. Ibid., p. 14.
11. Ibid.
12. See Rifkin, p. 14.
13. See Rifkin p. 16.
14. Ibid., p. 16.
15. Ibid., p. 17.
16. Ibid.
17. Ibid., p. 20.
18. Based on Rifkin p. 21.
19. Anil Rajimwale, *Environment versus Development,* Sunrise Publications, New Delhi, 2006, p. 183.
20. Anil Rajimwale, ibid., p. 186.
21. See Rifkin, p. 21.
22. See documents of World Climate Conference, Paris, 2015.
23. Rifkin, p. 37.
24. Rifkin, p. 39.
25. Ibid.
26. Rifkin, p. 44.
27. Ibid., p. 51.

28. *The Times of India* (TOI), May 28, 2014.
29. TOI May 28, 2014.
30. Rifkin, p. 110.
31. Ibid., p. 114.
32. See ibid., p. 115.
33. Ibid.
34. Ibid., p. 115.
35. Ibid., p. 116.
36. Based on Rifkin, ibid., p. 158.
37. Rifkin, p. 259.
38. Klaus Schwab, *Theme Paper* at the Davos World Economic Forum, 2016; from the internet: quoted in huffingtonpost.com, 'Davos Conference Misfires' on 2016 theme, by Jeremy Rifkin.
39. Jeremy Rifkin, "Davos Conference Misfires", ibid.

10

Mode of Information, Postmodernism and Subject-Object Relationship

It is interesting to note that according to J.D. Bernal, "Language is itself a means of production, possibly the first of all."[1] This is a profound concept, which helps us to go deeper into the question of the productive forces and unravel the contextual change in the nature of the subject and its relation with the object.

Mark Poster clarifies the nature of subject in the medium of the electronically mediated language and its impact on language, society and mode of information. The information revolution brings about the biggest transformation in the process of formation and dissolution of the modern subject, rendering it postmodern. This is done through the electronically mediated communication. According to Poster[2], electronic communication is *not just a new mode of transmission* that makes it easier and faster to send more information. More than that, it is a new phenomenon, with its own new structure. The electronically mediated communication *threatens the very existence of the individual and the society*. It leads to the formation of the mode of information. It is not a simple and usual communication in the existing sense simply amplified; it is a *challenge* to the society. It is a new language, which begins an age of symbolic exchange leading to the decentring of the individual and the subject. Communications in the form of and through electronics creates its own world of experiences and its own autonomous structures, which subvert the social structures.[3]

"Electronic mediation complicates the transmission of language and subverts the subject who would limit language to the role of a simple medium of expression."[4] "To copy an original means, in the mode of information, to create simulacra."[5]

Subject in Production and in Information

This brings us to the crucial question of difference between the two kinds of subject, their inter-relationship and their inter-changeability. In fact, it is the same subject evolving, changing, and transforming itself under the impact of electronics communications.

"The electronic mediation of musical information subverts the autonomous, rational subject for whom language is a direct translation of reality, instantiating instead an infinite play of mirror reflections, an abyss of indeterminate exchanges between subject and object in which the real and the fictional, the outside and the inside, the true and the false oscillate in an ambiguous shimmer of codes, languages and communications. In this world, the subject has no anchor, no fixed place, no point of perspective, no discreet centre, no clear boundary." The subject is disoriented in the mode of information. "In electronically mediated communications, subjects now float, suspended between points of objectivity, being constituted and reconstituted in different configurations in relation to the discursive arrangement of the occasion."[6]

This a very crucial point made by Poster; we need to draw certain conclusions and develop the concepts further. Unfortunately Poster has not given a totality of the picture because of his complex attitude towards what he calls 'totalization'.

Anyway, the point is that 'this subject' is floating between, is suspended between the points of objectivity. It becomes increasingly distant from objectivity because of the 'electronically mediated communication'. Here for the first time we meet the subject which is being dissected in the course of this particular kind of communication ('electronically mediated'). And the subject is being dispersed 'in the course of' communication'. This is because of the nature of communication, which is qualitatively different from all that was during the entire previous history. This is a very important point, even crucial. *It undoes the whole previous history*. 'The subject' was created in the course of human history. Today, it is destabilized, dispersed, made floating and suspended by the single act of communication which is *electronically* mediated. It is undermining history itself. One is reminded here of Francis Fukuyama[7], and he was right in this sense.

Thus this communication produces an effect *exactly opposite* of what was produced by the entire previous history. The whole of the previous communication consolidated the subject; the present, the electronically mediated one, *disperses* the same subject in no time and all over space.

This is what the industrial revolution did: consolidate the subject as never before. The subject came into full bloom. It was constituted and consolidated because it was the vehicle of reflection and interaction with the object. Such a subject was the product of the 'mode of production', *not* the mode of information, information a secondary factor. In fact there was no mode of information earlier, except accidentally. Information undoubtedly played a major role in fashioning the subject.

But now mode of information 'accidentally' has become the dominant factor constituting the subject. The previous subject had a direct and clear-cut ('Cartesian') relation with the objective world. Not any more. The subject is the 'mirror-image of the mirror-image', and therefore highly transitory, indirect and dispersed. It exists only for the moment when electronic signals are being communicated, thus appearing and disappearing every moment.

This is a new development in human history, particularly in the history of the evolution of the subject.

How Does it Happen?

"Changes in the configuration or wrapping of language alter the way the subject processes signs into meanings, that sensitive point of cultural production. The shift from oral and print wrapped language thus reconfigures the subject's relation to the world."[8]

Poster rightly states further that if the effects of the electronically mediated communications on the subject are demonstrated, then the field of the social will have to be theorized and the basic assumptions of critical theory and more generally of the social sciences will have to be questioned.

Change in the configuration of language is a crucial result of the electronics revolution. It changes the way signs are transformed into meanings and the way they change in the course of transmission. The above statement makes the important differentiation between the subject created by the oral and print media, and by the electronically mediated communication.

What is "the field of the mode of information"[9] that is constituted and which constitutes the subject? This is an important area of investigation. According to Poster there is a tendency to limit words to single meanings and to treat language as a transparent tool of action.[10] Thus according to him, the first obstacle to the constitution of the field of the mode of information is theoretical.[11]

As Poster elucidates, "social theory arose in a Cartesian culture of distinct objects and subjects."[12] In the context thus constituted, the subject, say social scientists, as Poster mentions, *is constituted as a knowing subject separate from the object of study*. The subject defines or develops univocal words to define the objective world.[13] It also means that the subject so constituted is dialectically contexted with the object, which demands or expects a particular kind of subject. This is an interesting development, as the evolution of the subject diverges considerably and increasingly from the necessities of the object, if the object changes qualitatively.

"In this theoretical context, language is nothing more than a transparent mediation, a representation of consciousness in writing and speech. Within this theoretical economy, electronic communications simply increase the representational power of language by reducing the temporal and spatial distancing of meaning."[14]

This is a very important point. The Cartesian subject is orderly, distinct, becoming ever more distinct with the development of the industrial revolution and its effects, takes a consolidated form and expresses the word clearly, to be interpreted through categories and laws. With the development of the technologies, and of the sciences, the distances and times become more defined, clearer, getting reduced, with the result that language develops along those lines. Words are communicated in their exact meaning, the endeavour is to represent the things as precisely as possible, to make words precise, to act as an intelligent subject.

At the same time, another, opposite tendency is taking shape. Distances, time and transmissions merge together to constitute:

1. One single entity with endless times and spaces, thus creating an objective world which loses its constituents. Therefore, it has a multi-spatial and multi-time relation with the subject. The objective world is thus changing, merging together as one. It is a new object, a result of the whole history of human society.
2. Consequently and independently, new subject, one which does not have a constellation of one-to-one relation with the objects of the objective world, but one which is in relation with the process of congealment and with the product of this congealment. Time and spaces of the object, of different objects, are congealed into one. It is with this less differentiated object that the subject enters into relation, and is thus transformed in the process. It is a new process of subject-creation, where identity is less conspicuous and the subject is rendered more temporary.

Electronically mediated communication and language play a crucial role by acting upon time and space of both the subject and the object. The communication establishes a relation between the two, which is itself congealed, crossing the barriers of the subjects and the objects. This crossing is reflected in the structure of the electronic language, which acquires a certain independence of its own because it is *electronically* transmitted. Electronics surpasses, transgresses and transcends the fixed structures of communication between fixed subjects and fixed objects. It is not them but their congealment that the communication represents. The established language collapses in every sense, and a new language comes into being. At the same time, it becomes an independent entity.

With the passing of time, the words become richer and loaded with more meaning/s, as also more flexible.

Thus emerges a subject-object relationship, a rich topic for philosophical studies and deliberations down the ages.

This state of affairs changes drastically with the introduction of 'electronically mediated communication'. This is a historic change, which is recognized only partially by Mark Poster. It is partial with him because he does not want to take a 'historical' view of things, which is quite strange. Yet he has been dealing with many historical trends in various fields in his present book.

Electronically Mediated Communication, and the Subject: A Discussion

What does the electronically mediated communication do to the subject? As we have already mentioned, the subject is dispersed for the first time in history. Instead of getting consolidated, it becomes fragile and insecure. This happens when the Cartesian world around the subject changes. In what way? The world *changes* because of the changes in the means of communication. The new communication penetrates the world deeper, revealing ever new features. The point here is that such communication, as the extension and amplification of the continued line, consolidates rather than disintegrates the subject. It enriches the subject with ever new information through the use of new kinds of transmissions and communications. But these communications basically do not create new linguistic or subjective structures.

Giving the example of money, Poster traces the growing distance between thing and commodity and its representation. From being represented by gold, money now has a fragile representation in the form of electronic signals in various forms. "The *correspondence* between word and thing was dropped in favour of a relation of *representation*."[15]

"The function of representation comes to grief when words lose their connection with things and come to stand in place of things, in short, when language stands for itself."[16] Poster argues that the power to represent now derives not from external sources but from something internal, from the linguistic structure itself.

We will quote in detail from Poster: "The crisis of representation derives, I suggest, not only from the information explosion noted by Jameson and Terdiman, but also from the new communicational structures in which that information circulates. Beyond a certain point, the increased distance between addressor and addressee allows a reconfiguration of the relation between the message and context, between the receiver/subject and representation of him or herself. These reconfigurations, which I call wrappings of language, in turn impose a new relation between science and power, between the state and the individual, between the individual and the community, between authority and law, between family members, between the consumer and the retailer. In sum the solid institutional routines that have characterized modern society for some two hundred years are being shaken by the earthquake of electronically mediated communication and recomposed into new routines whose outlines are as yet by no means clear."[17]

This is a very important point made by Poster, in which he traces the conversion of the subject, at least partially. In a sense, he is dealing with the transformation of quantity into quality. At a certain point in its development, the quantitative nature of information is transformed into a new quality due to the immense growth of it because of a change in the mode of transmission, which is now electronically mediated. It creates a different world of its own due to its changed nature. In this world the transmission is not that of simple information. It is not like saying 'I am coming' or 'he is reading' and so on. Transmitting this on the telephone or teleprinter does not change much. But being transmitted through electronic mediation and looking at it does begin certain changes in the information itself. It goes without saying that first of all there is an extraordinary growth in the amount of information, which affects the nature of transmission and brings about some changes in the subject.

The words and sentences begin to constitute a world of themselves, a separate world of their own. The subject begins to work upon this sphere, which assumes an independent existence.

Transmission through electronics makes certain changes in the information and its structure itself. What the subject confronts is not just particular information but its particular structure too. The text, for example, is a 'living' and *active* thing. It is not the same as on the paper, to take an example or comparison. It is surrounded by all sorts of commands and means of change. For example, there is the cursor, as if standing guard. Even the received matter can be manipulated and is of the temporary nature. What we simply write ('type') has a temporary nature, of which we are constantly aware. Suppose, we close the file and the computer; the matter is no more. It is actually out of our control, somewhere away in the hard disk or in the internet, out of our reach and in form that is not tangible, and therefore we cannot say: 'it is there'.

So, when I say (write), 'he is reading', the statement has no permanency about it. It is as transitory as the characters typed out. This is quite a different experience from that of the book or even a typed or printed page. It is more likely to be forgotten.

Vast numbers of people are shifting to the computer world. They are working and living their life more and more in the world of software, run and controlled by the computers. This brings about a rapid congealment of time and space in which we each exist. Thus the time-space relations within and outside the computer world are vastly different, and these differences are becoming vaster very quickly. The concept of the subject therefore is also becoming all inclusive rather than individual-centred.

"People with cell phones acquired what often seemed a new individuality—some would call it 'atomization'. 'It is not an individualism... forced by the actors', Ling wrote, 'but rather an individualism that arises out of the direction of the social order'.[18]

The computer page is surrounded by so many instructions, markers, type and font settings, means to scroll and so on. In other words, a whole 'press' is operating while we write. It is a collapse of various labour processes into one, a congealing of abstract labours. The abstract nature of labour is confirmed, yet its concrete nature is developed as never before.

The computer is *a world in itself*, and increasingly so. That world is displayed to us on the screen. Therefore, the screen is a new world for us. It is a world of images and not of reality. This world has to be analyzed for its growing complexity. It is constituted by a stream of electrons and other particles and waves in particular configuration. The software is its language. Hardware is its means. But it is to be noted that the hardware is just a means or medium of expression of the software, and this medium is disappearing fast. That is because it is superfluous due to the phase of development of society technology.

Hardware becoming superfluous is a milestone and a crucial event in the social development. It contains within itself the seeds of the future society. Through this event, the electronic signals connect themselves directly with our nervous system. The developments in the computer/brain interface and such other fields are indicative of these trends. It has a direct bearing on the formation of the new subject.

Therefore, the computer is both the small equipment that we open to start the software and a new world, as well as a key to the world that does not need hardware to enter that world. It is a world of images which we create and manipulate.

In this world, the text and the image occupy a transitory place. In fact, the world is being constituted by such images.

As a result, this information can be manipulated and changed. New meanings can be imparted. The subject for example, changes (manipulates) the images, creating a vast range of subject-oriented meanings. The meanings are determined by the medium woven by the electrons. Information acquires an independent existence. It becomes part of the subject as a new object. It does not reflect the object or less and less so; subject reflects subject.

What is a picture or art form on the screen? It is a temporary, and yet permanent, expression; it is independent of the object that it represents or is supposed to represent. It is an object in itself. It can create the object without really being in touch with it. It does not need the object that it wants to represent. When the subject receives it, the former can change it at will. A printed word or picture cannot be changed but something on the screen can be. These are two different things or images. So, we are not just writing but speaking as well, almost, talking to each other at the same time.

There is thus a complete disruption of the traditional and existing subject. The subject is becoming a structure, a construct of the signs and images that float on the screen and in the world of the internet. It is a break up of the object too.

In the course of this change the structure of the thing comes to the fore in many expressions. The meaning becomes the discretion of the subject, not of the object or the sender. The new meaning clashes with history, with the meanings created by and in the course of history. This can happen only when the 'sent' material assumes an independent existence. This may seem strange and even outrageous *but this is exactly what happens*. This happens with the newspapers and periodicals, with messages and mails. We are actually shifting to the configurations of the electrons (for example a message or an article or photo) from the printed matter, which of course is not losing its importance but which is being assigned a new place by electronic history.

The messages are sent in particular configurations of electrons (electronic signals). These structures can be changed because of their nature. They appear on our screens as series of waves and in glittering forms. Thus they are fragile and momentary, and therefore their meanings are momentary too.

As subject, the person concerned works with light signals displayed on the screen. They can acquire a permanent or a relatively permanent nature only after they are printed. They become something else in printed form. Then the relation with the subject changes at once. It is direct, clear, stable and Cartesian. But this Cartesian object is at once transformed and transfigured into something else through electronically mediated communication. The stability is gone. So, a new subject replaces the old, the Cartesian one.

Besides, when the signals are dispersed all over the globe, the subject is also dispersed. He/she is not tuned to a direct relationship of matter/idea relation. Pre-electronics subject-object relationship has a one-to-one relationship. The subject is constituted because the object is 'there'. It, the object, exists, as it is and in particular shape with a certain stability. The object exists in certain time and space. It is this that determines the nature of the subject, *which also, consequently, exists in certain time and space.* The subject is the realization of the object, while the object confirms its existence through the subject.

The electronic revolution and communication changes all this. To describe in rough contours, the information revolution disperses the object in time and space, rendering it amorphous and not confined to one place and becomes unstable. Consequently, basic changes are brought about in the subject.

Dramatic Changes at the Poles of Subject and Object

How does it happen and what is its significance for the mode of production and for the mode of information?

Dramatic events take place at the pole of ***the object***. It should be noted that the object is *dispersed*. By this we mean it is first converted into an image or images and then spread about, dispersed all over, everywhere on the surface of the globe. Therefore our relation with the object itself undergoes a fundamental change. We do not confront the 'thing' directly any more: it is lost for us! Every single object, thing and phenomenon is *first converted*, dissociated, into the binary language of the software, and only after that we 'see' it. *This is a fundamental transformation in the mode of production*. To that extent the objectivity of the object is lost. It is no longer in direct contact with the subject; rather its image is.

Thus the object is *represented* by its own image through electronic signals. These signals convert the thing/object into certain electronic configurations, which we see or look at as picture or writing and so on. The object is replaced by the image. It is the image that the subject is now in contact with.

The electronic signals represent both the subject and the object simultaneously as one and separate. Thus the signals have two opposite and contradictory sides. The words constituted by them, and the signals sent by them, are separate and at the same time merging into and as one. It leads to the creation of a new human being, particularly new consciousness. This is an interesting turn of events of history. To keep in contact with the thing existing out there, we must convert it *first* into an image. This is done, without our knowledge, so to say, by the electronic mediation or representation of the object. As soon as we introduce electronic communication, and information about the object is transmitted in electronic form, the subject-object relationship undergoes a drastic transformation. I see an event in a remote corner of the earth. It is independent of my time and space, and yet it enters into my time and space and becomes part and parcel of mine. Thus I am a rendered *a different subject* from one who is looking at it *direct on the spot*. These are two different subjects in relation with the same object, but the objectivities are qualitatively different.

I look at the signals and treat the object as having been looked at, while this is not really the case. Yet this also is the case. Even while treating the object having been disposed of, it is disposed of in a manner quite differently. It is object in non-object form, as representation. It is configured and put into contact with the subject, with me, for example. So, to be in contact with the subject and to be an object, the object has to be reconfigured, *without which the electronically mediated communication cannot communicate!* So, the object, the thing, is changed for the sake of and in the course of the communication by the electrons. This is an *unprecedented event of history*, destabilizing the existing social order.

At the pole of ***the subject***, the changes are equally dramatic and shocking, yet clinical and scientifically logical. The conversion and decentring of the object simultaneously decentres the subject. The consolidation of the subject is lost. The process reverses. The time and space of the subject is dispersed and spread over to reflect the objective reality of a similar nature. The subject is no more linear, orderly and step-by-step in terms of time and space. It is a unity, a growing and expanding unity, of various times and spaces, congealed into one. The object is everywhere and nowhere, now here, now there; therefore, the subject is transformed into an unstable entity with unstable reflective capacity; it is also everywhere and nowhere.

The subject reflects the *image* of the object, and therefore, is not the subject in the strict sense of the term; it is a subject with reservations, yet an expansive one. It is a subject, which by the very nature of the image, is nearer to and even one with what it reflects. It is in fact a process of merger with the image of the reality.

Thus, the subject reacts with what electronic images brings out of the word, and it brings what normally is unknown lying deep inside the reality. It is a new subject-object relationship, where the subject is both destabilized and expanded. The subject goes beyond the limits of the traditional/classical space-time relationships, and acquires new identity independent of these relationships.

The subject is being reconstituted by the electronically mediated communications.

Then there is another side to this transformation of the subject. Says Poster:

"While to some extent language is a tool for intentional action, ...language has another, very different, capacity. It is a figurative, structuring power that constitutes the subject who speaks as well as the one that is spoken to...By distancing the relation of the speaking body to the listening body, by abstracting from the connection between the reader or writer and palpable materiality of the printed or hand-written text, electronically mediated communication upsets the relation of the subject to the symbols it emits or receives and reconstitutes this relation in drastically new shapes. For the subject in electronically mediated communication, this subject tends to become not the material world as represented in language but the flow of signifiers itself. In the mode of information it becomes increasingly difficult, or even pointless, for the subject to distinguish a "real" existing "behind" the flow of signifiers, and as a consequence social life in part becomes a practice of positioning subjects to receive and interpret messages."[19]

Thus the language itself is changed in the course of transmission between the subject and the object. It drastically reconstitutes the relation. The language as a point, as a shifting point, between two poles has a changing structure, subject to independent interpretation.

In other words, language increasingly acquires an independent existence, to which meanings can be added and which at the same time is seen in *the internet*. It is an example of *the growing distance between the subject and the object* and of the independence of the pool of language. Simultaneously, it is a growing *merger and congealment* of the subject and the object.

It has to be realized that the internet is an independent sphere of growing layers of human consciousness, and is a crucial new factor in the changing relation between the subject and the object.

Here it would be in place to note that the use of the computer is forcing drastic changes in the traditional language and creating its own language. This one is run, besides, by the binary electronic language, upon which is built the software. Grammar is a particular victim of the electronics, a sitting duck. Rapid daily and hourly communication, communication even by the minute and the second, is forcing emergence of a new language completely different from the existing one, basically fashioned by the industrial age. It is also creating its own words and expressions.

"What the mode of information puts into question, however, is not simply the sensory apparatus but the very shape of subjectivity; its relation to the world of objects, its perspective on that world, its location in that world. We are confronted not so much by a change from a "hot" to a "cool" communications medium, ... but a generalized destabilization of the subject." In the mode of information, the subject is no longer located in a point in absolute time/space, fixed at a vantage point from which it rationally estimates its options. It is rather multiplied by databases, dispersed by computers messaging and conferencings, decontextualized and reidentified by TV ads, dissolved and materialized continuously in the electronic transmission of symbols. "In the perspective of Deleuze and Guattari we are being changed from "arborial" beings, to rooted in time and space, to "rhizomic" nomads who daily wander at will (whose will remains a question) across the globe, and even beyond it through communications satellites, without necessarily moving our bodies at all."[20]

It is a separation of the *subject from subject*. Even while being an individual subject, we become part of the larger, amorphous subject created through a congealing of so many subjects in time and space and simultaneously independent of them.

"The body then is no longer an effective limit of the subject's position. Or perhaps it would be better to say that communications facilities extend the nervous system throughout the earth to the point that it enwraps the planet in a noosphere, to use Teilhard de Chardin's term, of language." If one can speak directly or by electronic mail to a friend in Paris while sitting in California, if one can witness political and cultural events as they occur across the globe without leaving home, if government agencies make decisions affecting one's life without one's knowledge, "then where am I and who am I? In these circumstances, I cannot consider myself centred in my rational, autonomous subjectivity or bordered by a defined ego, but I am disrupted, subverted and dispersed across social space."[21]

The subject is dispersed all over the globe, the society, the object. A new subject is created, so also *a* new object. The mode of production cannot sustain such subjects and such objects. Things proceed beyond into the mode of information.

"Oddly enough poststructuralists call into question theory itself if by theory one means a set of concepts that open a terrain for investigation by strategy that produces discursive maps of the territory. My turn to poststructuralism thus precludes the development of a theory of the mode of information that displaces while mirroring the theory of the mode of production."[22]

Poster's 'Mode of Production' Clashes with Bell's Post-Industrialism

As we have seen, Mark Poster treats the mode of information as an explanation of the world of information. It deals with the results and structures of electronically mediated communication. With Poster, the concept of the mode of information has nothing to do with all round comprehensive changes in society and with the succession of societies. As such, it comes into conflict with the concept of post-industrial society advanced by Daniel Bell. That is why, Poster contradicts any suggestion that the concept of the mode of information shows evolution of past into present.

"But the problem is not to demonstrate the slow, continuous evolution of the past into the present, thereby creating a familiarity effect, an ideological haze of false recognition—one that posits that we have always already been in the mode of information—which celebrates and substantializes the phenomena in question; instead I see the issue as one of the configuring in theory certain phenomena so that their disruptive potential can be recognized and perhaps in time acted upon. I choose discontinuity over continuity, the newness of the new over the oldness of the new for political, not epistemological reasons. By doing so, as I believe Marx did with the concept of the mode of production, the prospects may be furthered for defining structures of domination and contributing to the process through which they may disrupted. Industrial capitalism was when Marx theorized it both as a minority phenomenon and the outcome of a long historical trajectory; the same emergent character may be attributed to the mode of information."[23]

According to Poster, Bell treats information in the manner of capitalist economic theory. But information is not subject to laws of commodity prices and market variations.

"Scarcity of material resources, the prime axiom of capitalist economic theory, does not apply to information. The edifice of capitalism appears to be threatened by the inexhaustibility of information, by its resistance to the commodity for. Instead of raising the theoretical question of the possibility of an economy beyond the limits of scarce commodities, Bell hurries to reconcile the new with the old. While information is not suited to spatial forms of scarcity, it initiates a new form of scarcity, he contends, the scarcity of time. Information becomes a commodity to the extent that the time needed to reproduce it falls within the principles of capitalist economic theory. Bell and capitalist theorists generally have discovered the information, like automobiles, can be sold and therefore may fall within the market system. The price of information is determined for them by the same laws of supply and demand that govern the distribution of material commodities."[24]

Electronic communication works against commodification. In fact, it is not an economic category at all.

"One feature of the electronic information works against its commodification. The new technologies advance considerably the reproductibility of information. The combination of electronic coding and recoding on plastic tape surfaced with oxides enables the speedy and accurate copying of many forms of information: words, numbers, music, visual images. As the technologies that process and reproduce information are integrated with the technologies that move information through space (telecommunication system) the prospects unfold for new patterns of communication, prospects that promise to introduce significant changes on the social order. The ease with which information can be reproduced or moved has already created havoc with the legal system that is articulated to protect the private ownership of material commodities."[25]

Information should be treated as a linguistic category, and not an economic one. Here the theory of post-industrial society fails to take notice of the linguistic novelty of electronic communication.

"By treating information as an economic rather than a linguistic fact the theory of post-industrial society obscures the question of the new communication possibilities of disseminating information opened up by the electronic technologies. While it is certainly true that capitalism engulfs as much information as it can under the net of the laws of the market, the new structures of information, treated as linguistic phenomena, introduce changes in the pattern of communication in society and destabilize the positions of the subject in that society.[26]

The problem with Poster here and elsewhere is that he and many others are trying imperceptibly to avoid the concrete implications of the information revolution upon the several aspects of capitalism/industrialism. Economics cannot be avoided, and the electronics revolution is having a deep impact upon the economics of capitalism itself, as Poster himself points out in many places. Information has to be examined in all its aspects, and not just in terms of the linguistic one. The point is that information as produced by the electronics revolution penetrates or cuts through both the capitalist and industrial structures. *And this precisely is what we are examining*. The transition from the capitalist to post-capitalist and from the industrial to the post-industrial societies is being made due to the emergence of a mode of production of information, and not of the tangible objects. At the same time, we have to examine the role of the new means of production, which generally speaking are moving towards the smaller scales.

A society based on the mode of information is quite a different matter from the one based on the mode of production. The mode of production turns out to be the base upon which the new society begins to be built. New linguistic configurations are among the major changes, but changes are not confined to them alone. Information and *the mode of its production* turn out to be the driving factor even for production of material goods or commodities. And this is what is novel in the history of social development. What we are witnessing is the society based on production of information and not on the production of goods.

Therefore, the concept of the post-industrial society advanced by Daniel Bell is a useful tool of knowledge to investigate the transition. Investigating economic and production bases would in fact be the key to identify the major changes. Capitalism has now to deal with something that does not fit in with itself. *Information is nowhere a capital sustaining and enhancing factor.* The contradiction puts capitalism in a position where it has to make a series of unsuccessful attempts, take several fruitless measures to keep itself in place and to keep its laws operating.

The very first results of the information revolution, of the means of production getting smaller, do not really fit in with the basic nature of modern industrial capitalism. That is why the modern has a tendency to become postmodern, the industrial post-industrial, and consequently capitalism tends to become post-capitalism. Capitalism, really speaking, is large-scale production, and such an event took place for the first time in history. And again for the first time on an almost universal scale, small and smaller scales of means of production are being created, which increasingly are driven by small or large amounts of information. Capitalism and industrialism as such cannot deal with or tackle these means. There must emerge social structures and relations that operate as well as produce these means.

What is also novel and unprecedented is that information is taking independent forms, independent of capitalism and industrialism.

What is actually taking place is something independent of social, economic and political development/s. This may sound strange and may be termed as 'technological determinism'. But the fact is that for the first time a technological revolution has taken place *overtaking social development*. The social structures have to fall in line with the needs and dictation of the logic of the electronics revolution, particularly due to the information revolution. The entry of information as the factor of social development has transformed the nature of social development.

The STR has forced the governments, states and nations to fall in line with its demands, and thus to suitably change their policies, programmes, concepts and formulations. This can be seen in the case of the EU (European Union), as also to some extent in the case of other regional groupings. For the first time in history, the barriers between the countries have come down considerably, and this cannot be attributed to the policies of the governments, parties and leaders alone. There are objective processes at play. The most important is the STR and the ICR. They have made it possible to increase the transmission of information and travel of human beings, materials, money etc so much that a huge qualitative change is going on.

The states and governments in Europe are more porous and transmitting than ever before. A European market has come into being, thanks mainly to the STR, which no government can ignore. Therefore the governments have to work out their policies accordingly.

This undoubtedly is no easy and smooth path, and is beset with contradictions and conflicts. Capitalism has reached a stage where much of the new is being treated and dealt with in the old manner. The justified and unjustified national feelings are rendered stronger particularly when they are sought to be deliberately suppressed, and here the subjective policies play an important role.

Yet, the trend is set by the objective processes, released by the unlimited information revolution. Information has forced the people and the governments as also the market to act in definite integrative ways. "What would have happened if every scavenger had been able to communicate with every other scavenger? The capacity of the 'lower orders' to know about the doings of their superiors would have been greatly enhanced. Freer movement of people and information contributes to egalitarian ideas and practices."[27]

The great process of world-wide integration has been unleashed all over the world. It is definitely an integrating and inclusive world, not one which is disintegrating. Other contradictions are part and parcel of this central process.

An adequate account of the forces of media must move beyond the behavioural aspects of conversations, the dramaturgical model, to confront the problem of communications practice at the level of language. As their proponents claim, the electronic media do alter the time-space parameters of social interactions, in principle rendering anyone capable of communicating with anyone else at any time."[28]

It is a world which is doing away with the traditional space-time relations and creating new ones, with the world emerging as a new space-time reference frame.

"To the extent that language is always contextual, that part of the meanings of the words derives from where they are uttered, the mode of information introduces a new language that occurs in places unrelated to the material limitations of everyday life. Hence words and gestures emitted by broadcasters and received by individuals are tele-language, a new form of English."[29]

The language is often loaded with outdated meanings, which were created in the space-time continuum of the past. This comes in conflict with the new paradigm shifts of space-time, with ever questionable meanings.

"The media promotes forms of self-constitution by viewers that profoundly engage them."[30]

"Third, the monologic context-less media language is self-referential. While all language is to some degree self-referential, media language is so to a greater degree than most in proportion to its distance from context and its monologic character. The more a language/practice is removed from a face-to-face context of daily life in a stable culture in which social relationships are reproduced through dialogue, the more language must generate and reproduce those features from within itself; in other words, the media must stimulate its context and ventriloquize its audience. The language/practice of TV absorbs the functions of culture to a greater degree than face-to-face conversations or print and its discursive effect is to constitute the subjects differently from speech or print. Speech constitutes subjects as members of a community by solidifying the ties between individuals. Print constitutes subjects as rational, autonomous egos, as stable interpreters of culture who, in isolation, make logical connections from linear symbols. Media language replaces the community of speakers and undermines the referentiality of discourse necessary for the rational ego. Media language—contextless, monologic, self-referential—invites the recipient to play with the process of self-constitution, continuously to remake the self in 'conversation' with different modes of discourse....the subject has no defined identity as a pole of a conversation."[31]

TV is now part and parcel of the biological existence of the individual, and yet in a growing contradiction with it. Disintegrating subject makes it liable to integrate with amorphous objectivity at higher levels.

"The TV ad is a performative semiotic phenomenon: it employs words and images in order to effect changes in the behaviour of the recipient of the message.[32]

The post-industrial social order is *kept alive* by a constant watching of TV and increasing use of the mobile. The conflicting contentions of Bell and Poster merge together to create the new reality of the post-industrial society.

"When an individual watches a TV ad, the chief social relation of the society is reproduced. "[33] "What happens when an individual watches a TV ad?... Ads are also in a central structural position in the economy, overlapping both the means and the relations of consumption. The major problem of the capitalist economy since the 1920s shifted from production to consumption. ... In the second half of the 20th century, this challenge has been fought in the diminutive arena of the 30 second ad on the 19–inch TV. When an individual watches a TV ad, the health of the economy is at stake. "[34]

This is nothing but a postmodern, post-industrial social order consequent upon the electronics revolution. As a result, the subject shifts historically.

References

1. J.D. Bernal, *Science in History* (in 4 volumes), Volume 1, Penguin, 1969, p. 72.
2. Mark Poster, *Mode of Information: Poststructuralism and Social Context*, Polity Press, 1990.
3. See, Poster, ibid., Introduction.
4. Poster, ibid., p. 10.
5. Ibid.
6. Ibid., p. 11.

7. Francis Fukuyama, *The End of History and the Last Man*, Penguin, 1992.
8. Poster, op. cit.
9. Poster, ibid.
10. Ibid., pp. 11–12.
11. Ibid., p. 12.
12. Ibid.
13. See Poster, ibid.
14. Ibid., p. 12
15. Ibid., p. 13; emphasis in the original.
16. Ibid.
17. Ibid., p. 14.
18. Robin Jeffrey and Assa Doron, *Cell Phone Nation*, Hachette India, 2013, p. 216.
19. Poster, op cit, pp. 14–15.
20. Ibid., p. 15.
21. Ibid., pp. 15–16.
22. Ibid., p. 18.
23. Ibid., p. 20.
24. Ibid., pp. 26–27.
25. Ibid., p. 27.
26. Ibid., p. 28.
27. Jeffrey and Doron, *Cell Phone Nation*, p. 37.
28. Poster, op cit, p. 28.
29. Ibid., p. 45.
30. Ibid., p. 45.
31. Ibid., p. 46.
32. Ibid., p. 47.
33. Ibid.
34. Ibid., pp. 47–48.

Conclusion

We have discussed various aspects of transition from the industrial to post-industrial era in the previous ten chapters. The discussion leaves us no doubt that we are witnessing *the great transition*. The industrial revolution was the greatest event to have happened at that time, and till recently it determined our life, ways and thought. But now it has been overtaken by a much greater, faster and deeper revolution, the STR. The STR has changed every aspect of our individual and social life in a very brief period of social motion.

We are witnessing an unprecedented event/process, whereby we ourselves are being transformed. We are most fortunate to live in such an era and to witness the great transition. It is our responsibility to grasp it and to contribute to its forward motion.

Production has lost its primacy; it has been overtaken by information and information-production. Information was supposed to be facilitating production, but the unforeseen has happened. It is information which now shapes production and our lives, so much so that we have begun to live in an information society, which undoubtedly is post-industrial and post-production. We are making a historic shift from the mode of production to the mode of information.

The industrial order of things, mills, factories, tools and machines are dissolving under the diluting powers of the electronics, in particular the software. The software has opened a whole new horizon of human and social development. We do not know the extent and nature of the future human/social development. The motion of electronics has taken the social motion by surprise, the latter has been overtaken by the former.

In many ways, the human and social evolution has begun anew. Till now it was based on fashioning tools. The tool reached its zenith in machines, to which the tool was attached and which was run by the powerful motive force brought into being by the steam power revolution resulting in the industrial revolution.

We no more use the tool; we use it only as a past habit. The tool has been replaced by the laser and other forces residing within the atom. The forces within the atom have transformed the entire social structure and direction of its development.

The tangible tools and machines have been replaced by the intangibles, by the imitation of the industrial age by the software, which makes it possible for the tools and the machines to 'grow' anywhere. Our body merges with the electron signals. It has become possible to create or 'manufacture' objects anywhere by small gadgets run by programmed software. The industrial age finally collapses with this event. Software negates the entire history of the human being and begins to 'write' it anew. A drastic turn has been taken in social development.

If the tool and the machine dissolve, then labour, labour process and labour power also dissolve, as also the production process; value disappears and labour theory of value loses relevance.

Capitalism is fast losing operation of its laws. Features of post-capitalism are discernible clearly.

We call the technological rearrangement of the society post-industrialism. It is a post-industrial society chiefly because it has lost or is losing the industrial features rapidly. It is a postmodern society in the sphere of thoughts, culture, social domain, philosophy, creation of the subject and its relationship with the object.

There are many trends, concepts and theories termed as postmodern. We do not necessarily agree with their interpretations and theories. In fact the book differs with most of them, with most of what goes by the name. Yet, through the mesh and jungle of postmodern theories a running thread appears. It is clear that a whole system of thought and approach is emerging, which drastically differs with the thought, consciousness and culture of the industrial age. If the industrial subject was created in direct reflection of matter (material objects) in the consciousness of the subject, now the post-industrial subject is created, for example, in the reflection of the reflection (image) (reflection of the reflected things). The information revolution and the mode of information make this possible.

Many interesting questions emerge and lines of investigation open up. They need to be followed in future. With the dissolution of the machine and the tool, a new era in human development begins. If we accept that the tool is disappearing, then we need to trace the new directions human development is about to take. The further development of society has to be reworked, giving up the existing dimensions taken as given or fixed.

If we have already entered a post-industrial phase of social development, then all the basic concepts and tools of knowledge worked out in the capitalist/industrial era have to be given up in their essentials, and a fresh beginning has to be made.

Marxism and Post-Industrialism

Marxism too needs drastic changes to be able to interpret the new turn in social and technological development. Marxism was the greatest height reached by the industrial thought. Nothing better has been written on nature, society and thought. Karl Marx reached the very limits, the very borders of his age and even went beyond. That is why Marxism has been such an influential thought-system. Its dialectical scientific method is still applicable. Our starting point in any analysis has to be the Marxist thought and Marxist conclusions.

Yet, Marxism itself is a production of the industrial age, expressing all its motions in a concentrated form. All its theories are scientific theories and Marxism itself is science. It is precisely for this reason that this science must evolve into the new age being created by the non-industrial forces residing within the atom. Marxism has to raise itself qualitatively to accord with the new era of STR and FTR (fourth technological revolution), to be able to guide scientific investigations.

A whole new world is emerging to be understood and to create a new praxis.

Capitalism Going Beyond Itself

It is clear that one law after another of the capitalist mode of production and society is becoming obsolete. These laws are unable to answer the new questions being posed by the transition to the post-industrial society. In an unexpected turn of events, technology and science have overtaken the social development, and they have begun to solve many of the problems of society. As an example, we may cite the law of value: the commodities are fast losing their value, which is going towards zero.

Mills and factories are becoming smaller, moving towards the miniature size, and consequently the classes and the collectives are disappearing rapidly. There are any number of industrial tendencies and phenomena under threat. Capitalism cannot exist at the level of the individual, a very small and miniature existence. Labour and production are transformed into electronic signals at this level. Consequently, social processes take the form of information, which drives the society.

Can there be a 'capitalism' which is based upon information? It is impossible.

Clearly, a mode of information is emerging as a system. We do not agree with Mark Poster when he says that the mode of information is confined only to the electronically mediated communication. In fact, this mode is becoming all-pervasive and is replacing the mode of production and the society based upon that mode.

The social development has fulfilled its historic task of equalizing production with society, and has potentially provided high levels of production and productivity. It is the task of the social beings and of the distribution system to struggle for egalitarian distribution. The material conditions for such a distributive system have already been provided by the STR and the electronics revolution.

The fourth technological revolution (FTR) provides the base from which the further development of society will take on. Virtually every individual has the means of communication, which potentially also are the means of production. This is an unprecedented event, a revolution. Revolution in information reaches every individual, who is connected with the internet.

The FTR has brought together various functions of the social technology together by converting each function into a part of the new electronic systems and gadgets. In other words, various forms of labour have become one.

Can there be a capitalism fully surrounded by and dependent on the internet? It is simply not possible. *It cannot remain an industrial capitalism, and information capitalism is no capitalism, simply because it is not based upon the production of value.*

Laws of Historical Materialism: STR and PIS

According to the laws of historical materialism or the materialist conception of history, socialism follows capitalism. Socialism is higher than and superior to capitalism. Capitalism is followed by another society and socio-economic formation when new productive forces become mature and cause changes in the production relations within the system.

STR has brought about certain modifications in this scheme of succession of social formations. The basic assumptions of historical materialism (materialist conception of history) are correct. They have been confirmed by the STR and associated developments. There is no better explanation of the causes and sources of social development and change.

Yet, the transition from capitalism to non-capitalism or post-capitalism has taken different routes and forms.

The transition from the industrial to the post-industrial stage fully accords with the materialist conception of history. The sudden explosion of productive forces through electronics is bringing about changes in the social structures.

The explosion of science and technology has caused a change in the order of developments in various aspects and indices.

The scientific concept of socialism was based upon large-scale industries, big factories and mills growing into giant industrial complexes, with associated giant sized infrastructures. Socialism was *industrial* socialism. Consequently, it was nearer to capitalism in many basic factors. Engels' scientific socialism, and other associated theories including by Marx and Lenin, assumed the existence of large-scale production run by large and larger scales of means of production and of fixed capital.

All this is now undergoing drastic changes. The trend has been reversed and the means of production are becoming smaller and smaller consequent upon the electronics revolution. Therefore the concept of socialism has to change.

That situation is changing now as the electronic revolution proceeds. The trend has been reversed due to the electronics and the computer revolution based upon the use of microchips. The size of the production units or centres, of the mills, factories, industries, and of the machines and tools, is on the whole reducing. This in our opinion is the *most important* factor affecting the very concept of both capitalism and socialism. The chips, the software programs and micro-electronics in general are causing the machines/tools to become compact, smaller and more efficient.

Consequently, the machine and the factory are becoming more suited to the individual rather than to the class and group. Potentially, it is more possible to buy and own the means of production.

In the latest, what may be called the fourth, stage of technological revolution, the means of production and communications are further being reduced in size and *are getting miniaturized*. 3-D printing is one of the latest developments, and is going to prove of great productive as well as social significance. It is an amazing technological event, in which the individual is the greatest beneficiary. The role of the individual and the subject is going to increase as never before. One can literally carry on manufacture on a table, almost single-handedly.

This development further disintegrates the group and the class. It also attacks the market, though initially immensely helping it. Every person can potentially produce his/her necessities, initially for the market, later increasingly for oneself. It has the potential to undermine thw entire social order.

If suppose on a table one creates an object with 3-D printing; there is a possibility that some bottles will be used in my house and another part sold in the market: watch, a bottle, pen, etc. In 3-D printing there is a tendency or potential tendency to go out of the market and to emphasize use value. It does not mean it is going to happen soon but it has the potential. If the production is for the individual, then it has a tendency of going away from the market. If production is by class, group or collective, it remains embedded in the market, but with a tendency to repulse away or shy away gradually. It is not necessary to remain connected to the market. The problem with individual production is that it could be made only up to a limit in industrial and capitalist production. When the role of the capitalist market is diminished, then use value will be produced more. It is not necessary for utility to go to the market.

Another revolutionary technology is nanotechnology. It can go anywhere, enter any part of a factory system, a machine and a living body. It will not need even an individual to assist it. This technology is going to unite the mechanical, the physical and the biological. The finer and the finest things can be made using nano machines and technology. It truly will be the dissolution of the machine: the 'giant' cannot stand before the minutely active nanos! Nothing industrial can survive.

The progressively small robots are another means helping the trend towards the smaller.

So, the point is that the small, miniature and microscopic means of production and communication are the basic building blocks, the trends, of a new society. They have begun to create their own structures to facilitate their work. The base upon which the existing industrial society and its structures were set up is disintegrating, with the new ones sprouting here and there. Classes, groups and such other formations/structures are unable to carry the weight of social development. They need a comprehensive reorganization.

It is for the first time in history that such a development has taken place. It is unprecedented. It is for the first time in history that the means used by human beings are fast getting smaller and reduced in size. Consequently, the new 'tools' are reaching every hand. It is actually the power to receive, create and send information to the producing and other systems that the human being is acquiring rapidly.

So, the ownership of the large means of production is threatened. This is a crucial development in the course of social development.

The development works both ways. It brings about a change in capitalism and it brings about a change in the way of transition to a new society.

Besides, production is no more the driving force; it is information now.

The objective forces of the socio-historical motion have opened new pathways to the future. This has resulted as a concentrated burst of science and technology. For the first time the motion of science and technology has left the social development behind. This is an extraordinary event.

It has become difficult for the monopolized and centralized capitalist tendencies and structures to remain in existence for any duration. Finance capital is under severe strain owing to the increase in productive capacities resulting from the STR.

Software versus Hardware, Tangible versus Intangible

These conflicts and contradictions are among the most decisive today in the social motion. As we have seen, software is dissolving and replacing hardware, creating new methods, means approaches and consciousness among humans. Henceforward, the motion and direction of social development will be determined by information created through software, which is taking over all the functions of hardware. Keyboard, screen, camera, and so on are all being made to function through the intangibles pathways of the software. All the tools of information and communication are being converted into the software, which can be 'invoked' as and when required.

The software has developed to a point where it is on the verge of merging with our biological body. This again is unprecedented. The domination of software is a qualitatively novel development. In fact, it provides a fresh basis for further social development, in which everything will have to be formulated anew. Human beings will live increasingly in the world of images and information about the tangible and intangible processes, and will manoeuvre the outside world through them.

The Cartesian world is being replaced by the particles and the waves, again an unprecedented event.

Scientific theory faces new and unparalleled challenges.

Index